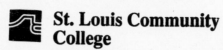

BLACK
AGED

OTHER RECENT VOLUMES IN THE
SAGE FOCUS EDITIONS

41. **Black Families (Second Edition)**
Harriette Pipes McAdoo
64. **Family Relationships in Later Life
(Second Edition)**
Timothy H. Brubaker
75. **Organizational Theory and Inquiry**
Yvonna S. Lincoln
76. **Men in Families**
Robert A. Lewis and Robert E. Salt
77. **Communication and Group
Decision-Making**
Randy Y. Hirokawa and
Marshall Scott Poole
79. **Community Power**
Robert J. Waste
80. **Intimate Relationships**
Daniel Perlman and Steve Duck
81. **Children's Ethnic Socialization**
Jean S. Phinney and Mary Jane Rotheram
82. **Power Elites and Organizations**
G. William Domhoff and Thomas R. Dye
83. **Responsible Journalism**
Deni Elliott
84. **Ethnic Conflict**
Jerry Boucher, Dan Landis, and
Karen Arnold Clark
85. **Aging, Health, and Family**
Timothy H. Brubaker
86. **Critical Issues in Aging Policy**
Edgar F. Borgatta and
Rhonda J. V. Montgomery
87. **The Homeless in Contemporary Society**
Richard D. Bingham, Roy E. Green, and
Sammis B. White
88. **Changing Men**
Michael S. Kimmel
89. **Popular Music and Communication**
James Lull
90. **Life Events and Psychological
Functioning**
Lawrence H. Cohen
91. **The Social Psychology of Time**
Joseph E. McGrath
92. **Measurement of Intergenerational
Relations**
David J. Mangen, Vern L. Bengtson,
and Pierre H. Landry, Jr.
93. **Feminist Perspectives on Wife Abuse**
Kersti Yllö and Michele Bograd
94. **Common Problems/Proper Solutions**
J. Scott Long
95. **Falling from the Faith**
David G. Bromley
96. **Biosocial Perspectives on the Family**
Erik E. Filsinger
97. **Measuring the Information Society**
Frederick Williams

98. **Behavior Therapy and Religion**
William R. Miller and John E. Martin
99. **Daily Life in Later Life**
Karen Altergott
100. **Lasting Effects of Child
Sexual Abuse**
Gail Elizabeth Wyatt and
Gloria Johnson Powell
101. **Violent Crime, Violent Criminals**
Neil Alan Weiner and Marvin F. Wolfgang
102. **Pathways to Criminal Violence**
Neil Alan Weiner and Marvin E. Wolfgang
103. **Older Adult Friendship**
Rebecca G. Adams and Rosemary Blieszner
104. **Aging and Health**
Kyriakos S. Markides
105. **The VCR Age**
Mark R. Levy
106. **Women in Mass Communication**
Pamela J. Creedon
107. **Midlife Loss**
Richard A. Kalish
108. **Cultivation Analysis**
Nancy Signorielli and Michael Morgan
109. **Black Students**
Gordon LaVern Berry and
Joy Keiko Asamen
110. **Aging and Caregiving**
David E. Biegel and Arthur Blum
111. **Societal Psychology**
Hilde T. Himmelweit and
George Gaskell
112. **Bilingual Education**
Amado M. Padilla, Halford H. Fairchild,
and Concepción M. Valadez
113. **Foreign Language Education**
Amado M. Padilla, Halford H. Fairchild,
and Concepción M. Valadez
114. **Teachers and Their Workplace**
Pedro Reyes
115. **Theories of Creativity**
Mark A. Runco and
Robert S. Albert
116. **Understanding Troubled and
Troubling Youth**
Peter E. Leone
117. **Preserving Families**
Ying-Ying T. Yuan and
Michele Rivest
118. **Fashioning Family Theory**
Jetse Sprey
119. **The Home Care Experience**
Jaber F. Gubrium and Andrea Sankar
120. **Black Aged**
Zev Harel, Edward A. McKinney,
and Michael Williams

BLACK
AGED

Understanding Diversity and Service Needs

Zev Harel
Edward A. McKinney
Michael Williams
editors

Published in cooperation with the
National Council on the Aging, Inc.

SAGE PUBLICATIONS
The International Professional Publishers
Newbury Park   London   New Delhi

For information address:

SAGE Publications, Inc.
2111 West Hillcrest Drive
Newbury Park, California 91320

SAGE Publications Ltd.
28 Banner Street
London EC1Y 8QE
England

SAGE Publications India Pvt. Ltd.
M-32 Market
Greater Kailash I
New Delhi 110 048 India

Printed in the United States of America

Library of Congress Cataloging-in-Publication Data

Black aged : understanding diversity and service needs / edited by Zev
   Harel, Edward A. McKinney, Michael Williams.
        p.   cm. — (Sage focus editions)
     Papers from the conference, Understanding and Serving the Black
   Aged, held in 1987 and sponsored primarily by the National Council
   on Aging and Cleveland State University in honor of Anna V. Brown.
     "Published in cooperation with the National Council on the Aging,
   Inc."
     Includes bibliographical references.
     ISBN 0-8039-3836-5. — ISBN 0-8039-3837-3 (pbk.)
     1. Afro-American aged—Services for—Congresses. 2. Brown, Anna
   V., d. 1985—Congresses;   I. Harel, Zev.   II. McKinney, Edward A.
   III. Williams, Michael, 1952-   . IV. National Council on the
   Aging.   V. Cleveland State University.   VI. Series.
   HQ1064.U5B387   1990
   305.26—dc20   90-33554
                                                                              CIP

FIRST PRINTING, 1990

Sage Production Editor: Susan McElroy

Anna V. Brown
This volume is dedicated to the memory of Anna V. Brown
and to the furtherance of her work.

Contents

Foreword
  LOUIS STOKES   9

Tribute to Anna V. Brown
  JACK OSSOFSKY   11

Preface   13

PART I: Understanding Diversity and Social Forces

Introduction
  EDWARD A. McKINNEY, ZEV HAREL,
  and MICHAEL WILLIAMS   19

  1. Diverse Black Aged
     E. PERCIL STANFORD   33

  2. Family Care, Economics, and Health
     WILBUR H. WATSON   50

  3. Health and Social Characteristics:
     Implications for Services
     HAROLD R. JOHNSON, ROSE C. GIBSON,
     and IRENE LUCKEY   69

4. Social Integration
   *LINDA M. CHATTERS and
   ROBERT JOSEPH TAYLOR*   82

5. Diversity Among Aged Black Males
   CARY S. KART   100

6. Understanding Diversity of the Urban Black Aged:
   Historical Perspectives
   SHARON E. MILLIGAN   114

PART II. Understanding Service Need and Use

Introduction
   *ZEV HAREL, EDWARD A. McKINNEY,
   and MICHAEL WILLIAMS*   131

7. African American Elderly Experiences with Title II:
   Program Assumptions and Economic Well-Being
   MICHAEL WILLIAMS   146

8. Targeting Benefits for the Black Elderly:
   The Older Americans Act
   JOHN H. SKINNER   165

9. Health Care Needs and Services
   WORNIE L. REED   183

10. The Health of the Black Aged Female
    MARY McKINNEY EDMONDS   205

11. Diversity in Black Family Caregiving
    CHARLES M. BARRESI and GEETA MENON   221

12. Clinical Social Work Practice with Black Elderly
    and Their Family Caregivers
    *CHERYL STEWART GERACE
    and LINDA S. NOELKER*   236

About the Authors   259

Foreword

We hear a lot today about how Americans are living longer than ever before, and how the quality of life for older Americans has significantly improved in the last two decades. This, however, is not the case for the Black aged population.

Recent studies have revealed some startling facts about the Black elderly. They are subject to poorer health, lower income, and a lower quality of housing than their White counterparts. They are three times as likely to be poor and are more likely to be sick and disabled.

In *Black Aged: Understanding Diversity and Service Needs*, the editors, Zev Harel, Ed McKinney, and Michael Williams give us the opportunity to look firsthand at the unique life-styles and circumstances of the Black elderly in the United States. While much of the literature on the Black aged has stressed the negative social forces that have an impact on this group, the chapter authors in this book highlight the rich diversity among the Black aged and illuminate the ways in which Black senior citizens demonstrate strength in the face of adversity. As the authors note, there is much that younger Blacks can learn from the strength of the Black aged in overcoming the effects of discrimination and poverty.

Moreover, this book is dedicated to a great pioneer in the field of aging, the late Anna V. Brown of Cleveland, Ohio. Ms. Brown was an inspiration to all who knew her, and, for her leadership role, she was respected not only in the Black community but in the White community as well. She was admired not just for her dedicated work in Cleveland but for her work in the state of Ohio and for her contributions to senior citizens nationwide, as President of the National Council on Aging and Vice President of the White House Conference on Aging.

This book is a fitting tribute to Anna V. Brown from the faculty at Cleveland State University, where she served as a frequent lecturer and often inspired students to seek careers in service of the aged.

The book represents an editing of presentations made at a conference held in Ms. Brown's honor and is an important addition to the body of scholarly work on the aged.

I congratulate the authors for such a noble and worthwhile effort and encourage all who are concerned about the problems of our Black senior citizens—the fastest-growing segment of our society—to read this important book.

—Louis Stokes
Member, U.S. Congress

Tribute to Anna V. Brown

Anna V. Brown, at the time of her death in 1985, was the President of the National Council on the Aging and its highest volunteer officer. She was also at that time Director of the Cleveland Department of Aging and a leader of many other local, state, and national organizations concerned with advancing quality services on behalf of older persons. Her training and broad experience, and especially her direct involvement with the aged, enabled her to gather information and data from a multitude of sources and apply it in her work. Anna Brown was also committed to sharing new intelligence with others to inform and motivate them to action. Applied gerontology was her field; service was her ideal; and progress, her goal. •

While she served all the aged, her interest in the Black aged reflected not only her own heritage but her concern for equity for those in the most vulnerable of circumstances and those society underserved. She was an advocate, and older Blacks, older women, and especially older Black women were the people on whose behalf she worked with special zeal.

These are the reasons for this volume in Anna's honor. It brings together the research and thinking of outstanding scholars, most of them Black, and points to new ways of understanding and serving the Black aged and, in many instances, all older persons.

Running through these pages is an understanding that, although the people reflected in the data have had many common experiences and lived similar long lives, their diversity and individuality call out for flexibility and a broad range of services, opportunities, and options. Most of all, it makes clear the special steps needed to be taken to assure that they benefit from existing programs as well as that new points of access and new modalities of service need to be established for them to be touched by the "aging network."

Anna contributed to growth of that network. She was a creative program developer and administrator. Her period of leadership spanned the early growth of the aging movement through the public spending constraints and cutbacks of the early 1980s. She was, however, a person of great enthusiasm and hope, who believed that this nation has the knowledge and resources to improve the quality of life of older people, to lift them from poverty, to assure health care, housing, and protection to those still untouched by the nation's programs. As she perceived the diminishing priority and resource allocations for the frail and poor, she called out for renewed commitment and reinvigorated response. "America," she said shortly before her death, "has placed a value on human life, on human dignity, on human decency—on older men and women—from which we will not retreat."

The conference, "Understanding and Serving the Black Aged," held in 1987, from which these chapters are drawn, carried forth Anna Brown's mission. It informed; it motivated; it advocated. The National Council on the Aging welcomed the opportunity to serve as a cosponsor. Now NCOA welcomes the opportunity to share the product of that event with a wider audience. The subject is not a new one for NCOA. Almost three decades ago, it worked with the National Urban League in the preparation and publication of *Double Jeopardy*, the landmark study of conditions facing Blacks as they grow older. During the intervening years, priority for the most needy and underserved among the old caused NCOA to give special attention in its programs and publications to the Black aged.

This publication is, however, more than a continuation of past efforts. It is a new step, taken jointly with the Cleveland State University and its Center on Applied Gerontological Research, to honor Anna Brown and to remind us anew of what remains to be done to advance her work and her cause, and to lift and empower the people described herein.

—Jack Ossofsky
Chief Executive Officer
National Council on the Aging, Inc.
1971-1987

Preface

This book has developed out of a collegeal relationship and a concern on the part of the authors for the well-being of all members of our society, including older Black Americans. The volume is significant for two major reasons. First, it addresses a topic of great scientific, professional, and general importance. Second, it is dedicated to the memory and legacy of a great pioneer in the field of applied gerontology, the late Anna V. Brown. The book is based on a conference and forum on the Black aged held at Cleveland State University.

Along with being a national pioneer, champion, and leader for various causes in the field of aging, Anna V. Brown was a friend and supporter of gerontology at Cleveland State University. It was fitting, therefore, for Cleveland State University to host a conference and forum on the Black aged in her honor. One of the major purposes of the event was to foster a better understanding on the CSU campus and in the community concerning the diversity and service needs of older Black Americans. After one year of planning, the conference became a reality on February 26-27, 1987.

There were three primary sponsors for the conference, and we wish to thank them for their institutional and financial support. First, the administration of Cleveland State University was both cooperative and generous in supporting the various activities of the conference. We are especially thankful to Dr. Georgia Lesh-Laurie, dean of the College of Arts and Sciences, for her consistent support. We are also thankful to Vice President Jeffrey Ford and Dr. Harry Andrist for their welcoming addresses and endorsement of the conference activities. Dan Meyer, director of conference services, was very diligent in overseeing all aspects of the planning and activities of the two-day event.

Second, thanks are due to the Cleveland Clinic Foundation, where Anna V. Brown served as a member of the Board of Trustees, for their interest in and generous support of the conference/forum. Special thanks are due to President (Chief Executive Officer) William S. Kaiser, M.D., and Vice President Shattuck W. Hartwell, Jr., M.D., and especially to Dr. Abraham Brickner, who, as member of the Conference Planning Committee, facilitated the financial support and helped with the planning and organization of the conference.

Thanks are also due to the Cleveland Foundation for its financial support of the conference/forum, and especially to Mr. Robert Eckardt for his attendance and contributions to the success of the conference.

During the planning and organization of this conference dedicated to older Black Americans, many national, state, and local organizations offered their sponsorship and assistance. Special thanks are due to Ms. Audrey Spencer, former director of Western Reserve Area Agency on Aging, and to Ms. Edwardina Riggans, Vice President of the Federation for Community Planning-Council on Older Persons. During the conference, students from the CSU Gerontological Studies Program volunteered to help with various tasks, thus ensuring that the conference would run smoothly. The goodwill and involvement of professionals, seniors, and students greatly helped to create friendship and respect for the legacy of Anna V. Brown.

This volume is the outgrowth of the presentations and exchanges that occurred at that conference and in its aftermath. Thanks are due to students of the Center on Applied Gerontological Research for assistance with the preparation of this book, Ms. Sharon Kryza, Ms. Giacoma Farhat, and Ms. Renee Wiltshire, and to Ms. Pam Milic of CSU Computer Services, for processing of the manuscript. All of them were dedicated to seeing that the work progressed and got done. A special acknowledgment is extended to Ms. Sarah Freeman, a student in gerontological studies, who assisted with the editing of the chapters and the completion of the manuscript.

We are greatly appreciative of the interest and support of Mr. Jack Ossofsky, then President of the National Council on the Aging, for his contribution at the conference and for arranging the publication of this book by the National Council on the Aging. Our thanks also to Mr. William Oriol, Director of Communication, and Ms. Louise Cleveland, Senior Editor at the National Council on the Aging, for their editing and preparation for print of this manuscript.

Finally, we thank all of the authors who contributed to the chapters in this book. Our goal to prepare a state-of-the-art book on understanding the diversity and service needs of older Black Americans was achieved by the interest and dedication to the topic of the authors. We hope that this book will further stimulate refinement of knowledge and more effective service planning to assure a safe, secure, and dignified existence for all older Americans, including the Black aged.

—Zev Harel
Edward A. McKinney
Michael Williams

PART I

Understanding Diversity
and Social Forces

Introduction

EDWARD A. McKINNEY
ZEV HAREL
MICHAEL WILLIAMS

The six chapters in Part I constitute an unprecedented coordinated effort to provide conceptual frameworks and extensive data for a better understanding of the Black elderly and the Black community. The chapters highlight the unique historical and collective experiences, as well as cultural values and symbols, of the current cohort of elderly Black Americans. This part of the book also provides critical dimensions and extensive data for understanding the diversity that characterizes the Black elderly and the social forces and resources found in the Black community. As such, these chapters break new ground. They remind us that if the growing number of Black elderly Americans are to participate as fully in our society and in their individual communities as they should, they must be regarded as members of a group with distinct cultural traditions, a group whose help-seeking behaviors have been shaped by history.

A better understanding of both the uniqueness of the Black aged and the diversity among them should be of considerable importance in shaping public and social policy meant to serve this significant segment of our older population. One way to improve such an understanding is to increase awareness of how Black aged individuals perceive problems and difficulties that have affected them during the course of their lives. Of equal interest are problem-solving strategies that have been used most effectively in the past as well as those used in the present to deal with such adverse experiences.

The lead chapter, by E. Percil Stanford, offers critical conceptual perspectives on the uniqueness of Black aged persons as a group and, at the same time, provides an analytical approach for understanding their diversity. Chapter 2, by Wilbur H. Watson, reviews empirical evidence on family care, personal economics, and health among Black Americans. It also suggests directions for economic and health care policies. In Chapter 3, Harold R. Johnson, Rose C. Gibson, and Irene Luckey offer additional empirical evidence about health and social characteristics of the Black aged, suggesting needed policy changes in the areas of income security and health care.

In Chapter 4, Linda M. Chatters and Robert Joseph Taylor provide data on the social integration of the Black aged, and in the fifth chapter Cary S. Kart documents diversity among older Black males. The sixth and final chapter is by Sharon E. Milligan, who draws from a rich store of oral history narratives to describe the experiences of Black migrants to a midwestern urban community. This chapter provides keen insights into a great social change that has concrete consequences today.

Overcoming Prior Biases

A goal of this book, as well as the goal of the conference on which it is based, is to provide a fresh view, free from research and professional biases that affect not only members of minority groups but all of the older population. Until fairly recent times, researchers, policymakers, and human service professionals have tended to regard the elderly from a monolithic viewpoint. By so doing, they ignored the distinctiveness and/or uniqueness of the life experiences of groups such as the Black elderly. Furthermore, researchers have been inclined to study differences between two or more groups, ignoring intragroup diversity. Even when researchers have focused on the Black elderly as a group, males have been frequently ignored.

In the past, much of the research on aging has been based on studies of White middle-class subjects, from whom generalizations were made. For this reason, limited data and information have been available on differing cultural patterns and life-styles of ethnically diverse aged groups. In particular, there has been limited understanding not only of how ethnic group status affects the aging process, but of how culture influences a person's perception of need and help-seeking behaviors.

One of the most serious problems with past research has been the array of conceptual approaches that have failed to take into account the diversity of various ethnic populations, such as Black Americans. Only in recent years have researchers come to realize that culture and social class are not synonymous because of a mere sharing of group membership (Green, 1982, p. 7). In formulating policies, and in the planning and delivery of services to the Black elderly, cultural diversity *must* be taken into consideration. Unfortunately, too many studies of Black Americans generally, and especially studies of Black aged, have failed to recognize not only ethnic diversity, but also minority status. The term *minority status*, for the purpose of its use here, implies diminished power—the degree to which individuals who are identified with some group may be denied access to privileges and opportunities available to others (Green, 1982, p. 7). Bias has been built into studies, in that *situational factors* (such as poor housing, low income, overcrowding, and negative help-seeking behaviors) often brought on by years of discrimination and/or racism have been viewed as culturally acceptable on the part of the Black aged. Therefore, many factors identified as cultural may be no more than what could best be described as situational adaptation, or the consequences of years of exclusion and discrimination.

The chapters in Part I address such problems. They offer directions for a better understanding of the effects of unique historical experiences and shared collective experiences at the present time on current adjustment and well-being. They also offer directions for observation, analysis, and discussion of the diversity that characterizes Black aged in personal, social, and economic well-being. A better understanding of both uniqueness and diversity in the Black aged will help efforts to develop more effective policies and programs. These chapters also further our understanding of how problems are perceived by various members of this group, and what problem-solving strategies are currently being used and have been used most effectively in the past in resolving those problems.

The Meanings of Diversity

Stanford states in Chapter 1, "Collectively, Black older persons should be viewed from the perspective of their own history, without having to suffer the indignity of being compared with those older persons who have, for the most part, had entirely different social, political, and economic experiences." Kart, the author of Chapter 5, reinforces Stanford's perspective: "Recognition of the diversity within the population should lead us away from the comparison . . . and toward a sharper focus on minority aging itself." This is most important if we are to understand the behaviors and actions of the Black elderly and, more specifically, how Black elderly people perceive their problems and solutions within a service delivery context. Help-seeking initiatives of the Black elderly, after all, have been greatly influenced by their past experiences with public and private institutions, and these experiences have been different from those of other groups.

Stanford identifies what he describes as a relatively new phenomenon among Black Americans: a long-range trend toward increased life expectancy. Although they may not be in the very best of health, as discussed in other chapters, Blacks are living longer. The overall improvement in the quality of life, including increased access to health care and improved nutrition, contributes to this new phenomenon among elderly Black Americans. It is suggested by Stanford that we need to rethink many issues resulting from this change, especially how to involve this population in a productive way.

Today's Black elderly, using age 65 as a benchmark, were born prior to the Depression and at the peak of the great South-to-North migration. They are the grandchildren of former slaves, and have been scarred by a history of discrimination, racism, and surviving in hostile environments for the greater part of their lives. So this population brings a very rich heritage of survival knowledge and skills that could prove to be quite useful for the understanding of difficulties experienced by other elderly Americans. The current and future cohorts of Black elderly citizens are well represented by those who have been in the forefront of the battle for equality. They can be great allies as coalitions are formed, for example, in the battle for comprehensive health services, increased and improved housing, and refinements in income maintenance programs for the elderly. Those involved in community organizing with elderly groups cannot ignore this wealth of knowledge, skills, and experience.

As Stanford points out, we can anticipate that the growing number of Black elderly Americans will become an essential and productive part of their communities. Therefore, they should not be seen just as members of the growing elderly population, but as members of a group whose distinct cultural traditions and problem-solving strategies—as well as their help-seeking behaviors—have been shaped by history.

Stanford strongly suggests that the current focus on the diversity in the Black aged should not be viewed in negative terms. There has been a tendency for scholars "to equate diversity with negative action and meaning." Diversity in regard to elderly Black Americans should be viewed from a positive perspective. Because of their unique history in this country, the Black elderly bring a cultural richness and problem-solving skills that cannot be claimed by members of any other group in our society. Cultural diversity and cultural pluralism have contributed to the overall richness of American life; therefore, we should be accepting of diversity as a positive force rather than a negative one.

A major focus in this country in recent years, especially during the Reagan administration, has been on the development of self-help skills. More and more people through small and large organizations have banded together to develop projects that will improve their overall quality of life. An important factor contributing to this movement has been the budget cuts in funding of human services. The reduction of government support for families in their day-to-day struggle to survive has necessitated greater reliance on self-help and mutual help.

Self-help is not new to many of the Black elderly. They have a history of a lack of resources for day-to-day survival. Therefore, Blacks as young adults and as older persons have had to create adaptive measures that would allow them to cope with needs for food, shelter, and clothing. The abilities to adapt, to develop strategies for survival, and to be resilient in a hostile environment have been ingrained in the elderly Black experience in America.

Historically, researchers may have prevented us from seeing the richness the Black elderly bring to the American culture because, as Stanford states, "essentially the Black older person has been viewed in juxtaposition to other older persons and has had the unfortunate circumstance of always being compared in unrealistic terms." From this perspective, the Black elderly have always been viewed from a deficit position in society. The primary focus has been on the weaknesses, rather than the strengths, they possess. For this reason, Stanford offers another conceptual framework for viewing elderly Black Americans: diverse life patterns. This approach allows researchers and scholars to view the Black elderly without comparing them with other elderly groups or trying to "justify whether their circumstances are better or worse than those of the majority elderly population." The diverse life pattern approach highlights the distinctiveness of the Black elderly experience in America. From this perspective we can begin to recognize the positive aspects of the Black experience, including a unique world-view and problem-solving strategies. We can gain greater insights into how elderly Black Americans have coped with and survived exclusionary practices and still contributed significantly to the overall American culture.

Economic Realities and Social Forces

Watson begins his chapter, "Family Care, Economics, and Health," with a discussion of projected demographic changes. He asserts that the population of persons 60 and older will double by the year 2025 and will represent approximately a third of the voting population in this country. He also indicates that the minority elderly population is projected to triple between now and 2025. This means that by the year 2025, the elderly population, including the Black aged, will have significant influence on a variety of public policy issues, much more than they have at the present time.

In his section on caretaking behavior in the Black family, Watson highlights a historical tradition in the Black family, where the expectation is for relatives as well as other members of the community to share in the responsibility of caring for the elderly who, due to a variety of disabling conditions, can no longer care for themselves. This supportive tradition, says Watson, has developed because of a unique culture and kinship pattern that has existed in the Black community for years. He refers to these patterns of kinship and loyalty as major strengths in the Black community that came about as a result of many years of discriminatory practices toward Blacks by White America. Because of these negative practices, "Black families had to rely more on themselves than on public agencies for support and assistance in times of trouble and illness." Consequently, there are strong expectations by the Black elderly that they will be cared for in the home by family rather than by public institutions. What this tells us is that the Black elderly have had little or no expectation that their needs would be provided for by public institutions.

Although discriminatory practices have excluded Blacks from public institutions in the past, Watson sees the enactment of the civil rights laws of 1963 and 1964, as well as the Supreme Court decisions of 1954 and 1955, as opening up public and private institutions for meeting the needs of the Black elderly. Without a doubt, these major decisions have had an impact on the service needs of the Black elderly. Also, the enactment of Medicare and Medicaid laws has helped to break down financial barriers for the Black elderly. It is anticipated that future cohorts of Black elderly will be less dependent on church, family, and other informal networks, as public and private institutions become more responsive to their needs. But we can also anticipate that these informal networks will continue to play a major role in the lives of the Black elderly.

Watson identifies a number of responsibilities held by Black families when an older person in the family becomes ill. He concludes that the family rather than the church has been the primary source of support in time of illness. However, the church also plays important roles, for example, by collecting money for the elderly infirm, and by friendly visiting and prayer services. Families have turned to physicians, or have taken ill members to hospitals, at times of illness, rather than turning to the church, but this should not be surprising, since the Black church has never identified itself as a health institution, and there is no research indicating that it is perceived as such.

Watson highlights the economic conditions of older Blacks and concludes that poverty remains a major problem for the Black elderly. He underscores the fact that women, especially Black women, are disproportionately represented among the poor. He cautions, however, about the use of the concept, "feminization of poverty," which has been used in the past in the context of "blaming the victim." Watson sees the concept as "a misnomer of a complex phenomenon and the multiple factors that help to explain membership of women among the poor. . . . It falsely suggests that there is something about the nature of women and/or femininity that explains the growing incidence of poverty among them." He asserts that there is a need to identify societal inequities and the nature of societal structures that oppress women, therefore denying them the necessary access to critical institutions for their overall growth and development, educationally as well as vocationally, resulting in their economic disadvantage.

In his chapter's section on health and health care of older Blacks, Watson focuses on the "crossover" phenomenon, which is a reversal in differential life expectancy occurring between Blacks and Whites after 70 to 75 years of age. Elderly Blacks, male and female, have shorter life expectancies than the White elderly up to approximately 60 to 65 years of age, but a reversal in this pattern takes place after 70 years of age, a reversal that has not been fully explained in the past by gerontological research. Watson offers a number of hypotheses for further study. Another health problem highlighted is bone loss among the Black elderly. Bone loss increases not only the risk of accidents due to musculoskeletal weaknesses, but the risk of death as well.

Watson asserts that, along with rapid growth in the population of older persons, including the Black elderly, there is an increasing risk of health- and life-threatening illnesses, and that poverty still poses a major threat to survival. He underscores the fact that families continue to be a major or primary source of support for older Black persons. He raises questions about the impact that major court decisions will have on the caretaking behavior of elderly Black Americans. He concludes his chapter by calling for social policies that will establish more preventive geriatric care, as well as for the enactment of a national health care system as part of a comprehensive health care package.

Economic Security of
the "Unretired-Retired"

In Chapter 3, Johnson, Gibson, and Luckey point out that, although Black elderly people are living longer, they "are more likely to be infirm, to die earlier, to have chronic diseases at earlier ages, and to be more physically limited by these illnesses." Therefore, one can expect this group to be less employable in the later stages of life, and to have a greater need for in-home types of social services.

One crucial highlight of this chapter is the authors' focus on a category of Black elderly they identify as "unretired-retired." According to Johnson et al., "Nearly 40% of nonworking Blacks aged 55 and over can be categorized as 'unretired-retired,' individuals who appear and behave as if they were retired, but do not call themselves retired." This is a crucial point because this group is excluded from retirement research and retirement planning, which are limited to those formally retired. Due to declining physical limitations and labor market and employment policies, this particular group gradually withdraws from the labor force. As a result, their needs are not identified or planned for within the framework of social welfare policy. The authors suggest that if this trend continues there may be some serious policy implications in the future. Should these individuals be entitled to benefits as a result of their preretirement due to physical impairments? This is a major area of concern for policy research as this population grows.

Johnson et al. make a very strong case for needed new and innovative social welfare policies that would enhance the overall health status of elderly Black Americans, as well as policies to increase their income supports.

Dynamics of Informal Networks

In Chapter 4, Chatters and Taylor focus on the social integration of older Black adults within the context of family, friends, and church. In Chapter 1, Stanford raises some issues about the survival skills of elderly Black Americans. How, considering the circumstances of exclusion, discriminatory practices, racism, and a very hostile environment, could this group survive? And why did it not only survive, but make a significant contribution to the growth of the American society? Chatters and Taylor provide some answers to these questions in their discussion of the social integration of the Black aged.

First, Chatters and Taylor remind us that due to historical discriminatory or exclusionary practices, the Black elderly have not had the option to rely on traditional social institutions, but have had to turn in times of need to family members, friends, and the Black church. This fact alone may very well help us to understand the help-seeking behavior of elderly Black Americans. Being well integrated within the fabric of these informal networks—the family system, friends, and the church—provided "the opportunity to both give and receive assistance." The authors point out that these informal networks have historically provided material as well as psychosocial supports. The Black elderly became very dependent on these informal social networks, but, at the same time, these networks played a major role in their development. Thus it is very important to understand the dynamics of these networks if one is to understand elderly Black Americans.

Being excluded from formal social institutions, including social services, Black Americans, say Chatters and Taylor, developed parallel institutions. These institutions have included burial societies, insurance companies, and social organizations designed to meet Black Americans' social and psychological needs. Black Americans pioneered the development of prepaid systems that would provide death benefits and meet needs in times of sickness as well as for day-to-day survival. In addition to the family and the church, these institutions became of primary importance.

There has been one major criticism of parallel institutions, according to Chatters and Taylor: "Unfortunately, it fosters the view that Black institutions are mere imitations of their counterparts in wider society. As such, Black institutions frequently have been characterized as, at best, inferior substitutes or caricatures of White institutions and, at worst, dysfunctional organizations that effectively impede the development of Black individuals and communities." Therein lies one of the major problems addressed in this book: the need to look at the Black elderly as members of a unique and distinct culture. It is critical to understand the historical circumstances under which these parallel institutions developed in the first place. If one looks at this development in the history of Black Americans by using, say, Stanford's diverse life patterns approach, one comes away with a positive appreciation for the insights and creative genius of Black Americans rather than the negative views implied in the above observation. What may be seen in this development is that when a group was excluded from the mainstream of life's opportunities, as in the case of Black Americans, they did not commit group suicide, but put their creative capacities together for survival. As social institutions become more and more accessible to Blacks, it is possible that they will become less dependent on parallel institutions. But until the arrival of such times, Black institutions will continue to be important in the lives of elderly Black Americans.

The discussion of parallel institutions may be of help in furthering understanding of some of the help-seeking behaviors of elderly Black Americans. This cohort of Black Americans was systematically excluded from traditional social institutions, and therefore became dependent on parallel institutions and informal networks. Although civil rights legislation passed in recent years guarantees them access to all forms of institutions, such as nursing homes and other social services, there may still be a lack of trust and assumptions that these institutions will not be responsive to their needs.

Chatters and Taylor clearly point out the significant role played by the church, family, and friends in the lives of older Black Americans. The church is seen as a kind of extended family. Not only has the church provided for spiritual needs, but it has historically provided an environment for leadership development, as well as for the meeting of social and emotional needs. Not only have the church and family provided a support network for the Black elderly, but unrelated individuals have been a major resource of support as well.

This chapter concludes by raising questions about future cohorts of Black elderly Americans. Can one expect the same level of support for the Black elderly from parallel institutions as from the informal networks? Can the Black elderly count on the more traditional institutions in our society to become more responsive to their needs? It may be suggested that parallel institutions and informal networks, which historically have been a major source of support for the Black elderly, will continue to be important for some time to come. It is anticipated, however, that the Black elderly will become less and less dependent on such arrangements as the more traditional institutions in our society become more and more responsive to their needs.

Elderly Black Males

In Chapter 5, Kart focuses on the diversity among Black aged males. This chapter is a welcome addition because, as Kart states, historically, "research literature on aging has generally focused upon the total Black population or upon Black women only; older Black males represent a relatively invisible minority within a minority." Ralph Ellison's *The Invisible Man* was appropriately titled as it relates to the real history of the Black male.

Historically, the Black male has been treated from a deficit perspective; researchers remind us constantly about the number of Black males who desert their families, who commit crimes or are serving time in penal institutions, or who are on public assistance or unemployed. As Kart points out, 60% of elderly Black males 65 and over are married and living with their spouses, a statistic rarely emphasized in published research or the media.

When we take a look at a profile of elderly Black men, a very diverse group emerges. As Kart states, "Some are young-old, others old-old; some work, others are retired; some are college graduates, others through no fault of their own had little formal schooling; some are well-to-do, others impoverished; some are married, others widowed and divorced; some maintain strong family ties, others do not; some are active participants in church activities, others are not."

Without any intent to compare, it may be pointed out that the Black male in American society has been the most victimized group in history.

The history books are full of accounts of lynchings, oppression, racism, and other forms of torture. Yet, many Black men have overcome these obstacles to become world leaders in science, politics, business, the arts, religion, and world peace. Kart calls our attention to the fact that this is not a monolithic group, but a diverse group with many strengths as well as weaknesses.

Insights from Oral Histories

Major insights can be drawn from Milligan's chapter on the historical perspectives of the understanding of diversity among the urban Black aged. The focus of this chapter is on the oral histories of elderly Black men and women residing in Cleveland, Ohio. An interesting feature is the sharing of experiences by elderly Black Americans who were part of one of the most significant movements in the history of the country: the great migration of Blacks from the South to the North between 1910 and 1920.

A crucial element in this chapter is not just the factual account of what happened, but the feelings behind the facts that are laid out by these elderly citizens of Cleveland. This aspect adds a different dimension to the research findings. What the chapter points out is that Blacks left the South in order to find better lives for themselves and their families in the North. It was their objective to leave behind lives made difficult by discriminatory practices, segregation, and a hostile environment. What they discovered in the North, however, was a form of racism in some ways similar to that in the South and in other ways quite different. As one listens to the narratives of this group, one realizes that the racism in the North was more subtle than they had experienced in the South, but it was very much present. Although the environment was not as hostile, and acts toward them not as overt, they still faced restrictions in housing, jobs, and education.

Milligan points out the social network that developed among the Blacks who came North. One person told her: "All my family came up, lot of my friends, lot of people I knew at the time." Networks formed among those who came from the same communities or the same towns. The circumstances they faced on arrival no doubt played a major role in their decision to form a variety of social networks. It is quite possible that some of the social networks that had been formed in the South, including fraternal and social organizations, were transplanted to the North. This was especially true of formal religious organizations.

For many of these early arrivals to northern cities, a steady job with a regular income was something new. Many had decent homes with running water for the first time, and the narrators in this chapter speak with pride about how sparkling clean these dwellings were kept. Although facing a different kind of racism—less overt, more subtle, than in the South—they took pride in the fact that this was a new beginning, somewhat different from the life left behind.

The narratives shared in this chapter also reinforce findings from more traditional research on the impact of the church in the lives of Black Americans. The church fulfilled not only the spiritual needs of these people, but their social and psychological needs as well.

On reading these narratives of elderly Black citizens, one has to be touched, especially by the woman who spoke about how she came to grips with her identity as a Black person while attending Wilberforce, an all-Black university. One comes away from this chapter with a better understanding of why the Black elderly up to this point in history developed such dependence on parallel institutions, the church, family, and friends for their day-to-day survival.

Toward a Better Understanding

The chapters that make up Part I of this volume contribute valuable insights for the understanding of diversity, resiliency, ways of deriving strength from adversity, social forces, and social resources, as well as disadvantage and needs among older Black aged. This part of the book offers new and needed conceptual frameworks that do not compare the Black elderly with other groups, but allow researchers, scholars, and others to see this group within its own historical and cultural experiences in American society. The chapters also highlight the diversity and social forces in the older Black population.

These chapters identify the strengths that generations of older Blacks gained through many years of encounters with institutional and individual racism. What is so important to underscore is how they derived strength from these negative experiences and carved out meaningful lives for themselves and for those who followed.

Solid empirical evidence on the social integration of the Black elderly within the context of family, friends, and the church provides valuable insights on how important informal support and parallel institutions have been in the lives of the Black elderly.

There is clear indication in the chapters of this book of the need for new social policy initiatives, especially for adequate income and health care policies. There is clear indication of the need to develop a comprehensive health care system, including national health insurance, to meet the health care needs of a growing aging population and to remove the financial barriers faced by elderly Black Americans in their struggle to gain access to health care. New income maintenance policies are also needed that will improve the incomes of elderly Black men and women living in single households. There is also a need for new policy initiatives for special population groups that have "fallen between the cracks," such as the "unretired-retired" and others who face extreme economic, health, and social hardships.

This book also highlights the importance of different research methodologies in the study of aging. Black elderly citizens who shared their experiences in the oral history project provide valuable insights about their reasons for leaving the South and the circumstances they encountered on their arrival in the "Promised Land." They also offer critical appraisals of the economic, educational, social, and residential hardships they had to face and overcome in their quest to establish themselves in their new environment.

Reference

Green, J. 1982. *Cultural Awareness in the Human Services.* Englewood Cliffs, NJ: Prentice-Hall.

1

Diverse Black Aged

E. PERCIL STANFORD

This chapter includes ideas and perspectives that have resulted from observations, listening, and living the Black experience. This chapter will highlight the following areas: (1) the historical experiences that have had a major impact on shaping the uniqueness of the Black elder, (2) the concept of diversity and related terms and the significance of understanding the proper utilization of this concept as applied to the Black elder, (3) the concept of diverse life patterns as a framework for better delineating the positive aspects of Black elders, (4) policy and social action areas that need amelioration if better equity for Black elders is to become a reality, and (5) social action measures and advocacy techniques that will facilitate the involvement of Black elders in acting more appropriately in their own behalf.

Increased life expectancy is a relatively new phenomenon for Black people in the United States. The increase in the number of Black older persons has brought about the need to rethink many issues related to the social, mental, economic, and health status of Black elderly. The increasing number of Black elderly makes it necessary to reconsider their inclusion and involvement in a productive way. Black elderly, to a great extent, have not been expected to be in good health or to be capable of being a productive part of the community as they reach the upper stages of life.

AUTHOR'S NOTE: This chapter was originally presented as a paper at "Understanding and Serving Black Aged: A Community Conference and Forum," sponsored by Cleveland State University and the Cleveland Clinic Foundation and cofunded by the Cleveland Foundation, Cleveland State University, Cleveland, Ohio, February 26-27, 1987.

As the older population, including Blacks, continues to live longer and to remain in relatively good health, it is expected that elderly people will be a more essential part of the community. Many older Blacks are finding that they are capable of being and have the opportunity to be productive in their environments in ways not previously experienced. Many of these changes resulted from the civil rights activities of the 1960s and 1970s. Because of these initiatives, today's Black elderly represent the first wave of Black older persons to be visible in the modern advocacy arena. Neither the society at large nor the Black community is accustomed to having this particular segment of the Black society involved as a meaningful and contributing catalyst for social change.

Prior to the civil rights amendments of the 1960s and 1970s, older persons in the Black community functioned, in large part, as gatekeepers of the culture that had been etched out by Blacks during the past century or more. It was not until the 1980s that older Blacks as a group were identified as persons who were taking responsibility for social and political changes that would have an impact on their lives. The current cohort of Black elderly have a tremendous sense of responsibility, but simultaneously they have exhibited a feeling of helplessness. This helplessness once felt by today's emerging cadre of Black elderly is now being removed temporarily by a feeling of political potency and support from other Blacks throughout society.

Recent legislation in the courts throughout the United States, including the Supreme Court, has made it possible for elder Blacks to express opinions they have held privately in previous decades but have not been willing to divulge publicly. For example, many Blacks since Reconstruction days have wanted to be much more involved in the political process, but have been denied the privilege. Since the passage of legislation in 1965 to enforce voting laws, there has been much more political involvement on the part of older Blacks than in any other period in our history. Another area that has received considerable attention is that of education. It was not until 1954, when the "separate but equal" doctrine was ruled unconstitutional, that Blacks were granted the right to an equal opportunity for education.

In short, the Black older adult of the 1960s and 1970s is very much a part of the "slave culture" that set the stage for the status of Blacks in our society during the nineteenth and thus far the twentieth century. Much has been written about the Black family in America. Very few scholars or casual observers stop to consider the fact that the Black person in America was originally prohibited from having a family in a formal sense. The "family" structure that emerged in the slave culture was constantly torn apart in a systematic and brutal fashion. Suffice it to say that the impact of the systematic deterrence of family life for Blacks had a profound impact on those persons who were and continue to be the older Blacks of the 1960s, 1970s, 1980s, and now 1990s. Realistically, we are dealing with older persons who are the grandchildren and great-grandchildren of former slaves. The distance between the reality of that cultural experience and that with which one is faced in today's world is not exceptionally great.

It matters little that our legal system formally substantiates that there are specific rights and responsibilities that have been accrued to Black individuals. The underlying social stigma perpetrated over the years is not easy to erase. Although many older Blacks fully understand that they can now exercise their rights within the law, they continue to doubt the sincerity of those in control of our economic and political systems. The assumption that older Blacks mistrust only non-Blacks must be carefully considered. There is some evidence that some Blacks are somewhat skeptical of anyone in a "power" position.

More recent avenues for involvement and the increased life expectancy of the Black elderly do not erase the historical experiences of the Black older person. History has helped shape the profile of today's old and very old Black person. Social and political forces have not served to eradicate the diverse nature of the older Black. There are multiple historical markers that have ensured that the Black elderly are different from other ethnic and racial cohorts. The differences have a very broad range; they go further than the pure racial aspects, from an anthropological perspective. Diverse Black older persons have been forced to cope in a society that has basically rejected them as free-thinking and participating human beings. They have been socially and politically imprisoned for the greater part of their lives. In recent years, they have been given the go-ahead to become more "responsible citizens" in a variety of areas, and many have accepted the challenge by expressing their political, social, and educational desires and preferences. At the same time, others have chosen to maintain the status quo.

Diversity should not carry a negative connotation. The tendency for many scholars has been to equate diversity with negative actions and meanings. Black elderly may be different in many ways, but they have a richness to offer that cannot be claimed by any other group of older persons. Their experiences stem from a life that has been culturally bound in ways that no other group of older persons can express or have experienced. Older Blacks of today bring a legacy that embodies the will to survive in a society that historically denied the Black person full human status. Much of the diverse nature of the Black elderly has stemmed from the cultural experiences that have structured the lifestyles of Blacks since the early stages of the development of our society.

The older Black in the United States is the product of an underclass citizenship. Most elderly Black people have not had the privilege of fully participating in decisions that shape their lives. They have had little or no opportunity to experience economic involvement that would afford meaningful participation in the marketplace. Due to restrictions related to travel, living environments, and employment, the majority of older Blacks have not been equal partners with others in shaping the environment in which they now find themselves. The lack of equitable exposure to and participation in the aforementioned areas makes it virtually impossible for them to have a qualitative impact on their environments.

From a positive perspective, Black elderly of today have the opportunity to use their life experiences to bolster the quality of life for all older persons. It is obvious that many older Black people have managed to live through extremely adverse situations and still carry on productive lives in their own environments. It has been said that age is a "leveler." This essentially means that as people age there is a tendency for the social, physical, and economic dimensions of their lives to become more similar, regardless of ethnicity and race.

Older Blacks have been major contributors to our society regardless of their diverse backgrounds and experiences. The richness of the Black culture as portrayed through literature, music, religion, and science substantiates the fact that imposed barriers have not prevented the growth and development of this segment of our population.

It is important to focus on the positive aspects of the diversity of the Black aged population. Considerable attention has been given to the negatives, which, for general purposes, have not been the handiwork of the Black aged themselves. The imposed restrictions have served to strengthen a group of people beyond what anyone imagined.

Social history has a long memory. The perpetrators of laws and norms that have restricted the growth, development, and meaningful involvement of the Black population over the years are not dead. The thoughts, philosophies, and deeds of many designers of our society with regard to the "place of the Black person" continue to be fostered. It is the positive diverse characteristics that will continue to play a major role in the strengthening of the position of the Black population and particularly the Black elderly in our society.

The spotlight has focused on the real or imagined melting-pot society. Indicators are that the depth of the diversity in our culture will force the light to shine on the richness of various entities of our culturally, socially, and ethnically pluralistic society rather than attempting to broaden the spectrum to view everyone in the same manner.

Social Significance:
Older Black Experiences

Older Blacks as social beings in our society continue, to a great extent, to live in social isolation. The ideal of our society becoming a melting pot of individuals of a variety of racial, ethnic, religious, and philosophical backgrounds has not materialized. As we move into the late twentieth century, the world has become a much smaller place; however, many decades will pass before the people of the world accept one another's modes of life and radically modify their own. Much of the literature points out that older people, regardless of racial background, are very steeped in their particular cultures and traditions.

From my own perspective, older Blacks are somewhat unique in that they have not had the benefit of carrying forward and fostering culturally specific artifacts, signs, and symbols that truly represent their uniqueness. Signs, symbols, language, and religion attributed to the current Black population and carried forward by older Blacks are an amalgam of what has been passed on or forced upon the Black society by majority cultures that have shaped our country politically and socially.

The original founders of the United States took the position that there was no reason to entertain the idea of using any of the "primitive" ways of the Negroes who were being transported to this country. In retrospect, there were some skills and attributes that could have been transferred to this society that were completely overlooked and denied. We fully understand the underlying purpose for denying Blacks the opportunity to continue to use the languages, religions, and basic traditions that represented their cultural backgrounds. To make Black slaves subservient, it was necessary to remove all the attributes that would have enabled them to sustain their familiar life-styles.

In spite of the indignities endured by older Blacks, many have been able to adapt with a high degree of effectiveness. For example, there are notable exceptions of individuals who have been able to obtain an advanced education in spite of the barriers. In most instances, the process of becoming literate was accomplished without the formal support of any social structure. Some received an education only because someone took an interest in their well-being. Others were able to get an education because they were able to pass for White or to otherwise break down prohibitive and restrictive barriers.

Black elderly have experienced a unique place in society not only by exclusion, but also by having to determine ways in which a satisfactory life-style could be developed to compete with the majority society in areas where skill, experience, resources, and sanctions were lacking. A good example of this type of deficiency is in the economic area. Few if any older Blacks had support for initiating businesses that would be able to compete in any way with other businesses in their communities. There are some Blacks who have been able to start small, family-type businesses, but the number who have been able to develop large, successful businesses is small.

Due to the many drawbacks of not being able to compete on an equitable level, Blacks as young adults and therefore as older persons have had to devise adaptive procedures to allow them at least a semblance of parity. They fully realize that there was no actual parity involved. These adaptive procedures have allowed older Blacks and others in the community to survive at a minimal level. Again, education as historically organized in the United States for Blacks is a good example. Another example is the manner in which Blacks have established a variety of social support organizations, fraternities, and sororities. This type of adaptive behavior can also be seen in religion, in that parallel or separate religious systems have developed to accommodate the religious preferences and styles of Black individuals.

Barbara Solomon (1974) has observed that our society is made up of smaller groups or collectives of individuals whose ethnicity serves to define them and their relationship to the larger society. She has pointed out that much of our behavioral science research and the literature emanating from this research have not acknowledged the characteristics of our social structure. Moreover, the literature has described the basic social process as derived from a single ethnic perspective—the Anglo perspective—in regard to social, cultural, and historical reality. Many minority groups have survived in the social system, but they have often been forced into an alienated, and sometimes separate, existence.

Scholars and laypersons alike have spent considerable time addressing the meanings of the terms *race, ethnicity,* and *minority status.* Each refers to a classification of individuals in our society. In turn, each has connotations that sometimes go unexplained and that are beset with negativism. There is no harm in identifying or designating members of a society according to physical or biological characteristics; the danger is in having these identifying symbols serve as detractors from what the individual may contribute to the society from a qualitative perspective.

There are numerous issues that warrant discussion and delineation in the effort to understand the ethnic and racial elements that stymie progress in bringing groups of Blacks together for meaningful causes. This discussion will point out some of the poignant issues that must be examined if we are to gain a reasonable perspective on the important contributions that have been and will be made by the Black elderly. Older persons in our society have made major contributions toward closing the gap in interpersonal relationships among various groups. Meaningful relationships have emerged, not so much because of individual interest or curiosity about each other, but because of the need to come together in mutual support efforts. Older adult programs established during the past 10 to 15 years have directly and indirectly contributed to the interaction of ethnic individuals far beyond the imagination of political leaders and social planners.

To provide a perspective for much of the discussion that follows, it is essential to delineate what is meant by *ethnicity* and related terms (Davis, 1981). The term *ethnicity* carries the connotation that a group is defined or set off by race, religion, national origin, or some combination of these categories—yet these do not mean the same thing. *Race* technically refers to differential concentrations of gene frequencies responsible for traits that seem to be confined to physical manifestations such as skin color or hair form. There is no intimate connection between race and cultural patterns and institutions. *Religion* and *national origin* are distinctly different institutions that do not necessarily vary in like manner. These categories have a common social psychological referent in that they all serve to create through historical circumstances a sense of cohesiveness for groups within this country. The object is to acknowledge the common social psychological core categories of race, religion, and national origin. The term *ethnic group* is useful for observing these elements and is a semantic convention for describing individuals. As used here, *ethnic group* refers to a group of persons who have common racial and cultural backgrounds and are people of color (Gordon, 1978).

Even though the older population had been recognized as the newest and fastest proliferating group in our society, Donald Kent (1971) was one of the first sociologists/gerontologists to bring forcefully to our attention the need to consider cultural diversity among older people. Previously, there was little attention given to the vast differences among the persons in that group. Kent has forced us to recognize and appropriately consider cultural variations among the aged. Age designations do not provide information regarding how people have evolved or who they are based on cultural traditions and experiences. Kent also indicates that we should keep in mind that not all differences are the result of dissimilar cultural backgrounds; further, our society, more than most, differentially rewards groups and individuals. Most significant is the fact that cultural dissimilarities among groups may have been dictated by their positions in society.

As we move into the 1990s, there is a conscious effort to meet the social, psychological, and material needs of Black older persons. It is essential to acknowledge the increasing importance of older Blacks in our society.

Diversity: An Understanding

Gerontologists who are proponents of ethnic minority gerontology continue to struggle with the notion that ethnic minority older people are fully worthy of consideration from three perspectives: social, political, and economic. Protagonists continue to insist that the Black elderly, along with other ethnic minority older individuals, have very little or no special claim in regard to cultural differences and variances. Gerontologists who firmly believe that there are significant variances must provide leadership in disseminating unbiased information to assure basic understanding of the characteristics and needs of older people.

The concept of the Black elderly being a diverse group is one that has been stated in many ways. In recent years, discussions have centered on the similarities and differences between older Blacks and other older persons. It is certainly appropriate to cast our thinking in the direction of similarities and differences; however, the issue is not that clear-cut. Turning our attention to the diverse nature of the older Black person begins to help sharpen the social, economic, and political profile of those under consideration. Formal definitions of *diverse* or *diversity* help clarify the direction in which we should be moving. *Diverse* is often put forth as meaning (1) varied, (2) different, or (3) dissimilar. To go a step further, it is necessary to examine yet another description provided by Webster's *New World Thesaurus*. One of the options offered is *distinct,* a word that has the strength and depth to help sustain the intensity of thought needed as we pursue an understanding of the older Black person in today's world.

When diversity is examined from the point of view that the Black elder is one who is unique in his or her own right, it provides dimensions that are sometimes not available when the issue is approached in other ways. Essentially, the Black older person has been viewed in juxtaposition to other older persons and has had the unfortunate circumstance of always being compared in unrealistic terms. The moment it is agreed upon that the Black elder is in fact distinct, the need to compare is removed. Older Blacks must be seen as self-contained individuals. Collectively, Black older persons should be viewed from the perspective of their own history, without having to suffer the indignity of being compared with those older persons who have, for the most part, had entirely different social, political, and economic experiences.

Diversity as a concept should not be burdened with negative connotations. The social and historical facts are that the Black older person of today continues to be viewed as an inferior being when compared with other older people. This distinctly different person being discussed continues to suffer due to verbal and nonverbal actions manifested on a daily basis in both formal and informal settings. From a sociological standpoint, I see the institutionalization of the nonverbal and informal degradation of older Blacks continuing. It continues on both macro and micro levels, which means that Black older persons are faced with the struggle of being recognized as contributing individuals in our society on an interpersonal level as well as on an institutional level.

Practical or daily social relationships between Black elders and others are much more tangible at this time than at any other point in history. The tangibility of relationships, however, does not connote the sense that relationships are more positive. There should be a close examination of the current status as well as the evolution of these relationships. More important, one needs only to examine the diverse nature of the Black elderly in comparison to the majority to begin to understand the potential for sustained and equitable participation in the economic and political arenas of our society.

As I have pointed out in an article in the *Black Scholar*, there is no well-developed theoretical framework to explain the relationships between minority older persons and others (Stanford, 1982). However, in the context of considerations put forth by other gerontologists and social scientists, constructs such as double jeopardy, triple jeopardy, and multiple hazards provide exceptional frameworks for explaining the circumstances and relationships between and among Black older persons and other elderly in our society. Such constructs allow an examination of the plight of Blacks as well as other ethnic minority older people. Hence it is reasonable to use the concepts of multiple hazards, double jeopardy, and triple jeopardy as starting points to build further conceptual notions regarding the experience of the Black older person.

I would like to offer another conceptual approach to considering older Blacks in a social and historical context, that is unique to them. The specific conceptual idea will be referred to here as *diverse life patterns*. Diverse life patterns are a culmination of the multiple effects of the unique experiences of the Black older person. The primary ingredient flowing from the diverse life patterns concept is the notion that there is a distinctiveness and uniqueness about the Black elderly experience that is not an integral part of the social, economic, or political experience of any other group of older persons.

The concept of diverse life patterns provides the opportunity for researchers and others to examine the life circumstances of Black elders without the burden of having to prove that there are significant differences between Black elders and others. The diverse life patterns concept assumes that differences are prevalent based primarily on race. The remaining task is to begin looking at the status of the Black elder within the context of his or her environment without having to justify whether the person's circumstances are better or worse than those of the majority elderly population. A greater concern is whether or not, based on diverse life patterns, the individual is functioning at the highest possible level, given the available resources in the total environment.

The diverse life pattern concept may also help explain why it is quite reasonable and logical for most Black elders to express great satisfaction with their particular life situations. Perhaps they, more so than any of us, have for some time realized their distinctiveness and have learned to appreciate their accomplishments within the constraints of the society in which they live. The positive aspect is that diverse life patterns have made it necessary for the Black elderly to draw on their emotional and physical strengths to maximize life situations and achieve the highest possible quality of life attainable given their means.

The dramatic increase in the number of Black older persons living longer in good health sets the stage for them to participate more meaningfully and to expect access to resources heretofore not readily available. Black elderly will continue to be at the center of older client groups needing services. Below, some special areas are delineated to which attention should be given if older Blacks are to be given a reasonable chance to achieve equity while taking diversity into consideration. These are also areas that highlight the need to consider the circumstances of the Black elderly by using the diverse life pattern concept as a primary variable.

Topical areas such as living arrangements, employment, and health care are clearly related when viewed from the perspective of the diverse life pattern concept. In each of these areas, Black older people have had to overcome life experiences that are unique to them. Employment, living arrangements, and health status share a common thread: Employment serves to generate income, which influences the ability of the individual to obtain reasonable housing and health services of reasonable quality.

Living Arrangements

One of the major issues to be brought to the forefront is living arrangements, an area that includes everything from lodging to psychological environment. Many Black older persons find themselves living in structures that are not only undesirable, but that are situated in physical surroundings that are virtually prohibitive. An immediate major undertaking is to improve the structural quality of single dwellings and other housing in which Black older persons reside. Without doubt, housing is one of the primary problem areas for older Blacks. Economically, many cannot afford adequate housing. Urban renewal has been one of the culprits deterring many Black elderly from having reasonably affordable housing in areas close to bus lines, shopping, and places of worship. Policy and political barriers have hampered efforts to bring about an environment that provides affordable housing.

Bryon C. Walters (1980) points out that approximately 43% of the total Black population are homeowners, and, because homeownership increases with age, it is reasonable to assume that more than 43% of Black elderly are homeowners. Neither Black nor White elderly, in large numbers, seem to reside with their adult children. The vast majority of elderly minorities who do not own their own homes live in rental units, and some reside in institutional settings, such as nursing homes, hospitals, and board-and-care facilities.

Health

Most people do not fear growing old, but do fear growing old in bad health. Many older Blacks have not had the luxury of good health care. Consequently, when they reach old age, they are apt to have problems identified of which they were not previously aware. Many have diseases that have reached a stage beyond hope of cure. Large numbers of Black elderly have worked in jobs where health care was not provided as a benefit.

Racial minority and ethnic older people have devised ways of ensuring that they have some protection as they age. These individuals have worked in situations where chronic diseases may be contracted more easily than those who work in more benign situations; they have carried the load with regard to menial jobs performed in hostile environments. In recent years, a trend has been observed whereby some racial minority and ethnic older people have been forced to claim disabilities at a relatively young age. Once on disability, many tend not to go back into their old work environments. As a result of this practice, many of these individuals consider themselves retired, even though they do not receive formal retirement benefits. There is an acceptance of the notion that disability benefits substitute for what may be traditionally thought of as a retirement pension. The primary observation in this instance is that many of these older people suffer from diseases and health problems that keep them out of the work force for several years. Most are too afraid to take the chance of going back into environments that may further harm their health.

Public health programs may be available, but the awareness of the benefits of those programs continues to be vague for many Black elderly. There has been an ongoing misunderstanding regarding benefits and the right to participation. Many feel that participating in public programs constitutes receiving welfare, and therefore they opt to disassociate themselves from the programs.

Employment

Another issue that helps explain diverse life patterns in relation to the Black elderly is employment. Most Black older persons have not been trained in technical or skilled professions and have worked in labor-intensive areas or domestic settings. Ongoing employment is essential for the majority of Black older people. They have not been able to amass reasonable sums of money to carry them into their later years, nor have they been given an opportunity to work in situations that provide substantial pensions. Those who have had the opportunity to work in occupations with pensions often find the level of compensation too meager to sustain them. Since most have not been in the upper echelons of management, or even middle management, they find themselves in need of part-time employment.

Many employers in the past have felt that older people cannot fulfill job expectations in a satisfactory manner. This, however, is beginning to change, and the trend now is toward giving older persons more employment opportunities, at least on a part-time basis. Unfortunately, Black older people are often not among those who are being hired. Some young-old who may have acquired some of the skills needed in the types of jobs available may get a chance, but the pattern of distinction due to lack of job equity is destined to continue for the foreseeable future.

Policy

Establishment of the Older Americans Act in 1965 brought about the first real national policy effort to develop programs exclusively for older people. The implemented Older Americans Act was culturally bland in that little or no consideration was given to the cultures and traditions of those who were not of Euro-American backgrounds. Those involved in the development of the law indicated that they were striving to address the needs of older people from a generic perspective. Experience to date has shown that the generic approach is not necessarily effective. Therefore, the implementation of the law had shortcomings. At least, it did not speak to the diverse life patterns of Black elders.

Even when older people have been served in accordance with the law, many gaps remain.

To ensure that each Black older person has an opportunity for input in policy development situations, special activities need to be developed to enhance diverse life patterns. There are examples of elder advocacy groups that have formed to speak for and act on behalf of Black and other ethnic older people. A model worth considering is one developed in San Diego, California, where a group identified as the Council for Minority Aging has been chartered. This group was developed as a result of a program to encourage minority older people to become more proactive on issues that affect their lives. A major purpose of the council is to work on behalf of and with older people to enhance their visibility and status. The global intent is to make it possible for elder Blacks and their cohorts to contribute to their own welfare in meaningful and productive ways.

In order to form a council for minority older people, it is necessary to identify a core group of individuals from a variety of backgrounds, religious groups, professions, and service organizations. Once the core body has been identified, the primary task is one of recruiting others who are willing to work in the community. It is recommended that no fewer than 5 individuals from each of the major ethnic and racial groups in the community be involved as steering committee members. This provides a nucleus of approximately 20 persons. It is not recommended that the group be larger than 25. The steering committee is the focal point for determining what is needed in the community and functions to bring in information and provides the background for pursuing items of interest. This group then provides the nucleus for recruiting others to become members of the council.

Councils for minority older persons serve as a tremendous link for older people who have not had avenues for input into the mainstream. Through these councils, not only can they have input into political decisions and help to shape directions taken by service agencies, they can also be responsive by providing leadership training for members of their particular councils. In general, councils provide a power base that can be persuasive in ensuring that Black older people receive equitable services at a quality level.

Councils should choose individuals with strong leadership qualities who are willing to take time to interface with individuals not only from their own backgrounds, but also from different racial and ethnic backgrounds. The success of a council for minority aging depends on diverse input and support from individuals in the community.

Community involvement and advocacy go hand in hand. Appropriate and sufficient community involvement in any planning process is somewhat narrowly defined. It is not easy to determine the extent to which a particular set of ideas and concepts represents normative factors involved in decision making and planning for any social group. Various racial and ethnic groups are likely to have ideas and positions that represent some persons more than others. It is often stated that a particular idea or stance on an issue is representative of "the Black community," without proof that this is so. Community involvement usually comes about through a structured phenomenon such as an organization or an institution. Black older people have for many years been on the fringes of these structures. It is true that Blacks have had their own social and religious organizations, but these organizations have not had the same impact on public policy as the larger and more economically secure Euro-American organizations.

To enhance their quality of life, elder Blacks must join the battle against ever-present deficiencies in a variety of areas. An area mentioned previously is that of housing. From an environmental perspective, housing is a good example of an area that must be pursued on an ongoing basis. Walters (1980) explains that positive impacts from housing policies come about when Black elderly are provided with maintenance and care activities and are also provided with housing chore services. Other positive outcomes accrue when Black older persons are made aware of the availability of programs and services. Four ideas emerge that could have a positive impact on providing reasonable living arrangements for Black older people:

(1) *code enforcement and zoning:* Housing code enforcement and zoning changes should be structured in order to do as little harm as possible to persons residing in those areas.

(2) *participation in housing assistance programs:* Assistance and subsidy housing programs should have regulations that restrict their use by persons who can afford to live in nonsubsidized facilities.

(3) *equality in real estate assessment:* Care should be taken not to establish low sales markets when assessing property owned by Black elderly.

(4) *deferred payments:* Special procedures and regulations should be provided to assure that Black elderly homeowners are not forced to sell their homes upon the death of a spouse.

Housing and living arrangements are diverse and complex. Maximum effort must be put forth to involve Black elderly persons in identifying alternatives for resolution.

The degree of community involvement has been limited and has often met with resistance. Church groups and social organizations in the Black community have been proactive on behalf of older people. The result is that older Blacks have benefited from organized efforts to enhance their quality of life and to justify diverse life patterns.

Summary

This chapter has emphasized the fact that Black Americans will continue to live longer and will continue to have a greater impact on the resource pool for older people. The major concern is that we do not try to compare the older Black person with others for the purposes of meeting the needs of the Black elder. The significant point is that older Blacks should be looked at in a distinct manner and should be judged based on their particular social, economic, and political circumstances. It has been and continues to be unfair and unreasonable to judge groups of older people as if they have had the same exposure to experiences and opportunities throughout their lifetimes. It is more appropriate to judge older people's needs and ways of meeting those needs based on what they have experienced and can contribute to today's marketplace. Today's old and very old Blacks are undoubtedly products of a second-class citizenship.

In spite of their many deprivations in comparison to the majority culture, older Blacks have made many contributions. The tragedy is that the positive contributions they have made have not been duly recognized or attributed to the Black elders themselves. What follows is that the status, prestige, and dignity that would have accompanied the recognitions of contributions to society have not been forthcoming; this situation has left a tremendous gap in the ego structure of the Black elder. In essence, there has been little external positive reinforcement to encourage the Black elder to succeed and become the true determinant of his or her destiny. The diverse Black elder is minimally a complex being. There is no simple way to explain the plight or destiny of Black older people.

It is my hope that the foregoing ideas and observations will provide a framework for better understanding of the Black elderly and a structure for beginning to understand the future of the Black elderly in our society. If we accept the idea that diverse life patterns are reasonable and can provide a functional framework for observing the Black elder in our society, some of the need for debating whether or not there are differences and/or similarities between Black elders and other elders will be eliminated. Rather, the focus will be on how to maximize the input of Black older people to society in order to benefit themselves and others. In addition, the focus can be directed toward enhancing the needs of the Black elderly without having to justify their uniqueness or distinctiveness.

The strength of the diverse life patterns concept is that the burden of eternally having to prove that there are differences is removed. The beginning point for service providers, researchers, legislators, and others will be that there is variance and that variance must be taken into consideration within the context of the total social, political, and economic history of the Black elder.

References

Davis, R. H., ed. 1981. *Aging Prospects and Issues.* Los Angeles: University of Southern California Press.

Gordon, M. M. 1978. *Human Nature, Class and Ethnicity.* New York: Oxford University Press.

Kent, D. P. 1971. "The Elderly in Minority Groups." *Gerontologist* 11(1, Part 2):26-29.

Solomon, B. 1974. "Growing Older in the Ethno System." Pp. 9-13 in *Minority Aging: Policy Issues for the 80s,* edited by E. P. Stanford. San Diego: San Diego State University, School of Social Work, University Center on Aging.

Stanford, E. P. 1982. "Theoretical and Practical Relationships Among Aged Blacks and Other Minorities." *Black Scholar* 13(1):49-57.

Walters, B. C. The Negative Impact of Housing Policies on Minority Elderly Homemakers." Pp. 83-87 in *Minority Aging: Policy Issues for the 80s,* edited by E. P. Stanford. San Diego: San Diego State University, School of Social Work, University Center on Aging.

2

Family Care,
Economics, and Health

WILBUR H. WATSON

Any discussion of the aging of America's population inevitably includes the question, How many older persons will there be in the future? (Fowles, 1984). According to Fowles, the older population, age 60 years and over, which currently numbers about 39 million, is projected to double by the year 2025. The proportion of the population in this age group will increase from one in every six Americans (16%) in 1980 to one in every four (26%) between 1980 and 2025.

The older population itself will continue to get older. The 85+ population (the old-old) will more than double in number between 1980 and 2000, growing at a rate over four times as high as the rate for the 60+ population as a whole (Fowles, 1984). Rapid growth of the old-old, however, is expected to slow down in the early years of the next century as the baby boom generation (born following World War II) enters the 60+ population, causing the younger segments of the older population to grow more rapidly than the older segments. Then, by the year 2030 and for the following 50 years, population patterns are expected to show new accelerated growth in the 85+ age group. It is projected that this group will grow ten times as fast as the 60+ population generally

AUTHOR'S NOTE: This chapter was presented as the Keynote Address at "Understanding and Serving Black Aged: A Community Conference and Forum," sponsored by Cleveland State University and the Cleveland Clinic Foundation and cofunded by the Cleveland Foundation, Cleveland State University, Cleveland, Ohio, February 26-27, 1987.

(Fowles, 1984). By 2025, old Americans will represent one-third (33%) of the voting age population, compared with about one-fifth (22%) today (Watson et al., 1987).

The older minority population, which numbered about 3.8 million, or 10% of the nation's 60+ population, in 1980 is projected to more than triple in number (to 11.9 million) by the year 2025 and to represent over 15% of the older population. The minority population as defined here includes Blacks, Native Americans, Asian and Pacific Islanders, and Hispanics, except those identified by the U.S. Bureau of the Census as White Hispanics. The latter are excluded because of the lack of comparable data with which to make projections for this group.

Against this background of demographic change in the general population of the aged, we now turn to a specific focus on older Blacks, with selected comparisons to their White counterparts. Special attention will be given to patterns of family care among older Blacks, the significance of church membership in coping with distress, selected economic differences between older Blacks and Whites, the crossover phenomenon, and health of older Blacks, with reference to osteoporosis, deaths due to accidental falls, and preventive geriatric care.

Caretaking Behavior in the Family

As an extension of the general respect for elders that has persisted among Blacks before, during, and since slavery, it has been traditional for kin and other members of Black communities to take part or full responsibility for elderly members whose infirmities have become so disabling that they can no longer care for themselves (Dancey, 1977; Genovese, 1974; Watson and Maxwell, 1977; Wylie, 1971). Even when severe disability of the individual and economic poverty of the family have required placement of the older person in a long-term care institution, frequent visits by family, friends, and members of the church have helped immeasurably to sustain the individual in spite of his or her infirmities.

The literature suggests that the culture and kinship patterns of many Black families create an environment that is naturally supportive of needy family members, especially the impaired older person (Billingsley, 1968; Hill, 1972). These patterns of kinship and loyalty are considered strengths among Black families in America (Hill, 1972), particularly in their social functions as buffers against the deleterious effects of racial discrimination and the social historical exclusion of Blacks from public and private social welfare and health services (Hill, 1972; Watson, 1983). As a result of segregation and discrimination in public accommodations during the adult years of many of today's older Blacks (1920-1960), their families had to rely more on themselves than on public agencies for support and assistance in times of illness and other crises (Fisher, 1969; Watson et al., 1978).

The literature also suggests strong sentiment among older Blacks that they should be cared for at home by their offspring, not in specialized institutions for the aged or necessarily through public service agencies (Watson, 1980). By contrast, in a comprehensive study of service utilization, the majority of elderly Whites felt that the government should provide care in old age, while 25% felt that adult offspring should provide care (Kent and Hirsch, 1971).

In a related study of filial responsibility—that is, adult children's obligations to meet their parents' basic needs—Seelback and Sauer (1977) have demonstrated once again the support of the Black family in relation to older members. Their data show that Black elderly parents experience much lower morale than White elderly parents when adult children do not meet their expectations for care. The authors interpret this finding to mean that the Black elderly express much higher expectations of filial responsibility than do the White elderly. It should be noted that this research did not take into account the socioeconomic and cultural diversity among Blacks and Whites, and that the results of these comparisons of aggregate data may not be externally valid when diversity is taken into account.

It seems apparent that the cultural and kinship patterns of the Black family provide a strong base of support for caring for ill or impaired elderly in the family home. This is a resource that has functioned for centuries with varying degrees of success and little or no assistance from formal agencies in the United States (Genovese, 1974). The fact is that racism and race discrimination in public accommodations have precluded access by Blacks to alternative resources during most of their history in the United States. In recent decades, however, major changes have occurred in race relations partly stimulated by the Supreme Court decisions of 1954 and 1955, which struck down the legal basis of the 58-year-old practices of public accommodations separated on the basis of race. Subsequently, the civil rights movement, the Civil Rights Acts of 1963 and 1964, and a variety of other changes in laws and customs have helped to bring about substantial improvements in access by

Blacks to public accommodations in the United States (Pinkney, 1984; Watson, 1986).

Low income, poor housing conditions, and overcrowding notwithstanding, Black families have managed in large numbers to keep their elderly infirm at home and to provide long-term care for them. Indirect evidence of this fact is the very small number of older Blacks found living in nursing homes during the nursing home surveys of the last two decades (U.S. Department of Health, Education and Welfare, 1979).

Some aspects of help-giving behavior have been demonstrated by Watson (1980, 1982, 1984, 1986, 1987) in an ongoing study focusing on older Blacks in the southern United States. This study helps to show the significance of family and church groups in caretaking of older Blacks in times of illness and other life challenges.

Family and Church Responses to Illness Among Older Blacks

Five different kinds of support lead the list of initiatives taken by Black families when illness occurs in an older member (Watson, 1980). It is surprising that the church is last on the list, following a doctor in the immediate neighborhood, doctors outside the neighborhood or village of residence, and local hospitals, in that order. Further study has shown that family caregiving is primary because most illnesses are sufficiently mild that family care is advisable, affordable, and sufficient to meet the needs of the older person (Watson, 1982, 1984) (see Table 2.1). Some crises, however, may involve acute illnesses that require the kind of technologically advanced and highly skilled services that are generally found only in hospitals and/or under the auspices of licensed medical doctors. If illnesses are too serious for the family to treat and require advanced medical care, the church is also relatively inconsequential as a source of informal support.

The absence of church intervention also seems to indicate that illnesses within families are regarded as a primary responsibility of the family, and the church usually does not intervene unless invited (Watson, 1982). Studying the response of the church to older infirm members of the congregation was one way to gain insight into the importance of the church as a caretaking group or organization in relation to older persons.

Table 2.1 Helpgiving by Black Families in the Rural South in Response to Illness of an Older Person

Support System	Frequency	Rank
Family is the primary caregiver	70	1
Family selects a local M.D.	53	2
Family selects M.D. outside community	19	3
Older person is taken to a hospital	18	4
Church offers support	9	5

SOURCE: Watson (1982, p. 147).

In another study by Watson et al. (1978), data from Mississippi showed a wide range of actions taken by the church when illness affects an older member (see Table 2.2). Perhaps as a reflection of the economic poverty of many older Blacks and the high costs of health care in the rural South, the surveyed churches in Mississippi used money collected from their members as the primary form of aid offered to the elderly infirm. Second, church members made friendly visits to the older person in his or her home. Closely following friendly visiting was the giving of aid by individual church members in association with their judgments about the needs of the infirm. Next were three types of activities that the church perhaps is best organized and able to perform: (1) visiting the home and praying for the infirm person, (2) serving communion, and (3) praying for the infirm by church members under the leadership of the minister. Providing material gifts for the infirm was the least frequent of all the responses initiated by church members on behalf of an older infirm person.

The foregoing discussion provides insight into selected aspects of community support that help to sustain older Blacks in their homes in the later year of life. Let us turn now to a discussion of selected aspects of the economics of older Blacks.

Economic Conditions of Older Blacks

The economic conditions of older Blacks have shown improvement since the turn of the century, but poverty is still a major problem. In 1982, the U.S. Bureau of the Census reported 38.2% of Blacks aged 65 and over with incomes below the poverty level (U.S. Department of

Table 2.2 Helpgiving Responses of the Church When Illness Strikes a Member

Type of Help	Frequency	Rank
Collection is taken in church to provide money for the infirm	97	1
Friendly visits to home	55	2
Individual church members give aid as needed	44	3
Visit home and pray for the infirm person	39	4
Serve communion	31	5
Minister leads the church in prayer	26	6
Gifts are sent to the infirm	11	7
Nothing special is done	1	8

SOURCE: Watson (1982, p. 147).

Commerce, 1982; also see Figure 2.1). While adjusted income figures for 1983 showed some improvement, with a poverty rate for older Blacks at 36.3%, this rate was still three times the poverty rate for older Whites, which was 12.1% in 1983 (U.S. Senate, 1985, p. 40). These deplorable economic conditions help to accent the social and psychological significance of family, kinship, and church groups as buffers between the older individual and his or her economic environment that would, in all likelihood, have devastating effects if the older poor Black person had to withstand those conditions alone.

Among all older Blacks 65 years and older, poverty is most pervasive among women. Older Black women single heads of households are especially and disproportionately represented among the poor (see, for example, Figure 2.1). The growth in the incidence of poverty among women since 1940 has become popularly known as the "feminization of poverty" (Dressel, 1988). A brief comment on this phenomenon is warranted here.

The term *feminization of poverty* is a misnomer of a complex phenomenon and the multiple factors that help to explain membership of women among the poor (Watson, 1987). It falsely suggests that there is something about the nature of women and/or femininity that explains the growing incidence of poverty among them. It is true that there are sex differences among the poor, but those differences, upon close analysis, point to various exogenous factors (outside sociosexual identity) that differentially affect women, especially older Blacks, and help to account for their growing numbers among the poor. Living arrangement, for example, is a crucial exogenous factor bearing on the incidence of poverty among women.

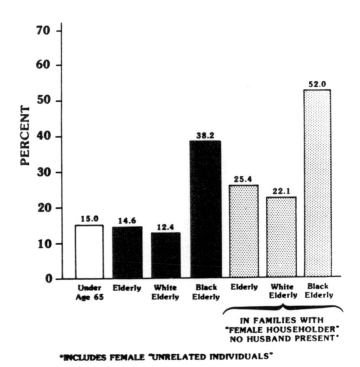

Figure 2.1. Persons Below the Poverty Level
SOURCE: U.S. Department of Commerce (1982).

Gender, Living Arrangements, and Economic Costs

From 1970 to 1981 the number of all families falling below the poverty line increased by 18.3%, or by 1.5 million, most of which were "female householder, no husband present" families. As shown in Figure 2.1, 52% of older Black female heads of households were below the poverty level in 1982.

Female family householders 65 and over in 1981 were twice as likely to be poor as their male counterparts—16% versus 8%, respectively (Williams, 1984). About 1 in 9 White female family householders 65 and over had incomes below the poverty level, compared with 3 out of 10 Black female family householders 65 and over. And finally, 3 out of 10 elderly females not living with any relative were poor.

Closely associated with the incidence of poverty among Black females in the 1980s was the disproportionate growth among them since 1940, including women over 60 years of age, as heads of households. As shown in Figure 2.2, Black women grew from an estimated 18% among Black heads of households in 1940 to 50% or more in 1980. By contrast, Black and White male heads of households with no wife present showed a slight decline from 1940 to 1960, then no change from 1960 to 1980. While there has been some growth among White female heads of households since 1960, that growth has been significantly smaller than that shown among their Black female counterparts.

The current incidence of poverty among female-headed households is partly accounted for by historical discrimination against women in the labor force, especially lower pay and less job security than their male counterparts (Dressel, 1986; Watson, 1986). Table 2.3 shows that women in the U.S. labor force in 1983 had significantly lower median incomes than did their male counterparts after 65 years of age. Exacerbating the economic woes of older Black single female heads of households is the fact that dependent children, other relatives, and/or nonrelatives often share their households.

In 1982, about half (46%) of all Black families with children were maintained by the mother alone, compared with about 15% for Whites (Williams, 1984). The proportion of children living with only one parent was 22% in 1982, up from 12% in 1970. Most of these one-parent families were among those on the lowest rung of the economic ladder.

In addition to low socioeconomic class and its constraints on the quality of life for older Blacks, there are other ways in which older Blacks are distinguished from their White counterparts, although not necessarily in a negative direction. I will focus, in particular, on two different but related health characteristics that signify positive rather than negative deviations of Blacks from Whites so far as longevity is concerned and in coping with the uncertainties of everyday life in later years. The objects of discussion will be (1) the crossover phenomenon and (2) bone loss as a risk factor in death due to accidental falls.

Health and Health Care of Older Blacks

Although there have been improvements in the health care of Blacks since the abolition of slavery in the United States, and measurable increases in longevity since 1850, older Blacks are still multiply jeop-

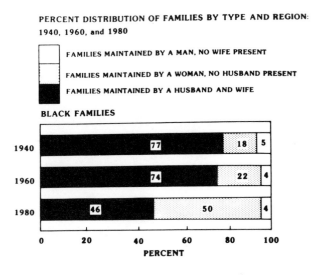

PERCENT DISTRIBUTION OF FAMILIES BY TYPE AND REGION:
1940, 1960, and 1980

☐ FAMILIES MAINTAINED BY A MAN, NO WIFE PRESENT

▨ FAMILIES MAINTAINED BY A WOMAN, NO HUSBAND PRESENT

■ FAMILIES MAINTAINED BY A HUSBAND AND WIFE

BLACK FAMILIES

1940	77	18	5
1960	74	22	4
1980	46	50	4

0   20   40   60   80   100
PERCENT

WHITE FAMILIES

1940	86	10	4
1960	89	8	3
1980	83	14	3

0   20   40   60   80   100
PERCENT

Figure 2.2. Percentage Distribution of Families by Type and Region: 1940, 1960, and 1980
SOURCE: U.S. Department of Commerce (1978); Williams (1984).

ardized in general when compared to their White counterparts (Jackson and Wood, 1976; Lindsay, 1975; Manuel, 1982). Taking this conclusion as a given that is well documented in the literature, I will focus my discussion on two anomalies that are less well known and less understood in the literature on the health of older Blacks.

Table 2.3 Median Income of Persons 65 and Older by Age, Race, and Sex, 1983

Race	Both sexes		Male		Female	
	65 to 69	70+	65 to 69	70+	65 to 69	70+
All races	$8,250	$6,556	$11,837	$8,663	$5,782	$5,540
White	8,665	6,889	12,180	9,109	5,966	5,765
Black	5,431	4,217	7,097	5,114	4,477	3,850
Hispanic	5,033	4,754	6,551	5,289	4,289	4,346

SOURCE: U.S. Senate (1985, p. 39).

The Crossover Phenomenon

Since the 1960 census of the population of the United States, vital statistics have shown that Black females and males who live to be 70-75 years of age or older have longer life expectancies than their White counterparts. This is referred to as the *crossover phenomenon*. Its name comes from the reversal in differential life expectancy that occurs between Blacks and Whites after 70-75 years of age. Both Black females and Black males tend to have shorter life expectancies than their White counterparts up to ages 65-70. Then, for reasons that are not entirely clear, there is a reversal in this pattern. When Blacks who are 70 years of age or older are compared to their White counterparts, there is an increasing difference in life expectancies, with Blacks more likely to live longer than Whites.

This phenomenon is puzzling, and, unfortunately, there has been very little research aimed at developing insights that might help to explain it. Some recent findings, however, and suggested hypotheses for further study are worth noting. In a recent study by Manton et al. (1979) focusing on age-specific patterns of mortality for five leading causes of death, marked differences were found between Blacks and Whites. For example, circulatory diseases (cerebrovascular disorders) show a consistent difference between Blacks and Whites from middle age through the later years of life. Among Blacks between 50 and 75 years of age, circulatory diseases produce a more rapid increase in mortality rates when compared to their White counterparts. The increase helps to explain the early Black mortality excess when compared to their White counterparts. By ages 75-80, however, the excess for Blacks is overshadowed by Whites, who show a more rapidly increas-

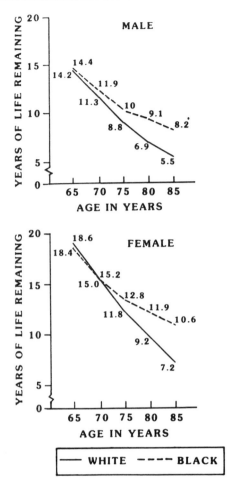

Figure 2.3. Years of Life Remaining for Elderly Age Groups, by Race and Sex, 1980

SOURCE: National Center for Health Statistics (1982).

ing rate of death due to circulatory diseases. Manton et al. (1979, pp. 297-99) have suggested a number of possible explanations for these apparent race-related differences in life expectancy after 75-80 years:

(1) Blacks may have a greater susceptibility to hypertensive disease that, if related to physical exertion, social position, or difference in medical care, would probably be most manifest among those 50 to 75 years of age, rather than the 80+ segment of the Black population.

(2) The simultaneous action of hypertension and atherosclerosis among Blacks between 50 and 75 years of age may help to explain the high rates of death among them due to circulatory disease in this age range. More recently, Savage (1988) has documented the significance of left-ventricular hypertrophy as a risk factor helping to differentiate Blacks from Whites further in mortalities due to heart disease.

(3) The greater susceptibility of Whites to atherosclerotic circulatory disease after 75 years of age may help to explain the crossover of Blacks, who suffer less from that condition and tend to live longer than Whites after 75 to 80 years of age.

Yet there are other points of view on this phenomenon. For example, Siegel (1972) suggests that the difference between Blacks and Whites at these higher ages may be explained by reporting errors in the census, especially with reference to the ages of Blacks. Moreover, some of the differences between the rates for Blacks and Whites may be explained by differential occupational, educational, and income factors (Kitagawa and Hauser, 1974; Siegel, 1972). Clearly, this is an area in which there are more questions than answers, pointing to a fertile area for further study in the development of social gerontology as a field of knowledge. For more recent discussions of the literature on this subject see Jackson (1988) and Manuel (1988).

Race, Bone Loss, and the
Risk of Death Due to Accidental Falls

Bone loss is another condition that seriously impairs the functional capacity of many older persons in the later years of life. Bone loss is sometimes used to help define osteoporosis: a gradual reduction in total bone density accompanied by an increasing porosity and brittleness (Albanese, 1977; Albanese et al., 1975; Wylie, 1977). Strong, healthy bones and neuromuscular balance are among the essential features of a sound body and the ability of a person to perform activities of daily living with confidence (Lawton, 1965).

With increasingly fragile bones, an unsteady gait, and the risk of accidental falls, the health of the older person is seriously jeopardized. Age-related increases in the incidence of bone loss and the risk of serious injury and death due to accidental falls are some of the major reasons for public concern about the frail elderly and the conditions under which they live. The risk of accidental falls and related fatalities are not, however, evenly distributed among the old-old.

Figure 2.4 shows that with advancing age, especially after 64 years of age, there is an accelerated increase in the incidence of death due to accidental falls. When we introduce the variables of race and sex, however, as shown in Figure 2.5, there are marked group differences in the incidence of death. For example, White women who suffer accidental falls after 65 years of age are far more likely to die than White males, Black females, and Black males in the same age group. Amazingly, Black males are the least likely to die under these circumstances. Like the crossover phenomenon illustrated in Figure 2.3, this finding is an anomaly that warrants further study.

The literature is clear that bone loss contributes directly to the frailty of the elderly person and increases the risk of falling accidents due to musculoskeletal weaknesses (Rodstein, 1972; Wylie, 1977). Further, bone loss increases the risk of death due to spontaneous fractures, such as those that may be due to falls and moving-vehicle accidents, occurring in individuals 45 years of age and older (Albanese, 1975). Since the incidence of osteoporosis increases with age, the old-old can be expected to show the most advanced signs of this condition and to be a group at much greater risk of serious injury or death due to spontaneous fractures.

To help illustrate differing sex- and age-related risks of fractures further, Wylie (1977) cites a study of hospital discharge rates for all fractures per 100,000 population in England and Wales in 1972. He found an increasing incidence of discharges for treatment of fractures among members of both sexes from 25 to 75 years of age and over. Although males showed a higher incidence than females up to age 64, females exceeded the rate for males in the later years. The earlier high rates for males were attributable to industrial accidents and other physically stressful events to which they were more likely to be exposed during their years of labor force participation (Wylie, 1977). By con-

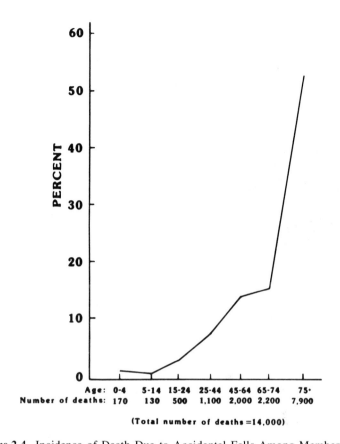

Figure 2.4. Incidence of Death Due to Accidental Falls Among Members of
Different Age Groups in the United States, 1977
SOURCE: Raw data from U.S. Department of Health, Education and Welfare
(1978, p. 6).

trast, males were decreasingly exposed to work-related socioenviron-
mental stressors after retirement, whereas females were increasingly
exposed to bone loss and the risk of fractures due, in part, to postmeno-
pausal calcium losses and rapidly declining bone density.

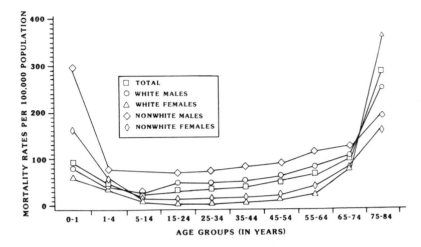

Figure 2.5. Age Patterns of Non-Motor Vehicle Accident Mortality Rates, by
Sex and Race, United States, 1900-1980
SOURCE: Holinger (1987, p. 88).

Preventive Geriatric Care and
Health Care Financing

Finally, there is a need for research on preventive geriatric care,
especially, but not exclusively, among aging Black persons. For example, community clinics or public health services aimed at pregeriatric
screening, early detection, and treatment of chronic illnesses can help
minimize the deleterious effects of many disorders that now prematurely end the lives of middle-aged and older Blacks. It is not clear,
however, to what extent middle-aged and older Blacks avail themselves
of these services to facilitate early detection and treatment of, for
example, Alzheimer's disease, hypertension, and other disorders. Research is needed on factors that function among Blacks to increase
and/or impede their uses of preventive geriatric care services.

An improved national health insurance program with comprehensive
benefits and supplementary provisions for the poor and socially disadvantaged elderly is also needed. It is well known that health service
utilization is closely associated with ability to pay the costs of care. For
the poor and socially disadvantaged, who are overrepresented among
the Black elderly, there is a decreasing likelihood of securing the kinds

of health services needed in the later years of life because of fixed income, few pensions or preretirement health benefit programs, and health insurance that they can draw upon after retirement. As a consequence, many often go without much-needed health care. In many instances, inability to pay the costs of health care may mean death at an earlier age than would have been the case had health care been affordable. Research is needed on health care financing among older Blacks, on class differentials in uses of health care services among them, and on strategies for resolving medical problems of near poor older Blacks.

Conclusions

Census projections have clearly shown rapid growth in the population of older Blacks and older members of other ethnic groups through the early decades of the twenty-first century. Of these special populations, persons 85 years of age and older are expected to show the most accelerated rates of growth well into the twenty-first century. Against this background of population change, this chapter has focused on selected social, economic, and health care characteristics of older Blacks in the 1980s, with implications for the years to come.

Families and kinship groups were shown to be major sources of informal support for most older Blacks in their everyday lives. While many live in residential settings, such as urban neighborhoods that are accessible by public and/or private transportation to modern medical centers, most older Blacks still turn first to informal caregivers in times of illness. Church membership groups continue also to be significant sources of support to older Blacks. The findings showed, however, that churches are secondary sources of support sought by older Blacks when compared to family and kinship groups.

Second, the discussion showed that economic poverty continues to be a major debilitating condition impeding opportunities for improvement in the quality of life of many older Blacks. Most deplorable has been the rapid growth since 1940 in the incidence of poverty among older Black women, especially those who have become single heads of households. The relationship between single female-headed households and poverty seems closely linked with a number of factors, not the least of which are historical patterns of discrimination against women and Blacks in hiring and pay in the world of work, and delinquent payments by ex-husbands and paramours of child support to ex-wives and lovers who became single heads of households after the dissolution of their relationships.

We also showed that, with advancing age, there is an increasing risk of health- and life-threatening illnesses and debilitating conditions, such as bone loss, that may require the intervention of health care specialists to minimize or reverse the deleterious effects. We also know that one of the most consistent differences between Black and White elderly in the utilization of health care services is the ability to pay, whether out of pocket, through public assistance, or through private health insurance. The high incidence of poverty among older Blacks and the low likelihood of private insurance to supplement public assistance programs sharply reduce their use of preventive health care, such as regular visits to health professionals for examinations and treatment. Clearly, this argues for major improvements in income maintenance and public health insurance for the elderly poor.

The foregoing discussion should leave no doubt about the disparities between the health statuses and access to health services that distinguish Black and White elderly persons in the United States. Black elderly tend to suffer earlier in their lives from debilitating chronic illnesses and to die earlier than Whites.

There is a need for more preventive geriatric care, especially, but not exclusively, for minority aging persons. For example, community clinics or public health services aimed at pregeriatric screening for early detection and treatment of hypertension and other chronic illnesses can help minimize the deleterious effects of many diseases that now end the lives of many middle-aged Blacks when they are in the prime of their careers and family lives. With the increasing numbers of older Blacks living to advanced old age, and the increasing incidence of poor and socially disadvantaged persons among them, the need for a comprehensive health care system—including national health insurance—that takes into account the plight of the elderly poor will become increasingly urgent in the years to come.

References

Albanese, Anthony A. 1977. "Osteoporosis." *Journal of the American Pharmaceutical Association* 17:252-53.

Albanese, A. A., A. H. Edelson, E. J. Lorenze, Jr., M. L. Woodhull, and E. H. Wein. 1975. "Problems of Bone Health in Elderly: Ten Year Study." *New York State Journal of Medicine* 75:326-36.

Billingsley, A. 1968. *Black Families in White America.* Englewood Cliffs, NJ: Prentice-Hall.

Dancey, Joseph, Jr. 1977. *The Black Elderly: A Guide for Practitioners.* Ann Arbor: University of Michigan/Wayne State University, Institute of Gerontology.

Dressel, P. 1986. "Civil Rights, Affirmative Action, and the Aged of the Future: Will Life Chances Be Different for Blacks, Hispanics, and Women: An Overview of Issues." *Gerontologist* 26:128-31.

————. 1988. "Gender, Race and Class: Beyond the Feminization of Poverty in Later Life." *Gerontologist* 28:177-80.

Fisher, W. 1969. "Physicians and Slavery in the Antebellum Southern Medical Journal." Pp. 152-64 in *The Making of Black America.* Vol. 1, *The Origins of Black Americans,* edited by August Meier and Elliot Rudwick. New York: Atheneum.

Fowles, Donald. 1984. "The Numbers Game: A Look at the Future." *Aging* 346:46-47.

Genovese, E. D. 1974. *Roll, Jordan, Roll: The World the Slaves Made.* New York: Pantheon.

Hill, R. B. 1972. *The Strength of Black Families.* New York: Emerson Hall.

Holinger, Paul C. 1987. *Violent Deaths in the United States: An Epidemiologic Study of Suicide, Homicide, and Accidents.* New York: Guilford.

Jackson, Jacquelyne J. 1988. "Social Determinants of the Health of Older Black Populations in the United States." Pp. 69-98 in *The Black American Elderly: Research of Physical and Psychosocial Health* edited by James S. Jackson. New York: Springer.

Jackson, M. and J. L. Wood. 1976. *Aging in America: Implications for the Black Aged.* Washington, DC: National Council on the Aging.

Kent, D. P. and C. Hirsch. 1971. *Needs and Use of Services Among Negro and White Aged.* College Park: Pennsylvania State University.

Kitagawa, E. M. and P. M. Hauser. 1974. *Social and Economic Differentials in Mortality.* Cambridge, MA: Harvard University Press.

Lawton, Alfred H. 1965. "Accidental Injuries to the Aged." *Gerontologist* 5(3):96-100.

Lindsay, Inabel, B. 1975. "Coping Capacities of the Black Aged." In *No Longer Young: The Older Women in America.* Ann Arbor: Institute of Gerontology, University of Michigan-Wayne State University.

Lutwak, L. 1964. "Osteoporosis: A Mineral Deficiency Disease." *Journal of the American Dietetic Association* 44:173.

Manton, K. G., P. Sandomirsky Poss, and S. Wing. 1979. "The Black/White Mortality Cross Over: Investigation from the Perspective of the Components of Aging." *Gerontologist* 19(June):291-300.

Manuel, Ron, C. 1982. *Minority Aging: Sociological and Social Psychological Issues.* Westport, CT: Greenwood.

————. 1988. "The Demography of Older Blacks in the United States." Pp. 25-49 in *The Black American Elderly: Research of Physical and Psychosocial Health* edited by James S. Jackson. New York: Springer.

National Center for Health Statistics. 1982. *Monthly Vital Statistics Report, Advance Report of Final Mortality Statistics.* Vol. 31, No. 6 (1979), Supplement, September 30.

Pinkney, A. 1984. *The Myth of Black Progress.* New York: Cambridge University Press.

Rodstein, M. 1972. "Interrelations of the Aging Process and Accidents." *Journal of the American Geriatric Society* 20(3):97-101.

Savage, D. 1988. "Cardiovascular Risk Factors Among Black Americans." Paper presented during a symposium at Howard University, School of Medicine, Department of Family Practice, January 26.

Seelback, W. C. and W. J. Sauer. 1977. "Filial Responsibility Expectations and Morale Among Aged Parents." *Gerontologist* 17:492-99.

Siegel, J. S. 1972. "Some Demographic Aspects of Aging in the United States." In *Epidemiology of Aging,* edited by A. Ostefed and D. C. Gibson. Washington, DC: Government Printing Office.

U.S. Department of Commerce, Bureau of the Census. 1978. "The Social and Economic Status of the Black Population in the United States: An Historical View, 1790-1978." In *Current Population Reports.* Special Studies, Series P-23, No. 80. Washington, DC: Government Printing Office.

———. 1982. "Money Income and Poverty Status of Families and Persons in the United States." In *Current Population Reports.* Series P-60, No. 140. Washington, DC: Government Printing Office.

U.S. Department of Health, Education and Welfare. 1978. *Accident Facts.* National Safety Council. Washington, DC: Government Printing Office.

———. 1979. "National Nursing Home Survey." In *1977 Summary for the United States, Vital and Health Statistics.* Data from the National Health Survey, Series 13, No. 43. Washington, DC: Government Printing Office.

U.S. Senate, Special Committee on Aging. 1985. *America in Transition: An Aging Society.* Serial No. 99-B. Washington, DC: Government Printing Office.

Watson, W. H. 1980. *Informal Social Networks in Support of Elderly Blacks in the Black Belt of the United States: Final Report.* Washington, DC: National Center on Black Aged.

———. 1982. *Aging and Social Behavior: An Introduction to Social Gerontology.* Monterey, CA: Wadsworth.

———. 1983. *Stress and Old Age: A Case Study of Black Aging and Transplantation Stock.* New Brunswick, NJ: Transaction.

———, ed. 1984. *Black Folk Medicine: The Therapeutic Significance of Faith and Trust.* New Brunswick, NJ: Transaction.

———. 1986. "Crystal Ball Gazing: Notes on Today's Middle Aged Blacks with Implications for Their Aging in the Twenty First Century." *Gerontologist* 26:136-39.

———. 1987. "Feminization of Poverty Among Older Blacks." Invited presentation at the conference, "Ethnic and Racial Variations Among Urban Women," Detroit Area Agency on Aging, Detroit, MI, May 15-16.

Watson, W. H., D. Knox, and C. Thorne. 1978. "Informal Social Supports for Older Blacks in the Rural South." Paper presented at the meetings of the Gerontological Society of America, Dallas, November.

Watson, W. H. and R. J. Maxwell. 1977. *Human Aging and Dying: A Study in Sociocultural Gerontology.* New York: St. Martin's.

Watson, W. H., N. McGhee, Jr., and W. L. Reed. 1987. "Health Policy and the Black Aged." *Urban League Review* 10(2):63-71.

Williams, J. D. 1984. *The State of Black America.* New York: National Urban League.

Wylie, C. M. 1977. "Hospitalization for Fracture and Bone Loss in Adults." *Public Health Reports* 92:33-38.

Wylie, Floyd M. 1971. "Attitudes Toward Aging and the Aged Among Black Americans: Some Historical Perspectives." *Aging and Human Development* 2:66-70.

3

Health and Social Characteristics

Implications for Services

HAROLD R. JOHNSON
ROSE C. GIBSON
IRENE LUCKEY

The elderly population (aged 65 and over) in the United States has been rising steadily. The number of elderly more than doubled between 1950 and 1984, growing to about 28 million; the number of those 85 and over more than quadrupled in the same period, to 2.6 million. The proportion of elderly rose from 8% in 1950 to 12% in 1984; by 2020, about 17% of the total population will be elderly (Siegel and Taeuber, 1986a). The number of Blacks aged 65 and over has been increasing faster than the number of Whites in that age group, but elderly Blacks constitute (and always will constitute) a smaller group of absolute numbers than comparable Whites. Based on sheer numbers, this means that Whites might fare better in competition with Blacks for benefits, services, and programs as our society ages (Gibson, 1986a, 1986c). The continuing disproportionate growth of the older Black population will have profound effects on the society's institutions. This chapter will concern itself with some mortality, health, social, and mental health character-

AUTHORS' NOTE: This chapter has been adapted from papers presented by Harold R. Johnson at the Gerontology Colloquium, Cleveland State University, May 29, 1986, and Rose C. Gibson at the Annual Conference of the National Association of State Units on Aging, Washington, D.C., 1983.

istics of the Black elderly and the implications of these factors for policy-making, planning, and services as we approach the twenty-first century.

Differential Mortality, Health, and Health Care

Life expectancy at birth, although increasing for both Blacks and Whites, is lower for Blacks. At current death rates, Blacks can expect to live 69.6 years and Whites can expect to live 72.2 years (Siegel and Taeuber, 1986a). Among individuals aged 75 and over, however, Black mortality rates are lower than those of Whites. This is the racial mortality crossover effect (Manton and Johnson, 1987). The Black age group 80 and older is, in fact, growing disproportionately. The most rapidly growing group within the Black elderly population is that of women aged 80 and over—they have the longest average remaining lifetime of the four race-gender groups. Race-by-gender differences were observable as early as 1900 (Gibson, 1986b).

The health status of Blacks historically has been worse than that of Whites. Excess deaths among Blacks aged 55 to 74 are mainly due to diseases of the heart, malignant neoplasms, and cerebrovascular diseases (Manton and Johnson, 1987). Blacks are more likely to get these diseases at earlier ages than their White counterparts. Incapacitating arthritis, although not a leading cause of death, is more prevalent among older Blacks. Large Black/White disparities are also found in diabetes, accidents, nephritis, and nephrosis (U.S. Department of Health and Human Services, 1982). Not only are chronic conditions more prevalent among Blacks at earlier ages, but they limit the activities of Blacks to a greater extent. According to unpublished data from the National Center for Health Statistics, in 1981 older Blacks spent 15.3 days of each year in bed per person, while their White counterparts spent 8.3 days. Almost half of Blacks aged 65 and over rate their health as fair or poor, in contrast to less than a third of Whites who do (U.S. Department of Health and Human Services, 1987).

In sum, health and mortality statistics indicate that the Black elderly, compared with the White elderly, are more likely to be infirm, to die (up to age 85), and to have chronic diseases at earlier ages and to be more physically limited by these illnesses. This means that, age for age, the Black elderly are less employable, less able to participate in out-of-home programs and activities, and, therefore, more likely to need in-home services.

Medicare and Medicaid have had positive effects on the quantity of health care available for older Blacks. It is less clear, however, that these programs have improved the quality of care for older Black Americans. Quality of health care encompasses prevention, community services, effective patient-physician relationships, and accessibility. Unfortunately, all of these aspects of good health care are infrequently found among older Blacks. The race disparity in quality of care manifests itself in at least two ways: Blacks are sicker when they first visit physicians, and, once hospitalized, have longer average lengths of stay. The greater tendency of older Blacks to use hospital outpatient and emergency services also contributes to their inferior health care (Ruiz and Herbert, 1984). More systematic and regular visits to private physicians' offices would result in more thorough delivery of care and would foster better patient-physician relationships. A lower ratio of physicians to patients in low-income areas (in which most elderly Black persons live) and discriminatory practices of practitioners and medical institutions exacerbate the problem. Bullough and Bullough (1972), in fact, identify discriminatory practices of medical institutions and practitioners as major factors in poor health care. Ruiz and Herbert (1984) similarly argue that the Black elderly are especially affected by the inadequacies of a health care system that does not address ineffective patient-physician relationships, differential distribution of physicians in high- and low-income areas, and the special needs of the elderly poor. Thus the quality of health care for older Blacks has not kept pace with the quantity.

Socioeconomic Status

Black/White disparities in social factors are widely recognized. Older Black Americans are poorer, less educated, and more apt to be separated, widowed, or divorced. And the gap widens with age. At mid-life, 14% of Blacks have family incomes of less than $5,000 per year, compared with 4% of Whites; 64% of Blacks have educational attainments of less than high school graduation, compared with 34% of Whites; and 55% of Blacks are married with their spouses present, compared with 79% of Whites. For the elderly, 27% of Blacks have annual family incomes of less than $5,000, 80% have less than a high school education, and only 38% are married and make homes with their spouses. The comparable figures for elderly Whites are 10%, 34%, and 54%, respectively (Gibson, 1982).

Living conditions of the Black elderly are inextricably bound with their poverty. Proportionately more Black than White elderly live in the inner city, creating a special set of problems that are different from those of elderly living outside central cities or in central-city gentrification areas. Those who live in the inner city are beset with problems of crime, deficient housing, and high costs of subsistence—food and medicines are more costly, for example, and the quality is poorer than in other areas. Some 13% of all Black elderly are victims of crimes of violence, and 9% fall victim to crimes of theft with bodily contact. Comparable figures for the White elderly are 7% and 2%, respectively (Gibson, 1983b). The fear of crime restricts the mobility of the Black elderly and threatens their well-being to the extent that they are less inclined to use public transportation to visit doctors and supermarkets. Inner-city residents are in greater need of special public transportation services than are others, but such services ironically are being curtailed in many of their communities.

The residences of older Blacks are likely to be substandard, because inner-city housing is more dilapidated. Fully 20% of the rental units occupied by Blacks are deficient. This is twice the national average of deficient rental housing units occupied in the United States. Combining rental and owner-occupied housing units, the rate of Blacks living in deficient housing is almost four times as great as the national average. Furthermore, 35% of all housing units occupied by the Black elderly (whether owner-occupied or rental) lack basic plumbing facilities, compared with 15% occupied by the White elderly (Wallace, 1981). In spite of the need, older Blacks are less likely to receive benefits under government housing programs targeted toward the poor. Three-fourths of poor Black elderly living alone, for example, do not live in either subsidized or public housing (Johnson, 1986).

Dilapidated housing gives rise to other problems: Repairs are more frequently needed, energy consumption is higher, and health problems are more common. Poor Black elderly homeowners have the additional problem of paying property taxes and mortgage installments from meager monthly incomes. Contrary to popular belief, older Blacks are deeply affected by such costs because a majority (61%) own their homes or are purchasing them (Newman, 1986). Taken together, these socioeconomic and housing statistics illustrate the increasing disadvantages of Black Americans on social factors in successively older age groups and the far-reaching implications of their flawed housing.

Labor Force Activities and Retirement

In this section, we summarize a study by Gibson (1987) that underscores the need to reconceptualize work and retirement for older Black Americans. According to Gibson, nearly 40% of nonworking Blacks aged 55 and over can be categorized as "unretired-retired," individuals who appear and behave as if they were retired, but do not call themselves retired. Because they do not meet the traditional retirement criteria—of chronological age, a clear line between work and nonwork, income from retirement sources, and their own realization that they are retired—this very needy group is screened out of major retirement research and the retirement-benefit planning and policy-making that stem from that research.

Who are these unretired-retired? They are older Black workers, many in early mid-life, who are making a gradual exodus out of the labor force mainly for reasons of physical disability. Among the middle-aged, disability in most categories increased more for Blacks than for Whites over a 12-year period, and over 26 years, decreases in labor force participation were more dramatic for Black men and increases more dramatic for White women (Gibson, 1986b). The disturbing possibility is that beginning at about age 55 and barring radical social intervention, such as equalizing employment opportunities and the creation of jobs that would accommodate their declining physical abilities, a large group of older Blacks may never work again in any systematic way; their work lives will effectively be over. In order to assure that they receive some type of benefits, retirement age may need to be moved back for older Blacks in the aging society—and eventually for other groups as well.

For many Blacks, the retirement years are often the happiest and most secure of their lives (Jackson and Gibson, 1985). This finding is in direct contrast to the results of several empirical studies of work and retirement that indicate that the elderly would benefit from remaining in the work force, and would in fact prefer to do so rather than to retire at the traditional age of 65. Parnes and Nestel (1981) found in their study of the retirement of Black and White men, for example, that the morale of White retirees was lower than that of older White workers even after controlling for income, age, and health. The Jackson and Gibson data from the National Survey of Black Americans (NSBA) (see the Appendix to this chapter), in contrast, suggest that the reverse is true for older Blacks: Retirees have higher morale than workers. There are at least two possible reasons for this. First, the combination of declining physical abilities of older Blacks and their restriction to strenuous and distasteful jobs at the bottom of the job hierarchy that do not accommodate their infirmities makes work as it is now structured more punishing than it is for Whites. Second, many Blacks in retirement can look forward for the first time in their lives to the reliability of a monthly check from social security and supplemental security income. For a majority of older Blacks it may not be work, but retirement, that promotes adjustment.

If current trends in disability and early labor force withdrawal continue, there is a distinct possibility that, by the middle of the twenty-first century, Blacks will cease working and begin retirement before midlife. This will pose problems at policy levels: Should those in this group be called "retired," in spite of the fact that they do not meet traditional criteria, so that some type of special benefits can be provided when their work lives are over? The problem is intensified by the fact that growing numbers of White retirees, who are living longer, will also need income supplements. New ways of supporting burgeoning numbers of Black and White nonworkers need investigation.

The lines between work and nonwork may become even more indistinct as older Blacks work more sporadically as a result of competition with growing numbers of older Whites for jobs that accommodate the declining physical capacities of older workers. Because disability pay is a mainstay of these middle-aged Blacks who are leaving the labor force, the disability identity may replace the retirement identity. The result could be an increase in importance of disability-pay legislation over social security legislation for the economic welfare of Blacks. When the age of eligibility changes under social security, there will be an even longer wait between the end of the work life and the beginning of benefits: Growing numbers of Black males simply will not live long enough to collect. Given the shorter life spans of Blacks, this raises an even more fundamental issue: Are age-based policies generally inappropriate for the masses of Blacks in an aging society?

Informal Support

Research findings on race differences in the quantity, quality, and type of social support are ambiguous (see Antonucci, 1985, for a thoughtful review of the literature on ethnic differences in social support). Some researchers hold that the social networks of ethnic minorities are quantitatively different from those of Whites; that is, they are more extensive, with more frequent interaction (Butler and Lewis, 1982; Cantor, 1979; Bengtson, 1979; Bengtson and Dowd, 1981; Dowd and Bengtson, 1978). Other researchers have found race-related differences in social interaction and support (Kernodle and Kernodle, 1979). Chatters et al. (1985), using the National Survey of Black Americans data, found several intra-Black group differences. For example, informal support increased as income and education increased. Gibson (1982), analyzing two waves of the Americans View Their Mental Health data, 19 years apart, found Blacks and Whites equally likely to seek help in their informal networks in times of distress, but they found that the help-seeking paradigms of Blacks and Whites are different. Blacks in middle and late life draw from a more varied pool of informal helpers than Whites and are more likely to reach for help beyond spouses and children to friends, neighbors, and church members. Blacks, in addition, are more versatile in substituting these helpers one for another as they approach old age. Whites, in contrast, are more likely to limit help seeking to spouses in mid-life and to replace spouses with a single family member as they approach old age. Gibson and Jackson (1988) found the informal networks of Blacks at extreme old ages characterized by a certain plasticity. The type, amount, and frequency of help seem to be on a sliding scale—the greater the disability, the larger the number of helpers, the higher the frequencies of contact and help, the more proximal the family members, and the more likely the increases in aid from adult children. Moreover, Harel and Deimling (1984) found the availability of social resources to be important in the mental health of the elderly.

Another consideration is that elderly Blacks receive less support than is commonly assumed. Three facts are notable here. First, the Black elderly are less likely than others to have spouses and living children, thus they are missing two important sources of informal support. Second, a large number of Blacks aged 55 and over live alone, are self-supporting (living almost exclusively on social security and supplemental security income payments), and are not receiving financial assistance from children (Jackson and Gibson, 1985). Finally, the Black elderly may be giving more than they are receiving from their informal systems, since they are more likely than others to be raising grandchildren. The popular assumption that elderly Blacks are less in need of formal supportive services because they receive more social and economic support from their families may be faulty. These informal support data indicate that much more needs to be known about the structure, size, function, and quality of the family, friend, church member, and neighbor networks of the Black elderly if services are to meet their needs efficiently. Wherever natural support systems are in place and functioning well, agencies might assist the helpers to encourage their continuing support of their elderly.

Mental Health Factors

Within the Black population, mental health status improves in successively older age groups. Being Black and 65, for example, is better than being Black and 45, and being Black and 80 is better than being Black and 65 (Gibson, 1983a). In the Gibson study, in fact, those at mid-life were the most likely of older Blacks to have serious personal problems and to have these problems affect them at nervous-breakdown levels and the least likely to take these problems in stride (interestingly, the death rate from stress-related diseases is also greatest during the middle years for Blacks). Comparing two older groups—the young-old (aged 65 to 74) and the oldest-old (aged 80 and over)—Gibson found the young-old more likely to have multiple stressors and to have problems that upset them. Similar patterns emerged in the morale measures: The oldest-old were more likely to be very satisfied with life and family, to have feelings of high personal efficacy, to have greater senses of life accomplishment, and to be very happy. These age group differences in mental health factors need further investigation. Younger age groups of the Black elderly might need preventive mental health services, while older age groups might serve as mental health resources. At any rate, these findings on mental health should not be construed to mean that the psychological well-being of the Black elderly is a substitute for their economic well-being.

Conclusions

We have discussed in this chapter some special health and social characteristics of the Black elderly. These conditions have implications for planning, policy-making, and services as our society ages. First, statistics indicate that Black elderly are physically less able than others, age for age, to participate in out-of-home programs. In-home services perhaps should be available to them at earlier ages, rather than at the traditional age of 65. A careful assessment of the appropriateness of age-based services and programs for the masses of Black elderly is needed.

Our review of housing statistics underscores the gravity of flawed housing for older Blacks. Independent living for the Black elderly depends upon the expansion of several types of programs and services: public transportation, home maintenance, installation of home safety devices, property tax breaks, and chore services. Additionally, older Blacks need greater access to existing and new government housing subsidy programs. Barriers that exclude the needy—lack of knowledge of programs and ways in which to apply—especially need attention.

Blacks at mid-life have serious problems of adjustment, but fully half do not seek help from professionals (social workers, psychologists, or psychiatrists); rather, they seek help from family and friends. Family and friends, however, in contrast to mental health professionals, do not have the objectivity, training, or potential for facilitating behavior change—particularly since many of the problems of older Blacks involve their family members. A challenge to mental health professionals is to identify these older Blacks in need through more effective targeting and outreach programs. These programs, however, necessitate a knowledge of older Blacks' milieu and social support networks. Informal network members should, in fact, be actively involved in the outreach process (Luckey and Nathan, 1989).

Our review of recent research on the Black oldest-old suggests that they are better off in mental health and morale than are younger groups of Blacks. Service providers should find ways in which to utilize some of these extraordinary strengths of the Black oldest-old as they grow more numerous in an aging society. The effectiveness of the informal support networks of the Black elderly seems to lie in their resilience and flexibility. Practitioners and those who design social programs might find ways in which to enhance these characteristics and functions. Overall, it is of paramount importance that policies and services build upon the personal strengths and resources of older Blacks, as well as address their lack of economic resources. Research is needed that identifies more precisely these strengths of older Blacks.

The findings presented in this chapter suggest that social action and policy-making in behalf of the Black American elderly should focus on their health care and income supplements. In regard to health, increases in Medicare coverage for in-home services, more preventive health care programs, and greater attention to the inaccessibility of high-quality health services are areas of particular concern. With respect to income supplements, incremental raises in minimum benefit levels under social security are needed more than are cost-of-living increases. As Kutza (1982) points out, cost-of-living increases under social security benefit the more advantaged; such increases benefit the elderly poor only marginally. These are difficult issues that require considerable thought as intergroup competition for such health and economic resources mounts as the population ages.

The elderly will be more numerous and more heterogeneous in an aging society. Future policies and programs should be developed with an eye to meeting the differing needs of subgroups of the elderly population. We urge those who would understand and serve the Black aged subgroup to replace stereotypes and generalizations with the findings of sound research. In this way, particular needs can be identified and services can be tailored to the reality of the circumstances.

Appendix:
The National Survey of Black Americans

The NSBA sample is a multistage probability sample of the Black population consisting of 2,107 respondents. The sampling design was based on the 1970 census, and each Black American residing in an individual household within the continental United States had an equal chance of being selected. The sample design is similar to that of most national surveys, but has unique features of primary area selection and stratification to make it responsive to the distribution of the Black population. Eligibility for selection into this household sample was based on citizenship and noninstitutional living quarters within the continental United States. Reflecting the nature of the distribution of the Black population, more than half (44) of the 76 primary areas used for final selection of households were located in the southern United States. Two methods of screening were developed to guarantee inclusion of Blacks (meeting selection criteria) in both high- and low-density areas (Jackson and Hatchett, 1986). The sample had a 69% response rate, and all face-to-face interviewing was conducted in 1979-1980 by Black interviewers trained through the Survey Research Center of the University of Michigan's Institute for Social Research.

The questionnaire used in the NSBA was developed especially for use in the Black population. Two years of pretesting and refinement preceded its actual use in the field. The instrument contained both open-ended and closed-ended items and took approximately 2 hours and 20 minutes to administer. Although the findings reported in this chapter were restricted to the retirement, work social support, mental and physical health, and demographic sections, the questionnaire also includes the broad areas of neighborhood life, racial and self-identity, religious experiences, and political participation. Thus the data available for analysis in the research reported here represent a rich, culturally relevant, and carefully collected source of information on the lives of the Black elderly.

References

Antonucci, T. C. 1985. "Personal Characteristics, Social Networks, and Social Behavior." Pp. 94-128 in *Handbook of Aging and the Social Sciences,* edited by R. H. Binstock and E. Shanas. 2nd ed. New York: Van Nostrand Reinhold.

Bengtson, V. L. 1979. *Ethnicity and Aging: Problems and Issues in Current Social Science Inquiry.* New York: Springer.

Bengtson, V. L. and J. J. Dowd. 1981. "Sociological Functionalism, Exchange Theory, and Life-Cycle Analysis: A Call for More Theoretical Bridges." *International Journal of Aging and Human Development* 12(1):55-73.

Bullough, B. and V. Bullough. 1972. *Poverty, Ethnic Identity and Health Care.* New York: Appleton-Century-Crofts.

Butler, R. N. and M. I. Lewis. 1982. *Aging and Mental Health.* 3rd ed. St. Louis: C. V. Mosby.

Cantor, M. H. 1979. "Neighbors and Friends: An Overlooked Resource in the Informal Support System." *Research on Aging* 1:434-63.

Chatters, L. M., R. J. Taylor, and J. S. Jackson. 1985. "Size and Composition of the Informal Helper Networks of Elderly Blacks." *Journal of Gerontology* 40:605-14.

Dowd, J. J. and V. B. Bengtson. 1978. "Aging in Minority Populations: Examination of the Double Jeopardy Hypothesis." *Journal of Gerontology* 33(3):427-36.

Gibson, R. C. 1982. "Blacks at Middle and Late Life: Resources and Coping." *Annals of the American Academy of Political and Social Science* 464:79-90.

―――. 1983a. *Coping in the 80's: New Research Findings from the National Survey of Black Americans.* Richmond: Virginia Union University, Black Family Institute.

―――. 1983b. *Special Social Needs of the Black Elderly: Recent Research Findings from the Panel Study of Income Dynamics and the National Survey of Black Americans.* National Association of Area Agencies on Aging Annual Conference. Washington, DC: National Association of State Units on Aging (NASUA).

―――. 1986a. "Perspectives on the Black Family." Pp. 181-98 in *Our Aging Society: Paradox and Promise,* edited by A. Pifer and D. L. Bronte. New York: Norton.

―――. 1986b. *Blacks in an Aging Society.* New York: Carnegie Corporation.

―――. 1986c. "Blacks in an Aging Society." *Daedalus* 115(1):349-71.

―――. 1987. "Reconceptualizing Retirement for Black Americans." *Gerontologist* 27:691-98.

Gibson, R. C. and J. S. Jackson. 1988. "The Health, Physical Functioning and Informal Supports of the Black Elderly." *Milbank Quarterly* 65(Supplement 2): 421-54.

―――. Forthcoming. "The Black Oldest Old: Health, Physical Functioning and Informal Support." In *The Oldest Old,* edited by R. Suzman et al. New York: Oxford University Press.

Harel, Z. and G. Deimling. 1984. "Social Resources and Mental Health: An Empirical Refinement." *Journal of Gerontology* 39(6):747-52.

Jackson, J. and R. C. Gibson. 1985. "Work and Retirement Among the Black Elderly." Pp. 193-222 in *Current Perspectives on Aging and the Life Cycle.* Vol. 1, edited by Zena Blau. Greenwich, CT: JAI.

Jackson, J. S. and S. J. Hatchett. 1986. "Intergenerational Research: Methodological Considerations." Pp. 51-76 in *Intergenerational Relations,* edited by N. Datan and H. W. Reese. Hillsdale, NJ: Lawrence Erlbaum.

Johnson, H. R. 1986. "Significant Characteristics of the Black Elderly and Their Implications for Services." Paper presented at the Gerontology Colloquium, Cleveland State University, Cleveland, OH, May 29.

Kernodle, R. W. and R. L. Kernodle. 1979. "A Comparison of the Social Networks of Blacks and Whites." Paper presented at the Gerontological Society 32nd Annual Scientific Meeting, Washington, DC, November.

Kutza, E. A. 1982. "The Impact of Federal Programs on Older Persons." *National Forum* 62(4):6-8, 14.

Luckey, I. and M. Nathan. 1989. "Outreach to the Black Aged in Rural Communities." *Human Services in the Rural Environment* 13(2):23-29.

Manton, K. Patrick and K. Johnson. 1987. "Health Differentials Between Blacks and Whites: Recent Trends in Mortality and Morbidity." *Milbank Quarterly* 65(Supplement 1):129-99.

Newman, S. J. 1986. "Demographic Influences on the Future Housing Demands of the Elderly. Pp. 21-32 in *Housing in an Aging Society,* edited by R. J. Newcomer et al. New York: Van Nostrand Reinhold.

Parnes, Herbert and Gilbert Nestel. 1981. "The Retirement Experience." Pp. 155-97 in *Work and Retirement: A National Longitudinal Study of Men,* edited by H. Parnes. Cambridge: MIT Press.

Ruiz, D. S. and T. A. Herbert. 1984. "The Economics of Health Care for Elderly Blacks." *Journal of the National Medical Association* 76(9):849-53.

Siegel, J. S. and C. M. Taeuber. 1986a. "Demographic Perspectives on the Long-Lived Society." *Daedalus* 115:77-118.

———. 1986b. "Demographic Dimensions of an Aging Population." In *Our Aging Society,* edited by A. Pifer and L. Bronte. New York: Norton.

U.S. Department of Commerce, Bureau of the Census. 1980. "Educational Attainment of the U.S.: March 1978-1979." In *Current Population Reports.* Series P-20, No. 356, August. Washington, DC: Government Printing Office.

———. 1982. "Population Profile of the United States: 1982." In *Current Population Reports.* Series P-23, No. 130. Washington, DC: Government Printing Office.

———. 1984. "Characteristics of the Population: Chapter D Detailed Population Characteristics." In *1980 Census of Population.* Vol. 1, March. Washington, DC: Government Printing Office.

———. 1985. "Money Income of Households, Families, and Persons in the United States: 1985." In *Current Population Reports.* Series P-60, No. 156. Washington, DC: Government Printing Office.

U.S. Department of Health and Human Services. 1982. *Health United States, 1982.* Public Health Service. Washington, DC: Government Printing Office.

———. 1987. "Vital and Health Statistics on Older Persons: United States, 1986." In *Analytical and Epidemiological Studies.* Series 3, No. 25. DHHS Publication No. (PHS) 87-1409. National Center for Health Statistics. Washington, DC: Government Printing Office.

Wallace, E. C. 1981. "Housing for the Black Elderly: The Need Remains." Pp. 59-64 in *Community Housing Choices for Older Americans,* edited by M. P. Lawton and S. L. Hoover. New York: Springer.

4

Social Integration

LINDA M. CHATTERS
ROBERT JOSEPH TAYLOR

Much of the research on Black aging in the social gerontology literature concerns itself with the social integration of older Black adults within a variety of social contexts. Specifically, this work addresses the relationships existing between older Black adults and social groups and settings such as the family, the workplace, peer groups, the church, and community and civic organizations. The impetus for these investigations originated from varied sources. First, social integration is prominent in several of the traditional theories of adjustment and well-being in older age (e.g., activity theory, social life space, role theory). Research addressing the relationship between social integration and personal well-being focuses on diverse forms of behavior such as social activity, social roles, and the nature of primary and secondary group relations.

A corollary interest in social integration arises from its potential for providing a context for supportive relationships for older Black adults. Social integration within family, church, and community settings allows the opportunity to both give and receive assistance from these informal networks. Informal networks and helpers provide a variety of instrumental, material, and socioemotional aid and services to older Black adults. The most widely investigated informal support networks

AUTHORS' NOTE: This chapter was originally presented as a paper at "Understanding and Serving Black Aged: A Community Conference and Forum," sponsored by Cleveland State University and the Cleveland Clinic Foundation and cofunded by the Cleveland Foundation, Cleveland State University, Cleveland, Ohio, February 26-27, 1987.

are those that are organized within the family, although church and neighborhood networks are receiving increasing attention in the literature (Chatters et al., 1985; Taylor and Chatters, 1986a, 1986b).

The focus of the present chapter is on the social integration of older Black adults within the contexts of family, friends, and church. Evidence regarding the integration of older Blacks in these settings will be reviewed. Following this, research on the well-being consequences of participation in these networks will be presented. Methodological limitations of previous work on this topic are discussed. Evidence regarding social integration within the spheres of family, church, and peer relationships is reviewed. The issue of intragroup variation within the older Black adult population and its influence on social integration and support will be included in this discussion. Finally, selected trends in the aging population will be examined and their potential effects on the integration and support of older Black adults will be explored.

Social Integration and Social Contexts

Social integration within informal networks and organizations has been a consistent theme in research and writing on Black Americans. Theory and research in the social sciences have documented the critical position and functions of these networks and institutions in the economic, social, and political development of Blacks. Informal networks and organizations developed as the result of a particular set of conditions in American society whereby Black Americans were systematically excluded from diverse spheres of economic, political, educational, and civic activity. Lacking access to social institutions and roles within larger society, Black communities developed parallel institutions and mechanisms to serve their needs. These supportive networks, organized within family, church, and neighborhood settings, exert diverse and far-reaching influences on individuals, families, and communities.

A negative aspect of this theoretical perspective is that unfortunately it fosters the view that Black institutions are mere imitations of their counterparts in wider society. As such, Black institutions have been frequently characterized as, at best, inferior substitutes or caricatures of White institutions and, at worst, dysfunctional organizations that effectively impede the development of Black individuals and communities. This perspective fails to appreciate the innovative and adaptive features of these networks and organizations.

Increased assimilation into the broader society and greater diversification within Black communities themselves (i.e., social class differentiation) have functioned to diminish the need and/or to alter the form and operation of these networks and organizations (e.g., educational, health care, and political institutions). However, in many instances these networks and institutions (e.g., family, church, civic and social groups) retain their distinctive position as the focal point for activity, involvement, and development within Black communities.

Social Integration and Personal Well-Being

The notion that social integration and personal well-being are intricately related in older age has had a long tradition in the field of social gerontology. It is generally recognized that with the coming of old age, the relationship between the individual and society is affected by a variety of circumstances and events that potentially result in a profound alteration in social roles and activities. Reversing a trend of increasing involvement in societal roles throughout the middle years, old age frequently involves relinquishing these roles and obligations. In particular, widowhood, retirement, and the loss of the active parental role often coincide in older age. Some writers have suggested that declining opportunities to obtain satisfactions from social roles results in a condition of rolelessness in old age, with its attendant problems of lowered morale and decreased personal well-being. This situation is counteracted by identifying and investing in roles and sources of satisfaction other than those that were relinquished. Related to work on social roles is the notion that activity (and more specifically, social activity and interaction) promotes personal well-being and adjustment (Diener, 1984; Horan and Belcher, 1982).

Early work profiling the activities of elderly Black adults indicated extensive participation in voluntary associations (e.g., church and civic) and leisure pursuits (Hearn, 1971), as well as involvement in a variety of social roles (Ehrlich, 1973). Research specifically examining social roles suggested that elderly Black adults had access to a number of roles that provided alternative outlets to the traditional roles of spouse and worker. Further, greater breadth and depth of existing roles were apparent, as well as more explicit behavioral expectations and norms for roles that were generally regarded as secondary (e.g., grandparent). Prominent among work on elderly Blacks is the significance attached to active participation in the roles of family elder and grandparent. Rather than a deemphasis on parental behaviors and the loss of the functional parent role, Black elderly are portrayed as being integral members of Black families (Mitchell and Register, 1984).

Research on secondary group relations and formal social organizations such as the church suggests that they similarly facilitate the social integration of older Blacks and contribute to personal well-being (Dowd and Bengtson, 1978; Ortega et al., 1983). The church has been described as a pseudo-extended family, mimicking many of the functions of the extended family (Ortega et al., 1983) and performing a variety of material, emotional, and spiritual functions (Taylor and Chatters, 1986a, 1986b; Taylor et al., 1987). Others have noted the significance of the church as a social institution and a context for primary group relations (Lindsay and Hawkins, 1974) as well as an outlet for social roles and activity. The structure and dynamics of social institutions such as the family and the church provide elderly Blacks with a context for the performance of meaningful and fulfilling social roles and allow their participation as active integral members of these groups.

With regard to older Black adults and their attitudes toward the work role, a history of labor market experiences marked by limited and unsatisfactory participation (i.e., under- and unemployment and discriminatory practices) may potentially modify elderly Blacks' retirement experiences and attitudes (Jackson and Gibson, 1985). Attachment to the work role is likely more tenuous and, under certain circumstances, its relinquishment is met with relief rather than concern. Additionally, given unsatisfactory experiences with traditional labor markets, older Blacks may participate in other informal market economies (i.e., social and underground) for the fulfillment of economic needs. Participation in these economic networks not only provides alternative role outlets but serves to strengthen the informal relationships that exist within these contexts (Jackson and Chatters, 1984).

Methodological Limitations of Research on Older Black Americans

Much of the early writings on the support networks and relationships of Black Americans were based on investigations involving small samples of adults. Many of these studies were locally or regionally based and examined select subgroups of the general Black population (e.g., urban Blacks residing in the North). A tradition of research adopted a qualitative approach to investigations of support relationships. Ethnographic studies of Black communities are representative of this work and provide us with the majority of available information in this area (Aschenbrenner, 1975; Kennedy, 1980; Liebow, 1967; Martin and Martin, 1978; Shimkin et al., 1978).

Quantitative assessments of support among Black adults are less numerous, and the literature has been dominated by the use of nonprobability samples (Jackson, 1972a, 1972b; McAdoo, 1978) and a reliance on the examination of percentage differences (Hirsch et al., 1972; Jackson, 1972a, 1972b; Martineau, 1977). Further, the use of multivariate analysis techniques to assess the independent contributions of factors to supportive behaviors is found in the work of only a few investigators (Cantor et al., 1979; Mutran, 1985; Taylor, 1985, 1986).

These methodological and analytic features of the available literature on the support relationships of older Black adults are significant for several reasons. First, despite the diversity of research approaches represented, there is a general paucity of data on this topic (Markides, 1983; Mindel, 1983). Work that is based on small and select subgroups of older Black adults provides a characterization of these behaviors that is not representative of the entire population. Related to this, several studies fail to provide adequate sample representation on a variety of demographic factors such as income and education. Given the restriction in the range of important status factors, their relationships to supportive behaviors are effectively obscured. Finally, the concentration on percentage differences and bivariate analyses means that the relative contributions of different factors to supportive behaviors cannot be discerned.

Taken together, the methodological and analytic limitations of much of the previous work argue for caution in generalizing these findings to the older Black adult population. The following sections detail the empirical findings regarding the nature of supportive relations that exist between older Black adults and their families, churches, and peers. The discussion focuses primarily on research based on representative samples of older Black adults and utilizes multivariate approaches to data analysis.

Social Integration
and Informal Social Support

Extended Families as a Source of Assistance

Research on living arrangements and household structures of older Black adults provides some indication of their level of social integration within family settings. Irrespective of socioeconomic status, Black adults of all ages are more likely to reside in extended households than are Whites (Allen, 1979; Angel and Tienda, 1982; Hofferth, 1984; Morgan, 1983; Sweet, 1973; Tienda and Angel, 1982). Work that examines the living arrangements of older adults also indicates that aged Blacks are more likely to reside in extended households than are aged Whites. Although they are less likely than older Whites to live with their spouses, older Black adults are less likely to live alone and more likely to live with more than one person (Rubenstein, 1971). Elderly Blacks are also more likely to reside with children and grandchildren (Mitchell and Register, 1984; Shanas, 1979) and to take children and grandchildren and nieces and nephews into their households (Mitchell and Register, 1984). Among spouseless elderly, Blacks have more children living with them (Lopata, 1979) and are more likely to raise the children of others (Hirsch et al., 1972).

The majority of work on the support networks of older adults has centered on the family as a source of assistance. Research in this area suggests that older persons exercise an ordered preference in their utilization of family assistance (Cantor, 1979; Shanas, 1979). Accordingly, spouse and adult children are employed first, followed by other relatives (e.g., siblings) and nonkin peers (e.g., friends and neighbors). Two studies that examined the use of informal helpers among older Blacks found evidence for demographic variation in the size of the informal network and the existence of a hierarchy of support (Chatters et al., 1985, 1986). In particular, women, married elderly, those with children, and southerners all had larger helper networks than did their counterparts. Reported closeness to one's family was also positively related to network size. Findings for the selection of individual helpers confirmed a preference for utilizing immediate family first, followed by other relatives and nonkin. Further, the absence of preferred helpers (i.e., through widowhood and childlessness) was directly related to smaller and more diverse helper networks.

Taylor (1985) examined the demographic and family factor correlates of the provision of aid to older Black adults. Women, persons with
few years of formal education, higher-income respondents, southerners,
and those who reported frequent contact with family all received support on a more frequent basis than did their counterparts. For childless
elderly, however, proximity of relatives was the only significant factor.

Social Structure Variability in Familial Support

Research that examines social integration and the nature of informal support relationships focuses on the attributes of both support
recipient and provider (e.g., in terms of demographic characteristics and
kin versus nonkin status), as well as the types of assistance that are
exchanged. Despite the paucity of information addressing the issue of
demographic variability in social integration and support among older
Black adults, several general trends and patterns can be discerned.

Age differences in social integration and support suggest that older
respondents are generally less likely than their younger counterparts to
receive assistance from immediate and extended family (Antonucci and
Depner, 1981). Investigations of Black families document the important
role of elderly Blacks in the family support system (Mitchell and
Register, 1984), but do not specifically address age differences in
assistance levels. Research among Black adults suggests that, in some
instances, the effects of age on support are conditioned by the presence
of children (Taylor, 1986).

A study on the entire age range found that income and age were
significant predictors of assistance from family among Black adults
(Taylor, 1986). The overall effect of increasing levels of age on support
was negative. However, the presence of a significant interaction between age and the presence of a child indicated that older persons
without children were much less likely to report receiving assistance
from their families than were older persons with children. Advanced
age has also been associated with the use of distant kin and unrelated
persons as support resources (Chatters et al., 1985). Other work indicates that, in terms of support from family, there is no specific advantage or disadvantage associated with age status (Chatters et al., 1986).

Consistent with other population groups, gender is an important
explanatory variable, and older Black women are more likely than
men to be participants in informal social groups and to do so at significantly higher levels. Greater sociability among older women is evident

in a variety of contexts related to affiliation and contact (i.e., family, friend, and church settings) as well as in the active supportive behaviors exhibited by women (Antonucci, 1985). Older Black women are important in maintaining the kinship networks of extended families (Aschenbrenner, 1975; Shimkin et al., 1978; Stack, 1974). Research on older Black adults indicates that level of assistance from the family are significantly higher among women (Taylor, 1985).

Socioeconomic status differences in social integration and support are not as clear as those for gender. Early ethnographic research on Black Americans suggested that persons of lower socioeconomic status exhibited considerably higher levels of family contact, interaction, and integration. As these studies were focused on specialized subgroups of the Black population, they were unable to address questions of demographic variability in these behaviors.

More recent work examining representative samples of older Black respondents suggests that in some instances socioeconomic status and support issues are unrelated (Chatters et al., 1985, 1986) or exhibit both positive and negative associations (Taylor, 1985). The absence of a relationship between socioeconomic status and support as well as the finding of greater levels of assistance among higher-SES respondents challenges the common assumption that apparent need for support triggers its provision. It may be the case that the need hypothesis of support operates within defined limits; the presence of too great a need may severely tax support providers and actually diminish potential resources for assistance.

Regional differences in social integration and support have not been investigated because of the lack of studies based on national samples of older Black adults. Emerging work suggests that southern residents are distinctive from older Blacks in other regions in that they have larger support networks (Chatters et al., 1985); are more likely to make use of the categories of sister, friend, and neighbor as informal helpers (Chatters et al., 1986); and receive assistance from extended family on a more frequent basis (Taylor, 1985).

Filial bonds and obligations emerge as potent motivators for the provision of aid to older adults, and both marital and parental statuses are important in differentiating levels of assistance (Shanas, 1979; Johnson and Catalano, 1981; Ward, 1979). In several studies of older Blacks, adult children (Chatters et al., 1985, 1986; Taylor, 1985) and spouses (Chatters et al., 1985, 1986), in particular, are noted as important sources of aid. Nonkin peer and sibling relationships figure prominently in the support networks of older adults who are without spouses and children (Chatters et al., 1985, 1986). However, several studies indicate that the presence of a spouse has no influence on level of assistance from extended family (Taylor, 1985) and church support networks (Taylor and Chatters, 1986a).

Churches and Social Support

Historically, religion and religious institutions have played a vital and primary role in Black communities (Hill, 1971). Evidence concerning the significance of the church stresses its role in providing for the material and psychological sustenance of older Black adults (Hill, 1971; Neighbors et al., 1982). Black Americans frequently exhibit lifelong attachments to the church. Religious institutions provide the context for a variety of important life events, such as marriages, births, and deaths, and constitute a stable environment for understanding these major life transitions.

With regard to older Blacks, religious institutions provide the opportunity to function in meaningful roles at a time when other traditional social roles—such as spouse, parent, and worker—are curtailed or nonexistent. Indeed, various aspects of the church, such as its similarity to extended families, allow for the participation of older Blacks in pseudokin relations with others. In fulfilling their social welfare functions, churches enlist older congregants as the actual providers of services to others. Consequently, religious institutions are important to elderly Black adults because they function as substitutes for many of the social roles that are lost or restricted with the coming of old age.

In addition to its social role functions, the church provides spiritual and religious meaning to the lives of older Black adults. Moral and religious traits and beliefs are ways in which older individuals, as well as others, define themselves and organize their personal lives. Religion has been viewed as a way of establishing meaning and order in life, particularly during times of distress (Hadaway, 1978). Among older persons in particular, religious pursuits are considered adaptive to the life crises of the later years (e.g., declining health, loss of loved ones, recognition of personal mortality) (Guy, 1982).

Emergent work suggests that the church is the focal point of supportive networks for older Blacks involving the exchange of material goods and services as well as emotional aid (Taylor and Chatters, 1986a, 1986b). Taylor and Chatters (1986a) examined the influence of church members as the providers of informal support to older Black adults. Frequency of church attendance emerged as a significant predictor of both the frequency of assistance and the amount of aid provided to older Black adults. The analyses also indicated that adult children facilitated the provision of assistance to older parents. For older persons with children, increasing age was associated with increases in the frequency of aid from church members. Among older persons without children, however, increasing age was associated with decreases in assistance. Church members provided a variety of assistance to older adults, including financial help, goods and services, and help during an illness.

A study of the patterns of assistance to older Black adults examined family, friends, and church members as sources of aid (Taylor and Chatters, 1986b). The vast majority of respondents received assistance from one or more of these groups; only a small minority were completely isolated from support resources. Individual support groups were distinctive in the types of aid they provided; family members tended to give instrumental assistance; church members provided advice and encouragement, prayer, and assistance when ill; and friends were more likely to provide companionship. Despite an overall tendency toward specificity in support source-type combinations, small percentages of respondents indicated that friends and church members played a substantial role in providing for their assistance needs.

Peer Relationships and Social Support

Ethnographic research suggests that individuals who are unrelated by blood or marriage are often represented in the informal support networks of Black families (Aschenbrenner, 1975; Kennedy, 1980; Martin and Martin, 1978; Shimkin et al., 1978; Stack, 1972, 1974). Several researchers have suggested that nonkin associates are particularly critical among certain subgroups of the Black population and assume a dominant and influential role in informal networks (e.g., Ladner, 1971; Liebow, 1967). Friend relationships are sometimes regarded in kinship terms, which serves to solidify feelings of mutual obligation and to extend the rights and responsibilities of kin status to support participants (Kennedy, 1980).

The majority of work on social integration and social support among older adults has examined the family as the major source and context for caregiving. The utilization of friends as caregivers typically occurs only under special circumstances and conditions. In this regard, the use of nonkin as support providers is evident among older persons who are without spouses and children. In addition, particular forms of support that emphasize affirmation and commonality of experience may be anticipated from age-peer associates such as friends, confidants, and neighbors. Limited research on this topic suggests that urban Black elders interact on a frequent basis with friends (Wolf et al., 1983), and older Black women express satisfaction with existing levels of frequent contact with close friends (Jackson, 1972a).

A limited amount of work examining the role of friends as support providers to older Black adults is found in the literature (Gibson, 1982; McAdoo, 1978; Taylor and Chatters, 1986b). In a comparison of middle- and late-life Black and White adults, Gibson (1982) found that Blacks at both life stages were more likely than Whites to utilize friends and neighbors in coping with psychological distress. Evidence from a representative sample of Black adults suggests that friends are represented in the support networks of older Black adults (Taylor and Chatters, 1986b). Among elderly Black adults who were without children and spouses, nonkin were particularly important (Chatters et al., 1985, 1986).

Diversity and Strength
Among the Black Aged

The collection of research findings presented here allows the opportunity to examine variability in the nature and form of social support provided to older Black adults. Particular areas of note include sociodemographic variability in relation to age, gender, marital and parental statuses, and region. Further, these results indicate that differences in attitudes toward the family and self-reports of involvement in the church are related to receiving assistance from these groups.

The demonstration of variability in these processes provides information with regard to the development of service models to older Black adults. By recognizing the diversity that exists in the older Black population, formal support agencies can more effectively serve their clients. Rather than simply accepting common assumptions regarding the support networks of older Blacks, emergent research is providing an accurate picture of how and under what conditions these networks function.

It is important to question the conventional wisdom that holds that the Black family provides for all the needs of its elderly members. The blind acceptance of this assumption implies that the informal support network is more than adequate to meet the needs of older Blacks and does not require the aid of formal agencies. Furthermore, in ignoring differences within the older Black population we fail to utilize extant strengths effectively.

Social Integration of Future Cohorts of Older Black Adults

In suggesting future areas of concern in relation to aging Black adults, it is critical to examine major demographic trends that will affect this group. One of the most striking is the anticipated "graying" of the general population. The proportion of the population made up of individuals who are age 55 years and over is expected to remain stable at just over one-fifth of the total population through the year 2000. By 2010, however, this group will constitute one-fourth of the total population, increasing to one-third of the population by 2050. Dramatic increases are expected in the number and proportion of the very old (85 years and over) elderly, so that by 2050 there will be 16 million in this category (compared with 2.2 million in 1982) (U.S. Department of Commerce, 1983). The sex composition of this future over-55 population will be overwhelmingly female. In 1982, older women outnumbered older men by 3 to 2, and the trend toward a female excess is expected to continue for approximately the next 20 years, to be followed by a leveling of rates (U.S. Department of Commerce, 1983).

These projected shifts in the aging population have implications for a variety of issues and concerns, including social integration and informal supports. Demographic trends evident among the general aging population in terms of increased longevity and increasing feminization will be apparent among older Blacks as well. The increasing female excess will be intensified among this group, which will lead to an exacerbation of the problems facing older Black women (i.e., low income, poor health, and decreasing social resources for care).

Current data on income levels among the elderly population as a whole indicate that Blacks and women are particularly disadvantaged. In 1981, 80% of older Black women had annual incomes below $5,000. Comparable figures for other race-sex groups indicate that 50% of

Black men and White women and 20% of White men had incomes below that level. Within the general aging population, income resources vary considerably by marital status and living arrangements, with elderly who are married and those who reside in family situations faring better.

Black women are consistently most likely to be widowed across all age levels of the older (over 55 years) population. This trend is especially pronounced at the later ages (75 years and above), where close to 80% of Black women are without spouses (U.S. Department of Commerce, 1983). Consistent with the effects of marital status and living arrangements, Black women who are widowed and those who live alone are most likely of all gender-race groups to live in poverty. Similar to their White counterparts, older Black women will continue to outlive older men and will constitute the large majority of future cohorts of "very old" Blacks. Coupled with reduced income resources, older Black women will increasingly have fewer personal resources for informal social support in the form of spouses.

Traditionally, the family and the church, through a variety of mechanisms, have been effective in providing for the social integration and informal support of older individuals. Projected demographic trends suggest that the coming years will present new challenges to Black elders, families, and churches. First, the increased longevity of older groups will not necessarily be accompanied by better physical health. Although medical science will be able to prolong the length of the life span, it is not clear that the quality of life in terms of physical health and morbidity will be improved. Further, while selective pressures have been suggested as producing current cohorts of hardy very old Black adults, medical advances will prolong the lives of emergent cohorts of old-old Black elders who will likely be less resilient.

These projected changes in the health profiles of future cohorts of older Blacks suggest that they may be at increased risk for receiving inadequate health care. These demographic and health changes will have direct significance for the informal support and care that elderly receive from families. The feminization of older groups of Blacks, along with imbalances in the male-female sex ratio evident across all age groups, will mean that, increasingly, those Black elders in need of care will be women. Due to a lack of marital partners, older Black women will have on average fewer family resources to draw on for caregivers, placing them at higher risk of institutional placement.

It is important to ask what the nature of caregiving responsibilities of families to their older members will be. Will one or more generations of older Blacks—for example, an elderly parent and grandparent—require family assistance? Who will have the major responsibility for the care of elders? Current patterns of care suggest that women, by and large, assume responsibility for caregiving. Increased demands for the provision of aid take their toll on the physical and mental health of caregivers. Caregiver burnout and a reduction in the quality of care are potential consequences of a situation in which the support provider is not being adequately supported in the caregiver role. As pressures for multiple caregiving arise, it will be necessary to employ new sources of assistance and/or to modify and adapt existing ones.

Summary and Conclusion

The emerging body of literature addressing the support networks of older Black adults focuses attention both on the nature of their relationships with family, friends, and social groups and on the conditions under which those relationships emerge and are maintained. The factors associated with the support networks of older Black adults are not unique to that group. However, these networks are distinctive with regard to the diversity of their composition and the prominence of affective bonds and long-term associations in the selection of particular helpers.

Both immediate and extended family members function as participants in the support networks of older Black adults. Immediate or nuclear family members (i.e., spouses and children) are the preferred providers of assistance to older Black adults, and their enlistment as care providers is supported by bonds of filial obligation and normative expectations to assist. In the absence of these individuals, however, extended family members are substituted as support providers. The willingness to employ extended family as members of the support network is fostered by the existence of extended household patterns and the involvement of extended family members in a shared history of reciprocal assistance. Questions as to the adequacy of support from these different sources, as well as the conditions and limitations of the assistance, remain unanswered.

For particular subgroups of the older Black population, friends are enlisted as participants in the support network. In general, the involvement of friends occurs in the absence of or in addition to that of immediate and distant family resources. The use of friends as support providers is facilitated by the intensification of friendship bonds to the status of pseudokin and the existence of enduring reciprocal relationships. Groups of older Blacks who tend to rely on peers for support include childless and widowed elderly and those who have never married.

As yet, there is little available information concerning the nature and extent of support provided by age peers. For example, research suggests that over the courses of their lives, never-married elderly have made considerable investments of time and emotional commitment in friendship relationships. Widowed individuals, on the other hand, may have focused attention on their marital relationships, to the exclusion of other associations. As a consequence, they may lack shared backgrounds with friends that would serve as a basis for a helping relationship. Clearly, there is much that we do not know about helping relationships with friends and those influences that affect their nature and functioning. Given the diversity of possible factors and circumstances, it is likely that there is considerable range in the forms and types of assistance provided by age peers.

The least examined topic in the area of informal helping relationships of older Black adults concerns the assistance provided by religious and social organizations. Available work suggests that Black churches, in particular, frequently provide considerable amounts of aid to members of their congregations. Similar to individual helping relationships, the provisions of assistance to older congregants is regulated by factors such as investment and length of tenure in the church (i.e., church attendance and membership). Individual attributes of the older person (i.e., age, region, and parental status) also influence the amount of assistance provided.

Further work is needed to explore more fully the role of Black churches in the social support networks of older Black adults. Relatively little is known concerning the use of complementary sources of assistance from family, friends, and church members. On the whole, this work suggests that most older Blacks receive support from one or more of these groups and that to a large degree there is specificity in the type of aid elicited from a particular group. Another unexplored area in relation to church support concerns the effect of institutional characteristics (i.e., religious denomination, size of congregation, organizational structure of the church) on the provision of support.

It is clear that despite the general perception of high levels of social integration among older Black adults, much more work needs to be completed if we are to understand fully the nature and functioning of the specific social contexts involved. The mechanisms of social integration are poorly understood, particularly as they relate to church and peer social networks. What sorts of factors govern participation in these settings? Do different groups of older Black adults (e.g., men versus women, southern versus nonsouthern) have differential access to these networks? How do different social networks (i.e., family, church, and peer) interface with one another? Continuing research in these areas will benefit the delivery of formal services and informal care to older Black adults.

References

Allen, W. R. 1979. "Class, Culture, and Family Organization: The Effects of Class and Race on Family Structure in Urban America." *Journal of Comparative Family Studies* 10:301-13.

Angel, R. and M. Tienda. 1982. "Determinants of Extended Household Structure: Cultural Patterns or Economic Model?" *American Journal of Sociology* 87:1360-83.

Antonucci, T. C. 1985. "Personal Characteristics, Social Support and Social Behavior." Pp. 94-128 in *Handbook of Aging and the Social Sciences,* edited by R. H. Binstock and E. Shanas. 2nd ed. New York: Van Nostrand Reinhold.

Antonucci, T. C. and C. E. Depner. 1981. "Social Support and Informal Helping Relationships." Pp. 235-54 in *Basic Processes in Helping Relationships,* edited by T. A. Willis. New York: Academic Press.

Aschenbrenner, J. 1975. *Lifelines: Black Families in Chicago.* New York: Holt, Rinehart & Winston.

Cantor, M. H. 1979. "Neighbors and Friends: An Overlooked Resource in the Informal Support System." *Research on Aging* 1:434-63.

Cantor, M. H., K. Rosenthal, and L. Wilker. 1979. "Social and Family Relationships of Black Aged Women in New York City." *Journal of Minority Aging* 4:50-61.

Chatters, L. M., R. J. Taylor, and J. S. Jackson. 1985. "Size and Composition of the Informal Helper Networks of Elderly Blacks." *Journal of Gerontology* 40:605-14.

———. 1986. "Aged Blacks' Choices for an Informal Helper Network." *Journal of Gerontology* 41:94-100.

Diener, E. 1984. "Subjective Well-Being." *Psychological Bulletin* 95:542-75.

Dowd, J. J. and V. L. Bengtson. 1978. "Aging in Minority Populations: An Examination of the Double Jeopardy Hypothesis." *Journal of Gerontology* 33:427-36.

Ehrlich, I. F. 1973. "Toward a Social Profile of the Aged Black Population in the U.S.: An Exploratory Study." *Aging and Human Development* 4:271-76.

Gibson, R. C. 1982. "Blacks at Middle and Late Life: Resources and Coping." *Annals of the American Academy of Political and Social Science* 464:79-90.

Guy, R. F. 1982. "Religion, Physical Disabilities, and Life Satisfaction in Older Age Cohorts." *International Journal of Aging and Human Development* 15:225-32.

Hadaway, C. K. 1978. "Life Satisfaction and Religion: A Reanalysis." *Social Forces* 57:636-43.

Hearn, H. L. 1971. "Career and Leisure Patterns of Middle-Aged Urban Blacks." *Gerontologist* 11:21-26.

Hill, R. B. 1971. *The Strengths of Black Families.* New York: Emerson Hall.

Hirsch, C., D. P. Kent, and S. L. Silverman. 1972. "Homogeneity and Heterogeneity Among Low-Income Negro and White Aged." Pp. 400-500 in *Research Planning and Action for the Elderly: The Power and Potential of Social Science,* edited by D. P. Kent et al. New York: Behavioral Publications.

Hofferth, S. L. 1984. "Kin Networks, Race, and Family Structure." *Journal of Marriage and the Family* 46:791-806.

Horan, P. M. and J. C. Belcher. 1982. "Lifestyle and Morale in the Southern Rural Aged." *Research on Aging* 4:523-49.

Jackson, J. J. 1972a. "Comparative Life Styles and Family and Friend Relationships Among Older Black Women." *Family Coordinator* 21:477-86.

———. 1972b. "Marital Life Among Older Black Couples." *Family Coordinator* 21:21-28.

Jackson, J. S. and L. M. Chatters. 1984. "Sociocultural Factors in the Productive Activities of Older Americans." Research proposal submitted to the National Institute on Aging, Washington, DC.

Jackson, J. S. and R. C. Gibson. 1985. "Work and Retirement Among the Black Elderly." Pp. 193-222 in *Current Perspectives on Aging and the Lifecycle,* edited by Zena Blau. Hartford, CT: JAI.

Johnson, C. L. and D. J. Catalano. 1981. "Childless Elderly and Their Family Support." *The Gerontologist* 21:610-18.

Kennedy, T. R. 1980. *You Gotta Deal with It: Black Family Relations in a Southern Community.* New York: Oxford University Press.

Ladner, J. 1971. *Tomorrow's Tomorrow: The Black Women.* Garden City, NY: Doubleday.

Liebow, E. 1967. *Tally's Corner: A Study of Negro Streetcorner Men.* Boston: Little, Brown.

Lindsay, I. B. and B. D. Hawkins. 1974. "Research Issues Relating to the Black Aged." Pp. 53-65 in *Social Research and the Black Community: Selected Issues and Priorities,* edited by L. E. Gary. Washington, DC: Howard University, Institute for Urban Affairs and Research.

Lopata, H. Z. 1979. *Women as Widows.* New York: Elsevier.

Markides, K. S. 1983. "Minority Aging." Pp. 115-37 in *Aging in Society: Selected Reviews of Recent Research,* edited by M. W. Riley et al. Hillsdale, NJ: Lawrence Erlbaum.

Martin, E. and J. Martin. 1978. *The Black Extended Family.* Chicago: University of Chicago Press.

Martineau, W. 1977. "Informal Social Ties Among Urban Black Americans." *Journal of Black Studies* 8:83-104.

McAdoo, H. P. 1978. "Factors Related to Stability in Upwardly Mobile Black Families." *Journal of Marriage and the Family* 40:762-78.

Mindel, C. H. 1983. "The Elderly in Minority Families." In *Family Relationships in Later Life,* edited by T. H. Brubaker. Beverly Hills, CA: Sage.

Mitchell, J. S. and J. C. Register. 1984. "An Exploration of Family Interaction with the Elderly by Race, Socioeconomic Status and Residence." *The Gerontologist* 24:48-54.

Morgan, J. N. 1983. "The Redistribution of Income by Families and Institutions and Emergency Help Patterns." Pp. 1-43 in *Five Thousand American Families—Patterns of Economic Progress.* Vol. 10, *Analyses of the First Thirteen Years of the Panel Study of Income Dynamics,* edited by G. J. Duncan and J. N. Morgan. Ann Arbor, MI: Institute for Social Research.

Mutran, E. 1985. "Intergenerational Family Support Among Blacks and Whites: Response to Culture or to Socioeconomic Differences." *Journal of Gerontology* 40:382-89.

Neighbors, H., J. S. Jackson, P. J. Bowman, and G. Gurin. 1982. "Stress, Coping and Black Mental Health: Preliminary Findings from a National Study." *Prevention in Human Services* 2:5-29.

Ortega, S. T., R. D. Crutchfield, and W. A. Rushing. 1983. "Race Differences in Elderly Personal Well-Being: Friendship, Family and Church." *Research on Aging* 5:101-18.

Rubenstein, D. I. 1971. "An Examination of Social Participation Found Among a National Sample of Black and White Elderly." *International Journal of Aging and Human Development* 2:172-88.

Shanas, E. 1979. *National Survey of the Elderly.* Report to the Administration on Aging. Washington, DC: Department of Health and Human Services.

Shimkin, D., E. Shimkin, and D. Frate. 1978. *The Extended Family in Black Societies.* Chicago: Aldine.

Stack, C. B. 1972. "Black Kindreds: Parenthood and Personal Kindreds Among Urban Blacks." *Journal of Comparative Family Studies* 3:194-206.

———. 1974. *All Our Kin.* New York: Harper & Row.

Sweet, J. A. 1973. *Women in the Labor Force.* New York: Seminar.

Taylor, R. J. 1985. "The Extended Family as a Source of Support to Elderly Blacks." *The Gerontologist* 25:488-95.

———. 1986. "Receipt of Support from Family Among Black Americans: Demographic and Familial Differences." *Journal of Marriage and the Family* 48:67-77.

Taylor, R. J. and L. M. Chatters. 1986a. "Church-Based Informal Support Among Elderly Blacks." *The Gerontologist* 26:637-42.

———. 1986b. "Patterns of Informal Support to Elderly Black Adults: Family, Friends and Church Members." *Social Work* 31:432-38.

Taylor, R. J., M. C. Thornton, and L. M. Chatters. 1987. "Black Americans' Perception of the Sociohistorical Role of the Church." *Journal of Black Studies* 18:123-38.

Tienda, M. and R. Angel. 1982. "Headship and Household Composition Among Blacks, Hispanics, and Other Whites." *Social Forces* 61:508-31.

U.S. Department of Commerce, Bureau of the Census. 1983. "America in Transition: An Aging Society." In *Current Population Reports.* Special Studies, Series P-23, No. 80. Washington, DC: Government Printing Office.

Ward, R. 1979. "The Never Married in Later Life." *Journal of Gerontology* 34(6):861-69.

Wolf, J. H., N. Breslaw, A. B. Ford, H. D. Ziegler, and A. Ward. 1983. "Distance and Contacts: Interactions of Black Urban Elderly Adults and Family and Friends." *Journal of Gerontology* 38:465-71.

5

Diversity Among Aged Black Males

CARY S. KART

Ethnogerontology is the study of the causes, processes, and consequences of race, national origin, and culture on individual and population aging (Jackson, 1985). Two issues prominent in the literature of this emerging subfield in gerontology are double jeopardy and the racial crossover in mortality. In this context, the term *double jeopardy* refers to the doubly difficult status of being both a minority group member and old. The phrase *racial crossover in mortality* describes the fact that the death rate of Blacks in virtually all age groups except the very aged is significantly higher than the rate of Whites. In the older years, the racial differential declines and, among people in their 80s, a crossover occurs in which the reported death rates of Blacks of both sexes fall below those of Whites (Zopf, 1986).

These concepts nicely capture the essence of ethnogerontology, with its characteristic focus on major sociodemographic differences between aged Whites and minorities. However, students of ethnogerontology have overlooked the issue of diversity or heterogeneity within specific minority aged populations. This may result from a concern with documenting social inequities between dominant and minority aged that is expressed at the expense of identifying diversity present within aged minority populations.

Research literature on Black aging has generally focused upon the total Black population or upon Black women only; older Black males represent a relatively invisible minority within a minority. In 1985, males 65 years of age and older constituted only about 40% of the total Black aged population. In part, this focus on Black women results from the expansion of the double jeopardy concept to triple jeopardy with the specification of gender (National Council on the Aging, 1971). But this focus also follows the increase in literature on various aspects of behavior in Black communities and, in particular, studies of the Black family with special attention given to Black women and their children (Gary, 1981).

According to Gary (1981), the roles Black men play in their families have at best received only marginal attention from social and behavioral scientists and practitioners. From his view, the attention given to the role and status of Black women has helped create "the impression in the minds of many people that the Black community functions primarily as a matriarchal family system" (p. 10). Cazenave (1979) agrees; he argues that even when the Black male has been studied, "there has been more emphasis on his absence than with his presence in the family" (p. 583). In fact, so little attention has been given to Black men as husbands and fathers that Cazenave believes they qualify "as phantoms of American family studies" (p. 583).

Are Black males phantoms in gerontological studies as well? Has the relative inattention Black males have received in the gerontological literature perpetuated assumptions of homogeneity in this population? What are the bases for diversity among aged Black males? And what policy and service issues make it essential that we recognize this diversity? I begin with a review of some basic demographic data to highlight the diversity within this population. A brief summary of the literature on the double jeopardy concept follows, with emphasis on how findings may pertain to Black males. Finally, selected policy and service issues are implicated in the need to recognize the diversity within this population group.

Demographic Considerations

Table 5.1 shows the age distribution of Black males 60 years and older in 1985. The "young-old" represent a majority of this population; 58% are between 60 and 69 years of age. Almost 11% of these elderly Black males are 80 years of age or older. It is worth noting that Black men are generally the most undercounted group in the United States (Parsons, 1972, p. 4). This is especially the case for younger Black males. The U.S. Census has estimated that nearly 20% of Black males between the ages of 25 and 40 were missed in 1970 (U.S. Department of Commerce, 1974, p. 11). Lieberson (1978) speculates that the influ-

Table 5.1 Age Distribution of Black Males in the United States, Aged 60 and Over, 1985

Age	Number (thousands)	Percentage
60-64	439	31.8
65-69	361	26.2
70-74	258	18.7
75-79	172	12.5
80-84	84	6.1
85+	65	4.7
Totals	1,379	100.0

SOURCE: U.S. Department of Commerce (1986).

ences of migrant status (e.g., born in the South and migrated to the North) and of low socioeconomic position on enumeration are interactive, so that low-income Black migrants are most likely to be overlooked.

The diversity of experience represented in the age distribution of older Black males cannot be overstated. Each cohort of Black males in the United States has been exposed to different cultural practices and social and political conditions (Green and Siegler, 1984). Wilson (1978) has identified three major stages that Blacks in the United States have experienced historically. The first stage includes slavery and the post-Civil War period. The second is the period of industrial expansion beginning in the last quarter of the nineteenth century and continuing through World War II. The third stage comprises the contemporary era since the end of World War II.

During the first two stages, racial barriers were explicit and designed to systematically deny Blacks access to economic, political, and social resources. Efforts to minimize, neutralize, and even negate the voting privileges of Blacks exemplify these barriers (Simon and Eitzen, 1982). According to Wilson (1978), very few Blacks were employed in industrial plants prior to World War I. In the South, Black labor was restricted largely to agricultural work and domestic services. The emergence of Jim Crow segregation effectively prevented the employment of Blacks in industry. Mechanization reduced the need for farm labor during the 1920s and 1930s, and Blacks suffered increased unemployment. Along with those in the working class, the self-employed, and recent immigrants, Blacks experienced particular hardship during the Great Depression.

The third stage brought change. World War II instigated a wave of Black migrants to the industrial cities of the North. Following the war, this concentration of Blacks in cities increased the likelihood of group actions in response to oppressive conditions in housing, employment, and the like. Increased educational opportunities allowed for the development of a cadre of Black leaders. The civil rights movement of the 1950s and 1960s helped reduce overt discrimination in employment and housing, education, and transportation, and provided Blacks with access to economic and social resources (Eitzen, 1986).

As Green and Siegler (1984) point out, gains that occurred during the post-World War II period came too late to make an appreciable impact on the educational level or economic condition of the oldest cohorts of Black elderly. A Black man who was 85 years of age in 1985 was already completing his work career by the time of the passage of the Civil Rights Act of 1964. Many in the younger cohorts of Black aged have benefited, however, so that social and economic differentiation is greater among the young-old than among the old-old. For example, in 1985, while 25.1% of Black males aged 60-64 had completed high school, only 18.9% of those 65 and older had done so. (This figure increases dramatically, to 44.8%, for those aged 55-59; in 1985, 57.6% of all Black males had high school diplomas). The median income of Black males aged 60-64 ($9,414) is 53.3% higher than that for their counterparts 70 years of age and older ($6,140). Whereas 10.8% of Black males aged 60-64 had incomes of $25,000 or above in 1985, less than 1% of those 70 and older had such high income. Some of this income difference results from the greater likelihood of younger aged men being employed. Almost four in ten (39.6%) Black males aged 60 to 64 were full-time workers in 1985. The comparable figure for those 65 years and over is 8.1% (U.S. Department of Commerce, 1987).

Wilson (1978) has argued that race is of declining significance in explaining the social and economic success of Blacks. Tate (1983) suggests instead that this argument holds only for a small percentage of affluent Blacks; most of the rest have been unaffected by this socioeconomic progress. It does seem, however, that the success Wilson describes is more likely to appear among younger rather than older aged Black males. Increasingly, the population of young-old Black males is made up of middle-class individuals who have experienced advances in employment, education, and income, and of a prominent underclass characterized by little education, low-wage and transient work careers, and impoverishment.

Table 5.2 Years of School Completed by Black Males in the United States, 65 Years of Age and Older, 1985

Years of School	Number (thousands)	Percentage	Percentage with Income Below Poverty Level
No school	43	4.7	53.5
Elementary grades			
1-5	263	29.0	31.6
6,7	187	20.6	27.8
8	110	12.1	26.4
High school			
1-3	133	14.6	21.8
4	103	11.3	20.4
College 1+	69	7.6	7.2
Totals	908	99.9	
Median	7.6 years		6.6 years

SOURCE: U.S. Department of Commerce (1987).

Table 5.2 shows the educational status of Black males 65 years of age and older in 1985. The median years of school completed is 7.6 (the median years of school completed for all Black males in 1985 was 12.2). Also presented for this population is the linear, though inverse, relationship between education and impoverishment; the more education, the lower the probability of having income below the poverty level. Among those with no formal schooling, 53.5% had income below the poverty level; only 7.2% of those with some college had poverty-level incomes.

Fewer than one in five (17.8%) Black males 65 years or older were employed in 1984 (U.S. Department of Commerce, 1987). Slightly more than half (54%) of these worked part-time. Among those who did not work, almost 71% reported being retired; 28% offered illness or disability as their reason for not being employed in 1984.

The total money income of Black males 60 years and older is shown in Table 5.3. Those 60 to 64 years show the greatest diversity: 18.4% have income of $20,000 or higher, while 10.6% have income below $2,000. The modal income category for this group is $10,000 to $14,999. Still, almost one of every two (49.5%) men of this age had income below $8,499. For those 65 to 69 years, this figure was 61.9%; for those 70 and over, the figure was 70.8%. In 1985, however, older Black males were slightly less likely than all Black males to have income below the poverty line; 27.4% of Black males were poor, compared with 26.6% of males 65 years and over. Among Black males

Table 5.3 Total Money Income for Black Males in the United States, 60 Years of Age and Older, 1985

	Age		
	60-64 (%)	64-69 (%)	70+ (%)
Without Income	5.4	0.9	3.6
With Income			
$1 to $1,999 or less	5.2	3.4	2.4
$2,000 to $3,999	5.9	11.0	13.1
$4,000 to $5,999	16.0	23.6	31.1
$6,000 to $8,499	17.0	23.0	20.6
$8,500 to $9,999	5.2	11.7	8.8
$10,000 to $14,999	18.9	14.7	15.3
$15,000 to $19,999	8.3	7.1	3.6
$20,000 to $24,999	7.5	3.4	0.9
$25,000 and over	10.9	1.5	0.9
Total (thousands)	424	326	582
Median ($)	9,414	7,215	6,140
Mean ($)	12,197	8,556	7,418

SOURCE: U.S. Department of Commerce (1987).

aged 55-59, only 18.6% had incomes below the poverty level (U.S. Department of Commerce, 1987).

Some 60% of aged Black males are married, with their spouses present (see Table 5.4). About as many have never married (5.7%) as are currently divorced (5.6%). One in five aged Black males (21.9%) are widowed and have not remarried. Marriage seems to offer some protection from impoverishment. Only 18.6% of those married with a spouse present had incomes below the poverty level in 1985. Widowers are also less likely than any other group to find themselves impoverished. More than half (55.8%) of those who have never married were poor.

Among Blacks, most married couples with a household head 65 years and over reside in owned homes (78.1%). There is only a modest difference in home ownership between young-old and old-old couples (78.7% versus 76.7%). About 15% of these aged married couples have family members 18 years of age or younger residing with them. For couples with household heads between 65 and 74 years of age, this figure is 15.7%; 13.3% of couples with household heads 75 years or

Table 5.4 Marital Status for Black Males in the United States, 65 Years of Age and Older, 1985

Marital Status	Number (thousands)	Percentage	Percentage with Income Below Poverty Level
Single	52	5.7	55.8
Married			
spouse present	544	59.9	18.6
separated	44	4.8	47.7
other	18	2.0	38.9
Widowed	199	21.9	30.2
Divorced	51	5.6	45.1
Total	908	99.9	

SOURCE: U.S. Department of Commerce (1987).

older have at least one young family member living with them. About 7% of the younger aged Black couples have one or more of their own children 18 years or younger residing with them.

Double Jeopardy

Jackson (1985) has provided a useful review of findings from ethnogerontological studies employing the double jeopardy concept. What is clear from this review is that questions of definition and operationalization continue to abound. The concept has been modified to include variants of triple and quadruple jeopardy (e.g., rural aged Blacks, aged Black women with low income) and expanded to include non-Black racial minorities, White Hispanics, and individuals with two or more undesirable traits that in combination subject them to prejudice and discrimination in the society (e.g., Crandall, 1980). Further, some researchers have employed objective measures of double jeopardy (e.g., gaps in socioecomonic indicators), while others have used subjective measures (e.g., differences in self-assessment of health or life satisfaction).

Inherent in the concept of double jeopardy is the idea of comparison. Overwhelmingly, researchers have employed the concept to determine whether Blacks are more disadvantaged than are Whites in the same age groupings, although different age comparisons are sometimes made (e.g., Blacks 65 years and over versus Whites 18 to 39 years). Gender has been used almost universally as a control to allow comparisons between older Whites and older Black women. Findings have not been consistent, even when independent investigators have employed the same data set (e.g., Jackson and Walls, 1978; Register, 1981; Ward and Kilburn, 1983). Generally, such inconsistencies seem the result of study differences in analytic approach.

Consistent or not, data on the comparative average disadvantage of the Black aged may not be particularly useful for recognizing diversity in the total Black aged population or within a specific subgroup such as aged Black males. In addition, to date, the concept has been employed in a fashion that suggests researcher insensitivity to issues of aging and social change. Most researchers interested in measuring double jeopardy have used cross-sectional data that confound age and cohort effects. For example, income differences between young-old and old-old Black males described above are not a function of age alone, but also of differences in educational achievement and occupational and wage histories of males in different birth cohorts. Further, although there is abundant literature on racial differences in patterns of aging, very little attention has been paid to the issue of how social change differentially affects racial groups.

Schaie and his colleagues (1982) offer the example of age changes in intellectual competence to highlight the importance of recognizing the differential impact of cohort and period effects upon racial groups. By and large, cross-sectional studies have shown early intelligence decrements. According to Schaie (1979), this was, in fact, no more than a substantial generational difference occasioned by dramatic changes in the educational system. But can we assume the generational differences among Blacks have proceeded at the same pace and on the same time scale as for Whites? And what of period effects? Does a dramatic period change permeate its effects equally throughout the society, or may one racial group experience change while another experiences stability or even stagnation? And what about generational and period effect within racial groups? Do these effects have equal consequences for Black males and females?

Too much attention in ethnogerontology continues to be focused on double jeopardy. At best, the concept may be period bound and unable to capture recent major social and political changes in the status of minority group members. At worst, investigators who have used the concept can be accused of providing very little useful information about age changes "in the statuses, roles, interpersonal relationships, attitudes, and values of adult minority individuals or populations as they age in their later years" (Jackson, 1985).

Schaie et al. (1982) used data on the life satisfaction of White and Black respondents in the 1973 and 1977 General Social Surveys to show "the interacting effect of race not only with age, but also with cohort and period effects." They determined that there were significant cohort effects in life satisfaction favoring earlier-born cohorts, regardless of race (even while controlling for health and income). However, there were race differences across the period studied, with life satisfaction increasing for Blacks while remaining stable for Whites. The authors speculate that this finding may result from Black respondents, on average, "beginning to perceive positive societal changes, which affect their overall levels of life satisfaction." This work may provide a model for moving beyond the double jeopardy concept.

Still, rather than focusing on minority *aging*, perhaps we should be focusing on *minority* aging. Manuel (1982) argues, for example, that we need to move beyond the assumption that application of a minority group label can be used as an indication that an individual has experienced the sociocultural events generally thought to be associated with the label. Given the complexity of racial and ethnic identity, the experience of some individuals may more closely resemble that of members of the majority than that of other members of what is only a nominal reference group. Clearly there may be diversity within a minority group with regard to the extent and manner in which group members have been victimized by their minority group status. To paraphrase a question asked by Manuel: Can we assume that all aged Black males have had significantly less of a chance than their White counterparts to participate fully in American institutions? On the contrary, he argues, it can be expected that there will be differential circumstances of aging within minority groups (Manuel, 1982).

Selected Service and Policy Issues

Many authors have stressed the importance of sensitivity on the part of policymakers and service providers to the life-styles and cultures of minority groups. This includes the recognition that minority groups have unique cultural beliefs and patterns. It also includes recognition of the diversity that exists within a minority group or within a specific subgroup such as aged Black males, and of the unique mechanisms employed by Blacks and others to meet the demands of what is often described as an essentially hostile environment (e.g., Myers, 1982). The concept of coping strategies is often used to describe the mechanisms that provide assistance with survival needs, as well as opportunities for meaningful social participation in the reference group (Moore, 1971). While the scope of this chapter does not allow for a comprehensive review of all coping strategies employed by aged Black males, two deserve some special mention: family and religion. In part, the Black family and the Black church represent strong natural support systems that responsible human service workers need to be aware of as they attempt intervention with aged minority clients.

The Black Family

It has become part of the conventional wisdom that family ties are a source of strength among Blacks. This should come as no surprise when applied to aged Black males. As reported earlier, according to 1985 census information, approximately 60% of Black males aged 65 and over are married and living with their spouses. Still, Watson's (1980) study of aged rural Blacks shows that males have a primary need for in-home services, such as help with meal preparation and household chores. Such needs are likely greatest among the 21.9% of aged Black males who are currently widowed and the 5.6% who are divorced and have not remarried.

Studies have shown that older Blacks interact with more extended kin and perceive them as more significant than do older Whites (e.g., Martin and Martin, 1978). Stack (1970) has shown how family functions are carried out for urban Blacks by clusters of kin who may or may not reside together. She offers the example of Viola Jackson's brother, who, after his wife died, "decided to raise his two sons himself. He kept the two boys and never remarried. His residence has been consistently close to one or another of his sisters who have fed and cared for his two sons."

Elderly Blacks play an important role in this extended kin network that so well characterizes the family life of many urban Blacks. For example, 15% of all aged Black couples have a child 18 years of age or under residing with them. About 45% of these cases involve the couple's own child or children; most of the rest of the cases involve taking grandchildren into their homes (e.g., Jackson and Wood, 1976). Presumably, the aged Black males in these families are active in the child- and grandchild-rearing activities of the families.

One reason Blacks may rely so heavily on family members is that they have minimal expectations for receiving effective service from social service agencies. This may especially be the case for older Blacks who have a painful history of inequality, rejection, and ejection when it comes to dealing with such agencies (Dancy, 1977). In addition, as Dancy (1977) points out, some elderly Blacks lack full knowledge or understanding of the services or benefits to which they are entitled, have no influence whatsoever on programs and the delivery of services, and find few meaningful and needed services located in their communities. Sainer et al. (1973) found that when Black elderly took an active role in establishing their own social service, utilization improved because the elderly were able to establish those programs they felt were needed most.

Family members often value their aged relations because they serve as important role models (e.g., Dancy, 1977). Some research suggests that young Blacks have more interest in and more esteem for their elders than do other young people. Tate (1983) cites evidence suggesting that minority group professionals are more inclined to work with the elderly than are their White counterparts. In one study she cites, 55% of Black student and registered nurses, compared with 41% of Whites, indicated a desire to work with the elderly. Race was the only personal trait that correlated with plans to enter geriatric nursing.

Clearly, not all aged Black males will be accessible through family support systems, although networks of "fictive" kin and friends may provide accessibility (Aschenbrenner, 1975). Fictive kin include unrelated individuals who are afforded status as family members. The push and pull factors of migration by young and old Blacks may reduce the availability of family supports and increase reliance on fictive kin and friends.

The Black Church

Religion is a source of strength to many Black elderly. Historically, the church has been a frame of reference for Blacks for coping with racial discrimination and has played a role in their survival and advancement. The church is one institution that Blacks control locally; it has remained relatively free from White authority. The so-called Black church is really many churches, including traditional Black Protestant denominations such as the Baptists and Methodists as well as fundamentalist groups. Religion is a main involvement of many Black elderly. For most, this reflects the continuation of a lifelong trend. Church attendance and participation in church activities were important early in life and continue to be so in later life.

Participation in church activities provides an opportunity for many to "be somebody." Black elderly receive high status and respect in the community as a function of such participation. Dancy (1977) offers the example of Mr. John Jordon, who worked for 25 years as a baggage handler for a large transportation company. He was often passed over for promotion; he was told that he was "not ready" or lacked the skills, or was given other excuses. Yet he saw Whites with the same education as his—tenth grade—get better opportunities.

> What kept Mr. Jordon from becoming demoralized and bitter was his church. In those same 25 years he had moved from a pew member to a deacon. Now he was also treasurer of the church—a job of enormous responsibility that required banking a thousand dollars weekly. Mr. Jordon's church appreciated his talents, and Mr. Jordon wa a faithful man and loved his church. There he was somebody.

Considering the influential position of the church in the Black community, it is essential that service providers understand the roles the church plays in the lives of Black elderly. The church is not only a place where large numbers of Black elderly can be reached, but also a place where needs can be assessed and services delivered.

Conclusions

Despite their relative invisibility, aged Black males are a diverse population. Some are young-old, others old-old; some work, others are retired; some are college graduates, others through no fault of their own had little formal schooling; some are well-to-do, others impoverished; some are married, others widowed and divorced; some maintain strong family ties, others do not; some are active participants in church activities, others are not. Additional dimensions along which the diversity of aged Black males can be measured are abundant. Physical and mental health, longevity, regional dispersion, and migrancy are just a few that have gained the attention of researchers.

Recognition of the diversity within the population should lead us away from the comparisons of double jeopardy and toward a sharper focus on minority aging itself. Efforts at teasing out how race interacts with age, cohort, and period effects may provide a greater understanding of the minority aging experience. Application of a life-span developmental approach to minority aging may also prove useful.

Policymakers and service providers should not view minority clients in homogeneous terms. This would invite disaster. Recognizing the diversity that exists within a minority group or within a specific subgroup such as aged Black males allows for greater understanding of the diversity of coping strategies minority clients employ. Family and religion represent two important mechanisms for dealing with what has been seen as a hostile environment. With such knowledge, the responsible human service worker will be in a better position to intervene effectively with aged minority clients.

References

Aschenbrenner, J. 1975. "Extended Families Among Black Americans." *Journal of Comparative Family Studies* 4(2):257-68.

Cazenave, N. A. 1979. "Middle-Income Black Fathers: An Analysis of the Provider Role." *Family Coordinator* 28:583-92.

Crandall, R. C. 1980. *Gerontology: A Behavioral Science Approach*. Reading, MA: Addison-Wesley.

Dancy, J., Jr. 1977. *The Black Elderly: A Guide for Practitioners*. Ann Arbor: University of Michigan/Wayne State University, Institute of Gerontology.

Eitzen, D. S. 1986. *Social Problems*. 3rd ed. Boston: Allyn & Bacon.

Gary, L. E. 1981. *Black Men*. Beverly Hills, CA: Sage.

Green, R. L. and I. C. Siegler. 1984. "Blacks." Pp. 219-33 in *Handbook on the Aged in the United States*, edited by E. B. Palmore. Westport, CT: Greenwood.

Jackson, J. J. 1985. "Race, National Origin, Ethnicity, and Aging." Pp. 264-303 in *Handbook on Aging and the Social Sciences*, edited by R. H. Binstock and E. Shanas. 2nd ed. New York: Van Nostrand Reinhold.

Jackson, J. J. and B. E. Walls. 1978. "Myths and Realities About Aged Blacks." Pp. 95-113 in *Readings in Gerontology*, edited by M. R. Brown. 2nd ed. St. Louis: C. V. Mosby.

Jackson, M. and J. Wood. 1976. *Aging in America*. Vol. 5, *Implications for the Black Aged*. Washington, DC: National Council on the Aging.

Lieberson, S. 1978. "A Reconsideration of the Income Differences Found Between Migrants and Northern-Born Blacks." *American Journal of Sociology* 83(4):940-66.

Manuel, R. C. 1982. "The Dimensions of Ethnic Minority Identification: An Exploratory Analysis Among Elderly Black Americans." Pp. 231-48 in *Minority Aging: Sociological and Social Psychological Issues*, edited by R. C. Manuel. Westport, CT: Greenwood.

Martin, E. and J. P. Martin. 1978. *The Black Extended Family.* Chicago: University of Chicago Press.

Moore, J. 1971. "Situational Factors Affecting Minority Aging." *Gerontologist* 11:88-91.

Myers, H. F. 1982. "Stress, Ethnicity and Social Class: A Model for Research with Black Populations." Pp. 128-48 in *Minority Mental Health,* edited by E. Jones and S. Korchin. New York: Praeger.

National Council on the Aging. 1971. *Employment Prospects of Aged Blacks, Chicanos, and Indians.* Washington, DC: Author.

Parsons, C. W. 1972. *America's Uncounted People.* Washington, DC: National Academy of Sciences.

Register, J. C. 1981. "Aging and Race: A Black-White Comparative Analysis." *Gerontologist* 21:438-43.

Sainer, J., L. Schwartz, and T. Jackson. 1973. "Steps in the Development of a Comprehensive Service Delivery System for the Elderly." *Gerontologist* 13(3):98.

Schaie, K. W. 1979. "The Primary Mental Abilities in Adulthood: An Exploration in the Development of Psychometric Intelligence." Pp. 68-117 in *Life-Span Development and Behavior.* Vol. 2, edited by P. B. Baltes and O. G. Brim. New York: Academic Press.

Schaie, K. W., S. Orchowsky, and I. A. Parham. 1982. "Measuring Age and Sociocultural Change: The Case of Race and Satisfaction." Pp. 223-30 in *Minority Aging: Sociological and Social Psychological Issues,* edited by R. C. Manuel. Westport, CT: Greenwood.

Simon, D. R. and D. S. Eitzen. 1982. *Elite Deviance.* Boston: Allyn & Bacon.

Stack C. 1970. "The Kindred of Viola Jackson: Residence and Family Organization of an Urban Black American Family." Pp. 303-12 in *Afro-American Anthropology,* edited by N. Whitten and J. Szwed. New York: Free Press.

Tate, N. 1983. "The Black Aging Experience." Pp. 95-107 in *Aging in Minority Groups,* edited by R. L. McNeely and J. N. Colen. Beverly Hills, CA: Sage.

U.S. Department of Commerce, Bureau of the Census. 1974. *Estimates of Coverage of Population by Sex, Race, and Age: Demographic Analysis.* Washington, DC: Government Printing Office.

———. 1986. *Estimates of the Population of the U.S. by Age, Sex and Race: 1980 to 1985.* Washington, DC: Government Printing Office.

———. 1987. "Poverty in the United States: 1985." In *Current Population Reports.* Series P-60, No. 158. Washington, DC: Government Printing Office.

Ward, R. A. and H. Kilburn. 1983. "Community Access and Life Satisfaction: Racial Differences in Later Life." *International Journal of Aging and Human Development* 16:209-19.

Watson, W. H. 1980. *Older Poor Blacks and Social Services in the Southern United States.* Washington, DC: Administration on Aging and National Center on Black Aged.

Wilson, W. J. 1978. *The Declining Significances of Race: Blacks and Changing American Institutions.* Chicago: University of Chicago Press.

Zopf, P. E., Jr. 1986. *America's Older Population.* Houston: Cap & Gown.

6

Understanding Diversity of the Urban Black Aged

Historical Perspectives

SHARON E. MILLIGAN

Conducting the Oral History Interviews

This chapter reports the personal reminiscences of elderly Black men and women living in Cleveland, Ohio. These personal accounts shed light on the Great Migration; on discrimination in employment, housing, and education; and on self-help activities that characterize life for urban Black aged. The story of the Great Migration, as told by the people who took part in it, provides an invaluable lesson about southern and northern Black society, about the manner in which the society survived, about the reasons that Blacks moved North, and about the early days in industrial Cleveland. The oral histories also describe the living conditions that were found in Cleveland, and the ways in which Blacks managed to earn their livelihood. The oral histories do not represent all Blacks; they document the diversity found in Black society by presenting the perspectives of one elderly group in an urban neighborhood.

AUTHOR'S NOTE: This chapter was originally presented as a paper at "Understanding and Serving Black Aged: A Community Conference and Forum," sponsored by Cleveland State University and the Cleveland Clinic Foundation and cofunded by the Cleveland Foundation, Cleveland State University, Cleveland, Ohio, February 26-27, 1987.

The Oral History Project emerged out of a casual conversation between two elderly members of the Sadie J. Anderson Women's Missionary Society at the St. James African Methodist Episcopal (AME) Church. They felt that the life experiences of elderly persons should be systematically collected and shared with the younger generation so that traditional values could be transmitted. From fall 1985 to summer 1987, 45 church volunteers planned and organized the collection and transcription of 55 life histories. Partial funding for the Oral History Project was provided by the Ohio Humanities Council, a state-based agency of the National Endowment for the Humanities, which allocates grants to nonprofit organizations in Ohio for public programs in the humanities.

The St. James AME Church is a part of the Connectional African Methodist Episcopal Church founded by Richard Allen in 1787 in Philadelphia. Church congregations are in North and South America, the Caribbean, Africa, and England (*St. James AME Church History,* 1984; Van Tassel and Grabowski, 1987). The St. James AME Church was established in Cleveland, Ohio, in 1894. Its current membership includes approximately 4,000 individuals living in the urban area known as the Fairfax community, where the church is located, and in other Greater Cleveland neighborhoods.

The elderly persons who allowed their life histories to be recorded were called *narrators.* Locating the older people was not difficult because of the centrality of the church to the Black community (Carter, 1982; Eng et al., 1985; Heisel and Faulkner, 1982; Taylor and Chatters, 1986). The narrators lived, worked, or attended church in the Fairfax area. Narrator selection was from individuals who seemed to typify the elderly in the area. The narrators were not selected from a representative sample in a statistical sense. Furthermore, since life histories were collected in tape-recorded interviews, those who were selected had to be verbal and willing to share life experiences. The narrators—from whom the personal histories were gathered—were born, for the most part, in the 40 years between 1880 and 1920. Thus in 1920 their ages ranged from infancy to around 40; at the end of World War II they were predominantly middle-aged, and in 1970, the youngest member of the group became 50 years old.

The interviewers were Black, had ongoing relationships with the narrators, and were readily accepted by the elderly individuals. Some of the interviewers were selected to do the tape-recording while some carried out other assignments, such as transcribing audiotapes. The interviewing was more conversational rather than formal, but the interviewers were asked to cover certain life events: childhood, church life, leisure activities, young adulthood, life during the Depression, work life, marriage and children, middle life, retirement, and changes over the life span. Similarly, the interviewers were asked to explore the manners in which the narrators coped with change and crisis. The actual interviews and tape-recording varied in content and length, depending on the comfort of the narrators. Some life histories were gathered in several tape-recorded sessions, while many were gathered in only two or three.

The Migration to Cleveland

Blacks have migrated to Cleveland in a slow but steady stream since the Civil War. Between 1890 and 1915, the beginnings of the mass migration from the South markedly increased Cleveland's Black population. The migration of southern Blacks to northern cities was one of the most important historic and demographic developments of U.S. history during this century. Between 1910 and 1920, Cleveland's Black population increased threefold, Detroit's population sixfold, and Chicago's almost doubled. Other northern cities experienced substantially fewer gains (Kusmer, 1976).

This mass movement altered the racial composition of the city of Cleveland and the lives of Blacks for decades to come. Similar to most mass movements, the causes of the Great Migration were numerous. Without World War I, the Great Migration would not have taken place. During the war, immigration from Europe fell off drastically, and with it the supply of cheap labor that U.S. manufacturers demanded. The draft drained off many U.S.-born workers. The need for workers in the North coincided with a period of economic depression in the South. It was under these circumstances that northern manufacturers began to realize the value of Black labor as an "industrial reserve" (Kusmer, 1976; Van Tassel and Grabowski, 1987).

An 87-year-old narrator who migrated from Virginia to Cleveland at the age of 16 explains why and how her family moved North:

> I didn't come to Cleveland because I was unhappy. All the flock followed me. I accepted being the leader. All my family came up, lot of my friends, lot of people I knew at the time when the war was declared and the Negroes were

leaving the South because there was a better world for them to work in, they could get work. They were coming up here in carloads at that time.

These words seem to summarize why a lot of Blacks came to Cleveland and how whole family systems relocated during the Great Migration. Some of the Black elders were born in the South; all lived in the North for decades.

These words begin to reveal how race and social inequality became a national issue through the Great Migration. To Black elders, moving North meant an opportunity to find status—to improve their own station in life. They made the radical choice to leave the toil of the South to move North to even more toil but better wages. Unlike the White European pioneers from the northern New England area, the Black elders were not able to load the family in the wagon and move North; instead, they had to steal away in the dead of the night, one by one. Leaving was dangerous, as southern officials tried desperately to slow the tide of Black labor forces moving North. Often family members were left behind. Once the migrants arrived in Cleveland, some of their families followed, but many stayed in the South. Many narrators related the financial hardship involved in visiting the South after moving to the North, and of saving money to bring family members from the South, one by one, to live in Cleveland.

Discrimination in Employment, Housing, and Education

The Great Migration was the first time in American history when employment opportunities for skilled and unskilled labor were offered to Black workers. Most male migrants found jobs in unskilled factory labor, but Blacks were also able to move up to semiskilled and skilled positions. Many of the migrants earned two to three times the wages they had received in the South. Before 1915, Cleveland workers, both Black and White, in similar industries received essentially the same pay, which averaged about $20 a week. By 1920, almost two-thirds of the Black males worked in the manufacturing industries, while only 12% were engaged in domestic or personal service. By 1930, the industrial work declined slightly, and the proportion of service occupations rose to 16%.

While the employment picture for Blacks had improved, there were still serious problems, especially in clerical work, domestic work, and the unionized skilled trades. Women had great difficulty with employment, and in fact most were engaged only in domestic or personal service work. An elderly female narrator who migrated from Alabama around 1922 recalled employment discrimination: "Housework—that was the extent of the employment. And that was really hard to find. In the newspaper ads, everybody wanted mulattoes. Nobody wanted dark-skinned people." A retired nurse also shared her experiences with racial and gender discrimination:

> After graduating from high school in Cleveland, I went to New York, where I was employed by a wealthy colored family and then later entered Lincoln School of Nursing, graduating in 1937. I returned to Cleveland and married but I had a difficult time in finding employment. I did know that hospitals did not hire colored nurses. The only place I did work after marriage was at Charity Hospital as a private duty nurse. There I worked until they too had to let go the married nurses. And then I did not work for a period of years—then Dunbar Insurance Company wanted a nurse with my experience. . . . I set up a kind of visitation for their sick patients who had insurance that paid for "sick and accident" and I investigated that. I set up the nursing system.

The Depression temporarily reversed much of the progress that Black Clevelanders made in the previous 15 years. Although both races were devastated by the economic collapse, Blacks suffered much higher rates of unemployment at an earlier stage, and many Black businesses went bankrupt. The New Deal relief programs helped to ease Black unemployment substantially.

As the Black population increased in Cleveland, the process of residential segregation accelerated. In 1910 no census tract in the city was greater than 25% Black, but ten years later ten tracts exceeded that number, and two tracts had become more than 50% Black (Green, 1931). The pattern of increasing concentration of the Black population in certain areas continued during the early 1920s. This is evident in the enrollment figures for Cleveland elementary schools at that time.

In the 1920s, Blacks moved into the Central-Fairfax community in large numbers. Black residential integration was resisted as late as the 1920s and then suddenly gave way. Italian immigrants shared the oldest section of the city with Blacks for two decades.

The increasing concentration of the Black population exacerbated the housing problem faced by Black Clevelanders. The housing shortage existed before the war, but during the Great Migration the housing shortage in the Black community reached crisis proportions. Landlords in White communities took advantage of the situation. Rents were 25% to 75% more for Black newcomers. Some Whites were torn between the desire to resist the "Negro invasion" and the opportunity to make money by dividing homes into kitchenette apartments and renting the "suites" to Black migrants clamoring for places to live (Kusmer, 1976). The promise of monetary gain, however, did not always prove sufficient as a deterrent to White hostility.

Narrators related racially motivated violence as Blacks moved to the Eastside areas of Cleveland, Ohio. In more specific terms, they described tactics used by Whites to keep Blacks out of homeownership. Many of the elders have been or are still homeowners in the Fairfax community. Whites tried to exclude Blacks from neighborhoods through mutual understanding or restrictive covenants that denied (in theory) the owner of the house the right to sell to Blacks.

> My parents bought this home in 1920. They had a real estate man who would take them up and down the streets trying to find an adequate home. They had been living on East 76th Street, where they had a two-family home which was too small; so they decided to move out past 79th Street. My parents passed this house and it was for sale. My mother said she wanted it; but the owner would not sell to any Blacks. There was a covenant here which stated, no Negroes and Mulattoes were allowed in this neighborhood; and that is on our deed to this day. My mother was able to get a White man, and paid him $500 for him to purchase the house; and she would purchase from him. She paid $8,500 for it through Society for Savings, as it was known then. They told her at the bank they did not feel, if the case came to court, that she would be allowed to live in the home.

> As a result of my parents moving in . . . being the first Blacks . . . people on either side of us put up for-sale signs. The house next door, the owner was an Irishman who had sons who were a fireman and a policeman, however, he was never able to sell his home and he and my parents later became friends. The people on the north side of the house . . . also put their house up for sale but they couldn't sell it either and they ended up having to move from their home because they lost it many years later. Across the street was a Jewish family . . . who was quite prominent in music in those days; and as time went on we found that the neighborhood improved as more Blacks moved in.

Another longtime resident commented that Blacks took pride in their homes: "When we were young, we swept the sidewalks and we had to take the hose and hose down the sidewalks. We even cleaned up around the curbs and everything." Still another narrator related how the Neighborhood Improvement Association provided standards for the beautification of the area: "All the people that lived in the area had a contest going every year—who had the best kept lawn and best kept property."

A longtime resident of the community summarized the housing history of the Fairfax community:

> It stayed status quo, as an integrated area, for many years; but as the years rolled the older Whites moved out, the Negroes stayed and the older Negroes who had bought at the very beginning, back in 1923, they died out. When fair housing came, a lot of the people deserted the area for, well, better housing and better neighborhoods. Being able to go, they moved. A few of the children of the original Blacks that moved in the area stayed in the area. Now we're trying to revitalize the area, . . . to see if we can't bring it back to what it was when we had all the trees, and when we were the Forest City.

Migrants came to the North for better education. Northern states allocated more money for education, and compulsory education laws encouraged students to stay in school longer. Between 1870 and 1915, Black students were not segregated in separate schools and classrooms in Cleveland, as they often were in other cities. However, between 1915 and 1930 discrimination affected the public schools. The growth of Fairfax as a predominantly Black residential area created segregated schools. The policy of allowing White students to transfer out of predominantly Black schools increased segregation. In the 1920s and 1930s, school administrators often altered the curriculum of the Black schools from liberal arts to an emphasis on manual training. This shift was a very controversial issue in the Black community.

Many of the narrators commented on social isolation in the White public and private schools. One woman recalled that in the schools the White students were pleasant but distant:

> At Addison Junior High School, I had one friend, White, who was a day-to-day friend of mine until the day she graduated from high school and never saw her again in life, which seems sort of odd. The boy-girl relationships were mostly among the Whites. In high school at East High, there were only 6 or 7 of us in my class, the social activity was very limited.

During the Depression, the narrator was admitted to Flora Mather College:

> At college in my freshman year . . . three Blacks in the freshman class, two Blacks in the sophomore class and one in the junior class. I stayed at Western Reserve College one year because the tuition was more than my family could handle . . . , it was only $300 a year. At that time, it was in the middle of the Depression.

During her sophomore year, she transferred to Wilberforce College for financial reasons. The same narrator compared the employment and personal growth opportunities of the two college experiences:

> At Wilberforce, although the school was both boys and girls, there was much more that I learned there than I would have learned at Flora Stone Mather College. In the first place, Flora Stone Mather was only going to give me a liberal arts degree; at Wilberforce I got a degree in education which gave me the ability to teach school when I came out. Many of my classmates from Flora Stone Mather were working at Halles [Department Store] when they graduated in 1937. Wilberforce taught me many other things, having gone all through school with a predominantly White group. I had very little contact with Blacks.
>
> I went to Christian Science Church, which was located then at 77th and Euclid, that was all White, so consequently, my concern was knowing more and more Blacks. Wilberforce turned me around and I will always be appreciative of my learning there. One of the advantages that I can say about a Black school then and now we had the best professors. Long ago, Blacks who were professors could not teach at White schools as they do today and get very good salaries.
>
> There was a history at Wilberforce that I had not known about, not having come up in the AME Church. Being in that environment with students who were concerned with education and who didn't have much money, who were in and out of school [because of lack of money], I learned to appreciate how smart all of those Black students were. . . . I appreciated how impressed they were with the professors. . . . After having been with these people [Black professors and students at Wilberforce University] I was able to recognize that Blacks made a great impact in our culture, which has never been accepted in the White schools, or taught in the White schools or in the White churches I went to. Consequently, my identity changed and I felt proud of being Black.

These data have illustrated the impact of discrimination on the social, economic, and educational lives of the Black elder. In many cases, discrimination in northern cities foreclosed better-paying employment opportunities. Work choices for men and especially for women were limited. In contrast to the jobs available to White workers, none of these jobs paid very well. However, for most, northern jobs paid more than the same jobs available in the South. With limited income, Blacks paid more, two to three times as much as their White counterparts, for housing. The housing difficulties and higher food prices contributed to overcrowding and other environmental problems. The chance for better education was part of the hope of migrating Blacks. Many found schools where they were isolated.

The Church, Self-Help, and the Family

In the lives of the Black aged, the church has played an important mediating role in the interest of the Black community's economic and social stability. As a long-standing tradition, the Black church has met not only the spiritual, but also the educational, physical, and social needs of its members and their families and friends (Carter, 1982; Eng et al., 1985; Taylor and Chatters, 1986). The church within the Black community often has initiated help-seeking, socially oriented groups. Black churches in Cleveland developed more slowly than in other northern cities, in that Blacks attended White churches in the early days of Cleveland. The first Black church, St. John's AME, founded in 1830, grew slowly for 25 years. Beginning in the 1860s-1890s, however, more Blacks became interested in setting up their own churches. Racism, coupled with the dispersal of many native Whites to newer parts of the city (and the building of new churches far removed from the major Black residential areas), led to a steady decline in the number of Blacks attending churches with predominantly White congregations (Kusmer, 1976).

The narrators commented on how the AME Church was a community resource. They related the special roles accorded them through church membership and participation in the usher board, deacon board, and other church organizations. These special roles provided Black elderly persons with an outlet for creativity and meaningful social positions in a society with increasing social inequities.

The St. James Literary Forum, founded on April 27, 1927, was mentioned by narrators more than any other community organization activity in the church. The Forum furnished a platform for the discussion of public questions by competent men and women. It was an important local institution and gained a national reputation. One narrator recalled several speakers at the Forum:

> It brought speakers here, nationally known speakers, from the South, from the East, and from the Midwest. The speakers included but were not limited to W.E.B DuBois, William Picken, and Walter White, the National Association for the Advancement of Colored People (NAACP), George C. Schyler, then associate editor of the *Pittsburgh Courier*, George Washington Carver, the scientist from Tuskegee Institute, Carter G. Woodson, the father of Black history.

The influx of migrants to Cleveland caused social problems that the Black churches were only partly able to deal with through church self-help organizations. A neighboring Baptist church was mentioned in that it had a social worker to help people in need. Narrators commented on and were members of numerous community organizations that were engaged in self-help activities to address the social and political problems of the day. The Phyllis Wheatley Association, a residential, job training, and recreation center for girls, was established by Jane Hunter, a Black nurse. As more and more young girls arrived in Cleveland to find jobs, the Phyllis Wheatley Association provided housing for homeless girls. The Future Outlook League, founded by John Holly, became the first Black organization to use the boycott successfully to combat discriminatory practices. This organization had as its slogan "Don't spend your money where you can't work," recalled one male narrator. Today, many of the narrators are members of self-help organizations like those mentioned above.

The value of the family was a very important theme for the narrators. When asked if they could pass on anything to the young, they mentioned a concern about the family. They recalled times when they had counseled the present generation about the importance of marriage and the importance of family life as a buffer against life's difficulties. Several of the female narrators had been married; the males had not. The elderly men were responsible for providing care for their parents (particularly mothers), disabled siblings, and the siblings of brothers and sisters. These caregiving responsibilities were the reasons the elderly men gave for never marrying. The women combined marriage with the care of the younger and older generations. The women commented that "back in the days" they would not have thought of letting their own mothers live physically alone because it was not proper to do so or because they could not afford it. Ironically, these elders took pride in living independently in the community without family members in the home. Many emphasized that even though they lived physically alone, they had frequent and satisfying contact with family and friends. Even children and other kin who were geographically mobile maintained contact across the miles. This is a community where many children live in the neighborhood or the Greater Cleveland area (Petchers and Milligan, 1987).

Another theme elders wanted to pass on to young Blacks pertained to self-help and freedom. One narrator captured the feeling of the group when she said, "I hope that Blacks will stop worrying about what other people [Whites] think and start thinking for themselves. You know freedom comes from within. No one can give it; we just have to be free."

Conclusion and Implications

This chapter has analyzed findings from oral histories of older Black men and women in Cleveland, Ohio. The Oral History Project was initiated and implemented by a Black church. The purpose of the project was to help preserve the history of elderly men and women who had experienced a unique time in American history—the migration of Blacks from the South in large numbers—and social, economic, and legal discrimination most of their lives. Many grew up in both the South and the North. Some were born in Cleveland and their parents were from the South. Narrators who migrated to Cleveland said that they came to the North for new opportunities in employment and education. All the narrators spoke about race relations in the 1920s, 1930s, and 1940s.

The oral histories provide a greater understanding of the Black aged in the Fairfax community. Repeatedly, the narrators and interviewers indicated that involvement in the project increased their self-esteem. They were tremendously proud of organizing, implementing, and locating funds for the Oral History Project. Moreover, they were proud of the common experiences of surviving in the hostile American environment of the 1920s and 1930s.

The narrators' life histories have major implications for understanding the urban Black elderly person. It is clear that history has shaped the profile of the Black elderly. The Great Migration was different for the Black person moving to Cleveland when compared to settlers from the northern New England area. In contrast to White northern New

England families, these Black migrants came one by one, without household goods, and were very poor and remained so most, if not all, of their lives. The uniqueness of the Black life-style is evident in the years of social, educational, and economic inequality they experienced in both the North and the South. There is also evidence that the Cleveland experience was different from the experiences of other northern cities. In Cleveland, there were more migrants and a delay in development of the Black church. In other northern cities, the church provided continuity with the southern culture as well as support in times of social and emotional need. Church activities, social clubs, self-help activities, and fraternal organizations were all a part of southern life and provided a sense of community. These activities served as a buffer in a hostile environment. The Black church developed out of the discrimination of the times and concurrently with the influx of Black settlers. The implications of this cultural continuity delay for the settlers in Cleveland are uncertain.

Given this historical background, it would not be surprising if Black elders expect less from formal social service institutions designed to meet their needs and depend on the church and kin or nonkin for assistance in times of need (Taylor and Chatters, 1986). The Black community has always been an agent of its own advancement. Action by government and other formal social institutions in addressing social, emotional, and economic needs, however important, has been both recent and modest. Blacks made the transition from slavery to a strong, vital community largely through individual effort and through the work of civil rights, cultural, fraternal, social, and service organizations in the Black community (Martin and Martin, 1985). Thus Black Americans have a proud history of self-initiated contributions to their own well-being. Past expectations and experiences may affect the social service utilization offered by public and voluntary agencies for Blacks (Martin and Martin, 1985; Taylor and Chatters, 1986).

It seems evident that informal support networks would be important elements of any social service system in the Black community. Social service agencies serving the urban Black aged should be aware of the social and political importance of the Black church and other informal support networks. The infusion of these networks may strengthen any attempt to provide access to some groups of elderly persons who traditionally underutilize social services. These networks should be worked with directly to plan and organize aging services. Efforts need to include strategies to develop methods of communicating with urban

Black elders, their families, and their churches. Black elders can be expected to be suspicious of programs not sanctioned by individuals and institutions that they trust. Social service agencies working with the urban Black aged should be sensitive to the elderly individuals' role in the informal network. The interdependency of family members and nonmembers should be considered in any assessment of the elderly.

In conclusion, the Oral History Project provides data to support the importance of historical forces on the lives of urban Black elders. Generally, these data document the social vitality that exists in a Black urban community and the people who worship and live there (Childs, 1986). The church, through the project, expanded the roles of the elderly in including them as narrators. The narrator role enabled the Black elders, the Black church, and the community to become their own historians and to gain a vital understanding of their past, and thus to acquire greater power to control their present and their future. Furthermore, research in the humanities fostered a relationship between the Black church as a community organization and other formal agencies and organizations in the larger community. Finally, the data have become available to the public: The transcripts and taped interviews of the St. James Oral History Project are located in the Black Archives at the Western Reserve Historical Society Library in Cleveland, Ohio.

References

Carter, A. 1982. "Religion and the Black Elderly: Historical Basis of Social and Psychological Concerns." Pp. 103-7 in *Minority Aging: Sociological and Social Psychological Issues,* edited by R. Manuel. Westport, CT: Greenwood.

Childs, J. B. 1986. "Policy Implications of Current Research on the Black Community." *Social Policy* 17(1):16.

Eng, E., J. Hatch, and A. Callan. 1985. "Institutionalizing Social Support Through the Church and into the Community." *Health Education Quarterly* 12(1):81-91.

Frazier, E. F. 1974. *The Negro Church in America.* New York: Schocken.

Green, H. W. 1931. *Population Characteristics by Census Tracts, Cleveland, 1930.* Cleveland.

Heisel, M. A. and A. Faulkner. 1982. "Religiosity in an Older Black Population." *Gerontologist* 22:354-58.

Kusmer, K. L. 1976. *A Ghetto Takes Shape: Black Cleveland, 1870-1930.* Chicago: University of Illinois Press.

Martin, J. and E. Martin. 1985. *The Helping Tradition in the Black Family and Community.* Silver Spring, MD: National Association of Social Workers.

Petchers, M. and S. Milligan. 1987. "Social Networks and Social Support Among Black Urban Elderly: A Health Care Resource." *Social Work in Health Care* 12(4):103-17.

St. James AME Church History. 1984. Unpublished manuscript.

Taylor, R. and L. Chatters. 1986. "Patterns of Informal Support to Elderly Black Adults: Family, Friends and Church Members." *Social Work* 31(6):432-38.

Van Tassel, D. D. and J. J. Grabowski. 1987. *The Encyclopedia of Cleveland History.* Bloomington: Indiana University Press.

PART II

Understanding Service Need and Use

Introduction

ZEV HAREL
EDWARD A. McKINNEY
MICHAEL WILLIAMS

The chapters in Part II aim to advance our understanding of service needs among Black aged and to offer directions for effective planning and utilization of services by older Black Americans. Only in recent years has there been an evolving interest in the well-being and service needs of minority aged in general, and the needs of Black aged in particular. Interest, to date, has been more likely to focus on differences between White and Black aged on sociodemographic characteristics, socioeconomic status, health and functional status, social resources, and psychological well-being. There has been scarce interest in examining the needs for service, service preferences, and service utilization issues among Black aged.

The six chapters in this section are intended to contribute toward a better understanding of service needs, service preferences, and service use among the Black aged. Chapter 7, by Michael Williams, examines the effects of Title II of the Social Security Act on the economic security of Black aged. Chapter 8, by John H. Skinner, addresses the issues of resource targeting and resource allocation and their impact on the availability of Older Americans Act-connected services for Black aged. In Chapter 9, Wornie L. Reed examines the issues of health status, health care need, and health service use among Black aged. Mary McKinney Edmonds focuses in Chapter 10 on the unique needs and experiences of aged Black women concerning health status, health care need, and use. In Chapter 11, Charles Barresi and Geeta Menon review theoretical perspectives and applied data on informal support and caregiving among Black aged. The sixth and last chapter in Part II, coauthored by Cheryl Stewart Gerace and Linda S. Noelker, reviews and addresses critical practice issues in serving Black aged.

A pragmatic concern with the service needs of the Black aged is indeed timely. Data indicate that, at present, about 8% of the Black population in the United States is 65 years of age or older, and, of these, approximately 8% are 85 or over. It has been predicted that by the year 2000, the Black aged population will reach 4 million and will exceed the rate of growth of the White aged population by 26% (U.S. Senate Special Committee on Aging, 1986). These demographic trends have significant implications for elected and appointed public officials, social and behavioral scientists, social gerontologists, and health and social service professionals concerned with the elderly.

It is becoming increasingly evident that social programs and policies that aim to enhance the well-being of our aging population will need to address the special needs and preferences of the older Black members of our society. Recent economic policies and budgetary practices on the national level have led the way in reducing government concern for the needs of our children, have shown disregard for adults who cannot fend for themselves, and have further reduced funding of services for vulnerable aged. In spite of these trends, it is important that scientists and professionals continue to address the basic needs of survival, security, and well-being for all Americans and to highlight the unique needs of special subgroups of our society. Black older Americans make up one of the groups that have had to endure consistently throughout their lives extensive economic, political, social, and psychological hardships. It is indeed appropriate that scientists and professionals understand better the needs and resources of Black older Americans in an effort to aid them in coping with the increasing demands and challenges of personal aging experiences and those of an aging contemporary society.

Social Security: A Critical Analysis

In his chapter on the effects of social security on the economic well-being of the Afro-American elderly, Michael Williams reviews the role and function of Title II of the Social Security Act on the lives of Black aged. The 1935 Social Security Act was designed to provide the nation's working population with a "supplemental means of support during retirement years." Quoting Frances Perkins, chair of the Committee on Economic Security, a leading architect of the 1935 Social Security Act, Williams reminds the reader that the general premise held out, at that time, was that the (Title II) program would play a vital role in allowing the elderly to grow old "without being haunted by the spectre of a poverty-ridden old-age or being a burden on our children" (Perkins, 1946, pp. 792-94). He concludes that, despite the fact that the proportion of the elderly population receiving some portion of their income from Title II of the Social Security Act has reached 93%, this program has not been meeting the economic needs of the elderly and has been even less successful at meeting the needs of the African American elderly. After a critical review of the impact of Title II on the economic well-being of the elderly, since its enactment to the present time, Williams reaches the conclusion that, given current projections of employment, underemployment, and unemployment, Title II will continue to be inadequate in eliminating or significantly reducing the likelihood of a poverty-ridden old age for most African Americans in the future.

It is important to underscore that the United States is the only country among the developed industrialized nations that does not have a national insurance program. Old Age Survivor Disability Insurance (OASDI), an employment-related insurance program, provides benefits in line with one's contributions over the working years. The benefits from this program are based exclusively on a separate tax paid by employers and employees. Elderly of low occupational background, those who had disrupted histories of employment, and the underemployed and the unemployed have very little economic security from this program in retirement years. Our supplemental insurance program (SSI), which addresses the needs of the economically deprived aged and disabled adults from general tax revenues, assures individuals and families little more than a starvation diet. It is indeed necessary that we address the economic security needs of all members of our society who need public support, our needy children, adults, and aged. Such a concern must be part of a comprehensive national economic security policy that would assure all Americans, including our Black aged, a secure existence in our affluent society.

Targeting Scarce Resources

In his chapter on issues in targeting the benefits of Older Americans Act (OAA) services for the elderly, John H. Skinner provides a critical review of service benefits for Black elderly under this program by examining the strategies of resource allocation and targeting of program funds. After a review of the experience of the aging network with targeting strategies, Skinner concludes that there is considerable room for improvement. To a great extent, the failure results as much from the formulation of the methods of distributing funds as from the ways these procedures are implemented. Skinner suggests new approaches in the search for better ways to assure that the old, the frail, and the poor among the aged generally, and among the Black aged in particular, are given better attention in the use of service program funds.

Skinner, who has served as an officer of the Administration on Aging, is keenly aware that the OAA has lofty goals, and that it has been sold as a "panacea for all and funded as a balm for a few." The U.S. Congress, however, has attempted to assure that attention is given to the needy through the use of formulas to assure the distribution of funds to targeted populations. These efforts, to date, have failed to assure effective targeting of OAA funds to the elderly in greatest need. A more effective targeting strategy, in Skinner's view, would assure that Black elderly in need of services would be assured a more equitable share of these and other resources.

Skinner is hopeful that with the increased interest of Congress in assuring greater attention to minorities, the 1987 amendments to the OAA will be a positive step toward improving the conditions and access to services of vulnerable populations. In his view, it may be anticipated that both states and Area Agencies on Aging, as a consequence of the more recent legislative mandates, will pay greater attention to the economic and social needs of low-income minorities. It may be reasonable to expect, therefore, that a more equitable share of OAA-funded services will be available to Black elderly.

We are keenly aware of the contradictions inherent in the Older Americans Act. On the one hand, elected political officials wanted to demonstrate, over the years, that they provided adequate funding of services for all seniors, while on the other hand they constructed funding formulas to target services to those in greatest economic and social need. To accomplish both sets of goals with less than 1% of the national budget was obviously impossible. Therefore, service planners and service providers have been facing a constant impossible challenge.

This challenge has been made more difficult in light of the growth in demand for services on the part of increasing numbers of vulnerable aged in need of services and the constant reduction in other funding sources for services for the elderly. Fluctuating commitments on the national level, coupled with recent budgetary reductions, have brought about a practical policy of constantly increased funding scarcity and, consequently, consistent reductions in availability of services. This de facto, even if not declared, national policy, which does not allow adequate funding for health and social services, places service planners and service providers in the position of facing a constant challenge of reducing services at a time of rising demand and need. The scarcity and inaccessibility of services affect the well-being of all vulnerable aged, including vulnerable older Black Americans.

Addressing Health Care Needs of Black Aged

In his chapter on issues in health care needs and services for the Black aged, Wornie L. Reed reviews and discusses health and medical care, two key concerns of elderly persons in general and the Black elderly in particular. He notes that old age is generally accompanied by deteriorating health and an increasing need for medical care. These attributes of old age are especially problematic for the Black elderly, as they suffer disadvantages in both health status and access to health care services.

Reed employs a needs-based measure of access to medical care to assess whether the Black elderly have equity of access to medical care. He examines the access measure across Black subgroups in an effort to determine which subgroups underutilize medical care services and under what conditions. He concludes that the current population of Black elderly are at great risk for acute as well as chronic diseases, and that Black elderly do not have equity of access to medical care services. He notes, following the application of a normed measure of service use relative to need, that the Black elderly are underutilizers of medical care.

Reed asserts that the consequence of underutilization of medical care services is undoubtedly poorer health. In his view, there are two primary consequences of the underutilization of medical care by the Black elderly. First, the general tendency to underutilize may be a function of their experiences with medical care services. Blacks tend to use public facilities and hospitals more readily than Whites, and the concomitant result is a greater dissatisfaction with this care. Second, many of the Black elderly do not have supplementary insurance to pay for visits to other places of care. Furthermore, Reed asserts that among Black elderly there are many individuals without regular sources of care, and they are likely not to have regular family physicians.

Reed also notes that social structural factors have direct effects on the medical care-seeking behavior of Blacks. In his view, the most critical of these barriers is that of financial resources. Since Medicare provides for only one-half to three-fourths of the costs of medical care, many elderly must depend upon Medicaid to pay the other costs. Yet many "near poor" elderly do not qualify for Medicaid. So almost 20% of the elderly's medical care costs must be paid out of pocket or by supplementary insurance. However, only one-third of the Black elderly have such insurance. Consequently, many of the Black elderly do not have any insurance in addition to Medicare.

Reed concludes that there are needs for attitudinal changes among health professionals and for structural changes in the organization of health care services, and an urgent need to address the issue of equity of access to care. In his view, broader-based efforts are needed on the national and state levels to solve the long-range problem of health care services for all. In the interim, Reed calls for increased emphasis on state-level approaches to solving health policy problems, including the establishment of programs to finance health services for "near poor" individuals who are unable to qualify for Medicaid. Other proposals would provide direct insurance to individuals as well as financial support to local hospitals. He hopes that such interim strategies will not detract from the effort to develop a national health plan that is more comprehensive than the current provisions of Medicare and Medicaid.

It is obvious from the review presented in Reed's chapter that many of the problems of poor health care services are exacerbated by the absence of a national health care policy and program. Again, the United States has the dubious distinction, along with South Africa, of not having a national health care and long-term care policy and service system.

While Medicare provides a certain coverage not available for other age groups in the United States, the structural and financial features of high deductibles and copayments make this program inadequate to address the health care needs of many, especially the chronic long-term health care needs of the elderly. The Medicare Catastrophic Coverage Act of 1988, which was repealed, was likely to reduce some of the burdens for the aged, but the health care needs of a significant number of older Americans, including a significant segment of the Black aged, would not have been adequately addressed by the addition of this law. Again, it is clear that we need a comprehensive national health care policy that will systematically address the health care needs of all members of our affluent society, including those of the Black elderly.

Whereas Reed reviews issues of health status and health care that concern all Black aged, Mary McKinney Edmonds focuses on the conditions of older Black women. Her chapter examines the health status, health care needs, and health care utilization of aged Black women in the context of their sociohistorical experiences, their present health status, and their coping strategies, in order to ascertain how these influence their health and illness behavior.

Edmonds asserts that the health status of the elderly in the United States has economic, social, health care, and political implications. Assessment of health status gives us one basis for understanding some interactions between health and the aging process. In answering the question, Why study aged Black females? Edmonds notes that the problem of myths is nowhere more apparent than in the area of the aging of minority women. She indicates that little is known about the process of Blacks growing old in America compared with what is known about growing old, in general, in America and in the world.

Limited empirical bases have led to an erroneous assumption of homogeneity in the Black population. Edmonds further notes that Black women have been subjected to discriminatory practices throughout their lives and, as a consequence, have had to develop coping strategies to maintain equilibrium in hostile and inconsiderate social and economic situations and environments. She states that older Black women have been constantly faced with the stigma of sexism and ageism. *Triple jeopardy* is a term attached to Black aged females, because they find themselves subjected to the negative stereotypes of ageism and sexism as well as racism.

Edmonds suggests that the health care needs of Black aged women can be better understood if more is known about (1) their unique characteristics, (2) their self-perceptions of their health status, (3) factors that account for their health care utilization patterns, and (4) the consequences of their illness behavior. A better understanding of these factors should provide health care planners and providers with directions for appropriate strategies to facilitate more effective utilization of health care services by aged Black women. Additionally, such insights could provide directions for policy formulation and decision making to counter and reverse the alarming mortality and morbidity figures for Blacks.

Two major task force reports, those of the National Task Force on Black Minority Health (U.S. Department of Health and Human Services, 1985) and the Ohio Governor's Task Force on Black and Minority Health (State of Ohio, 1987), which make similar recommendations, are used by Edmonds as bases for the following recommendations for improvement:

(1) Create outreach programs to disseminate information designed for specific minority groups.

(2) Increase the number of qualified applicants for medical schools and for allied health professional programs.

(3) Address the diverse health care needs of Black aged females in health care planning.

(4) Educate health care providers to increase their sensitivity to the needs and perceptions of Black aged females.

(5) Locate health care facilities and health care professionals closer to where Black aged females reside.

(6) Make financial resources available to supplement what Medicare does not cover for Black aged females.

(7) Improve health care policies, including long-term care policies, through the constant attention and concern of elected and appointed public officials.

(8) Work to enhance access, availability, and quality of health care services through health care professional organizations, academic institutions, senior organizations, and health service organizations.

In summary, Edmonds states that the health status of aged Black women has been affected by their lifelong experiences of disadvantage and discrimination. Therefore, health care planners and providers need to be more sensitive and need to work to allay the suspicions of Black women and encourage service use on their part. The consequences of inadequate financial resources, housing, nutrition, education, and life-style have converged to exacerbate the health problems of the aged in general, and of Black aged women in particular.

A national agenda to address the health care needs of all Americans, including the specific health concerns of older Black men and women, is called for. Quality health care service available to all members of our affluent society needs to be seen as a priority. The chapters by Reed and Edmonds challenge the health care delivery system to be understanding and respectful toward older Black men and women in aiding their access to and utilization of health care services they rightfully deserve and to which they are richly entitled.

Underutilization of Programs and Resources

In Chapter 11, Barresi and Menon assert that an essential source of emotional and general well-being of the elderly can be traced to their informal support networks. Informal supports are supplemented by the formal support networks of public and private agencies. A major source of support for Black elderly is provided by the family. Barresi and Menon note that much of what has been written about the Black family has assumed that there is only one family form, with little or no variation. They set out to examine in this chapter the diversity of the Black family as it is affected by socioeconomic status, region, urban or rural location, family size and type, and other characteristics. This chapter reviews the diversity of caregiving networks within the Black American family, and examines the impact this diversity has on the elderly in these families.

Barresi and Menon note that there is underutilization by Black elderly of programs such as multipurpose senior centers, housing, in-home services, adult day care, long-term care residences, crime prevention and legal assistance programs, and health and mental health services; this underutilization adversely affects the well-being of Black elderly. They suggest that a possible explanation for underutilization of services could be associated with lack of information and inadequate referral procedures. Inaccessibility of services and facilities could be another possible explanation. Barresi and Menon suggest a European model of service, the *Sozialstationen* in use in West Germany, as a way in which social services and facilities can be provided for the aged. Basic services such as nursing care, personal aides, and homemaker services are provided at public housing sites for the elderly. In the authors' view, a program of this type would also reduce the stress that primary caregivers tend to experience.

Another innovation suggested by the authors is the warden system used in Great Britain. A warden or "friendly visitor" is assigned to a block of dwelling units to look in on the occupants each day and help them. The warden is typically a middle-aged woman who acts much the same as would an interested neighbor. She arranges formal services, accompanies the elderly on medical and agency visits, and in general sees to their well-being. The British warden system could serve to extend the caregiving that is provided by family or other informal caregivers.

Barresi and Menon conclude that the informal support networks, both kin and nonkin, of the Black elderly tend to be willing but increasingly unable to provide for the needs of their elderly members. Policies and programs geared toward enhancing the quality of life and unique needs of Black elderly, who are expected to constitute a relatively large sector of the elderly population in coming years, need to consider this fact.

Clinical Practice with Black Aged

The primary purpose of Chapter 12, by Cheryl Stewart Gerace and Linda S. Noelker, is to review and adapt existing models for clinical social work practice with Black or minority clients to working with Black elderly clients and their family caregivers. In accordance with the principles of social work education and the profession's code of ethics, a key premise underlying the effort is that the culture and cultural values as well as the ethnic identity of any client system are central concerns in rendering service. These include a respect for human rights and the dignity and uniqueness of the individual, as well as adherence to the values of social responsibility and social equality.

Quoting Lum (1986), Gerace and Noelker indicate that social workers have an ethical responsibility to promote nondiscrimination, equal opportunity, and respect for cultural diversity. These responsibilities should guide and direct all social work activities with distinct ethnic/cultural group members. Relying on Lum, the authors further suggest that social work values must encompass both client rights and the collective values of the minority group. Among African-Americans retaining a southern cultural orientation, this collective value system emphasizes family unity, the leadership of older generations, kinship responsibilities, and the prominence of religious institutions and spirituality. Moreover, the collective value system of a culturally distinct group should guide social work practice rather than the more commonly used European-American value system.

Accordingly, Gerace and Noelker's first objective is to identify aspects of Black culture and aging that should structure social work practice with Black elderly and their families. Although culturally sensitive treatment programs and the ethnic sensitive model have been delineated previously, these authors focus on the special considerations that should be given to the joint effects of aging and Black culture on social work practice.

The second purpose of the authors is to use case material from clients served by the Benjamin Rose Institute's Community Services Division to illustrate the application of these practice principles to different types of elderly Black clients whose informal support systems vary in their structure and functioning. Third, the authors draw on clinical research from the institute's Client Information System to identify differences in elderly Blacks' family networks and their implications for social work services.

Gerace and Noelker delineate three major practice principles that should be applied in work with minority elderly to enhance the performance of an on-target assessment and the development of an appropriate service plan:

(1) being knowledgeable about and responsive to the minority culture as well as to elderly clients' cultural experiences related to their generation or cohort (termed *tuning in* or *being in tune*)

(2) understanding the communication patterns and techniques in minority groups and how communication is affected by age-related changes, and adapting communication with the client accordingly

(3) completing a comprehensive assessment utilizing the life model or eco-systems approach and the ethnic sensitive practice principles

The authors underscore the need for practitioners to recognize the special stresses experienced by Black elderly who become chronically ill and functionally impaired. While a portion of this group is bereft of informal caregivers, the majority requiring assistance receive it from kin, primarily wives and daughters. At the same time, the demands of caregiving can resurrect and exacerbate long-standing problems in family relationships or exhaust the resources of well-functioning, stable family networks. For these reasons, the authors suggest that the special needs and care-related burdens of family members should be a focus of social work intervention in the assessment, care planning, and counseling process. This approach can help to forestall or prevent institutional placement of the aged client, alleviate the strain on family caregivers, and improve the functioning of family support networks.

As Gerace and Noelker note, attention to the special needs of Black aged and their family caregivers has been limited. Their chapter will most certainly enhance the ethnic sensitivity of social workers serving Black aged by considering how Black culture affects the stresses encountered by minority elderly and how cultural values and forms (family, church) can be used effectively to attenuate these stresses. In view of the projected growth in the Black aged population and consequent increased demands on younger family members for care, continued work is needed to refine practice techniques with various groups of elderly and their support networks.

Determinants of Service Use

A review of the health and social services literature reveals that planning and practice efforts of health and human service professionals in the field of aging are guided by the following objectives: (1) providing older individuals and families with effective services that are efficiently delivered; (2) allowing older service consumers as much discretion as possible concerning the services they use and enhancing their participation in the planning and provision of services; (3) encouraging and supporting family members, friends, neighbors, and volunteers in caring for older persons; and (4) enhancing the coping resources of older service consumers and their informal caregivers (Harel et al., 1985).

Implicit in these professional objectives is a commitment to the promotion of survival, security, and well-being of the aged, including older Black Americans. These objectives imply the need to reduce stress and enhance coping resources of the aged's informal caregivers. In addition, these objectives imply the need for information and preferences from the perspective of service planners and service providers.

Research indicates that there is a great deal of variation among older people generally concerning the extent of information about social resources and services that might directly enhance the quality of their lives (Harel et al., 1987). Recent research on Older Americans Act-funded services has found considerable variation in knowledge about and access to services among nutrition site and homebound Black service users (Harel, 1985, 1986). Lack of knowledge about resources and services is likely to reduce both the search for benefits and the search for information about services. Even when people have a general knowledge about available services, they may not be able to relate them to their own needs or to the needs of others around them (Harel et al., 1985). Ralston (1984) found that the senior center participation of Black aged was related to a commitment to become involved in senior centers, perception of senior centers, and contact with family and friends. Research also indicates that most older Black Americans have viable and functioning informal support systems. Older persons and their informal caregivers turn to formal organizations for assistance when the nature of their problems becomes such that they are too difficult for them to handle alone. For the older population in general, 50% of all in-home services are provided by the family; for those who are severely impaired, the rate climbs to 80% (Comptroller General of the United States, 1977).

The consequences of lack of knowledge and service accessibility may include physical and mental isolation. This isolation may be most severe among those elderly left behind by their culturally and geographically mobile children. The limitations in economic and social resources will result in situations where Black aged are likely to be homebound without needed services or to become candidates for institutionalization. We are convinced that the organized Black community needs to play a meaningful role in accessing services for elderly members of their respective communities.

Needs, Resources, and Services

Several points need to be restated in considering the service needs of Black aged. First, older Black Americans constitute a heterogeneous population. Recognition and consideration of this diversity is essential for any serious attempt to plan interventions on behalf of the aged. Respect and understanding of the needs and preferences of service consumers, coupled with effective communication with the elderly and members of their informal support systems, are essential in working with Black aged.

Second, informal support systems are of central importance in the lives of all elderly, including the Black aged. These systems include children, other family members, friends, and neighbors. In addition, churches, civic groups, and other organizations play significant roles in the lives of elderly Blacks. Black institutions provide opportunities for involvement and affiliation and sources of support for the aged. While informal caregivers play an important role, they cannot alone shoulder all the responsibility and meet all the service needs of elderly family members. Service planners and providers need to be cognizant of the potential and actual involvement of the informal support system in the care of Black aged.

Third, while potentially they may play an important role, most Black communities simply do not have the expertise, resources, or services needed by their elderly members. It is also important to underscore the fluctuations in public commitment and the fragmented nature of the health and social service system in the United States. The availability of needs-based benefits and services in the United States varies across and within different states and changes from year to year. The extent to which benefits and services may be available for Black aged may, therefore, vary considerably in different locations.

Fourth, it is important to underscore the need for a national economic policy that is likely to assure personal security and a national health care policy that will assure the survival and security needs of all Americans, including those of older Black aged.

Fifth and finally, it is important to underscore the importance of adequate funding for health and social services to assure the rational planning, organization, and delivery of services to meet the needs of all aged, including older Black Americans, effectively.

References

Comptroller General of the United States. 1977. *The Well-Being of Older People in Cleveland, Ohio.* Washington, DC: U.S. General Accounting Office.

Harel, Z. 1985. "Nutrition Site Service Users: Does Racial Background Make a Difference?" *Gerontologist* 25:286-91.

———. 1986. "Homebound Aged: Does Racial Background Make a Difference?" *Journal of Gerontological Social Work* 9:133-43.

Harel, Z., E. McKinney, and M. Williams. 1987. "Aging, Ethnicity and Services." Pp. 196-210 in *Ethnicity and Aging,* edited by D. Gelfand and C. Barresi. New York: Springer.

Harel, Z., L. Noelker, and B. Blake. 1985. "Planning Services for the Aged: Theoretical and Empirical Perspectives." *Gerontologist* 25:644-49.

Lum, D. 1986. *Social Work Practice and People of Color: A Process-Stage Approach.* Monterey, CA: Brooks/Cole.

Perkins, Frances. 1946. *The Roosevelt I Knew.* New York: Viking.

Ralston, P. A. 1984. "Senior Center Utilization by Black Elderly Adults: Social, Attitudinal, and Knowledge Correlates." *Journal of Gerontology* 39:224-29.

State of Ohio. 1987. *The Ohio Governor's Task Force on Black and Minority Health: Final Report.* Columbus: Author.

U.S. Department of Health and Human Services, Task Force on Black and Minority Health. 1985. *Report of the Secretary's Task Force on Black and Minority Health.* Washington, DC: Author.

U.S. Senate Special Committee on Aging. 1986. *Aging America: Trends and Projections.* DHHS No. 498-116-814/42395. Washington, DC: Government Printing Office.

7

African American Elderly Experiences with Title II

Program Assumptions and Economic Well-Being

MICHAEL WILLIAMS

The Title II Federal Pension Program celebrated its fifty-fourth birthday on August 14, 1989. Enacted as an integral part of the 1935 Social Security Act, the program was designed to provide the nation's working population with a "supplemental" means of support during their retirement years. Frances Perkins (1946), chair of the Committee on Economic Security, architect of the 1935 Social Security Act, believed that the Title II program would play a vital role in allowing the elderly to grow old "without being haunted by the spectre of a poverty-ridden old-age or being a burden on our children" (pp. 792-94).

Since becoming operational in 1942, the Title II program has provided economic benefits for millions of the nation's elderly. In 1984, for example, 14,169,379 individuals over the age of 62 received such benefits. To understand the vital importance of Title II as an income source, one has only to recognize that 93% of the elderly population receive some portion of their income from Title II-related programs (Social Security Administration, 1986).

Despite the number of elderly individuals participating in the program and receiving benefits, it is clear that Title II is not meeting the economic needs of the nation's elderly population. Recent census data point out that 13% of the elderly population live in poverty. Another 16% of the elderly population have incomes between poverty and 125% of the poverty level. Over 50% of African American elderly find themselves living in or near poverty (U.S. House of Representatives, 1987).

As a result of having insufficient economic resources, many of society's elderly individuals find themselves unable to meet their basic needs. A substantial number are forced to live in substandard housing. Many cannot afford to meet their health and nutritional needs (U.S. House of Representatives, 1987). Contrary to Perkins's high expectations, many of the nation's elderly are still haunted by the specter of a poverty-ridden old age and being a burden on their children.

Why is the Title II Federal Pension Program failing to meet Perkins's economic expectations? Why are so many of the nation's elderly finding it increasingly difficult to make ends meet? The answers to these questions can be found by examining the assumptions upon which the Title II program was developed. It is my contention that the Title II program was well thought out from a political standpoint but not from a social welfare vantage point, hence its ineffectiveness in meeting the economic needs of the nation's elderly population.

The purpose of this chapter is to examine the major assumptions behind the Title II program and their effect upon the economic well-being of the retired African American elderly. I will seek to determine how well the African American elderly fare under the Title II Federal Pension Program. It is my position that through such an analysis the flaws of the program will become apparent. It is my hope that the exposure of these Title II flaws will spur social welfare policy experts to take corrective measures resulting in a much improved program.

The Past: 1935-1954

African Americans have had a unique experience under the Title II program. It is imperative that we understand this experience if we wish to grasp how African Americans have been affected by the operation of Title II over the years. With this in mind, a brief summary of the early African American experience under the Title II provisions is provided. Initial discussion is focused on the years 1935-1954. It was during this period that a number of critical events occurred that had both positive and negative effects upon the economic well-being of the African American elderly.

Bonita Harrison (1936), upon reviewing the 1935 Social Security Act, declared, "Verily, the Negro has the need, but no one believes that he will secure his full share of benefits under the Act" (p. 10). Harvard Sitkoff (1978) concurred with Harrison's assessment when he stated: "No group needed social security more than Negroes and none got less of it" (p. 52). What led two distinguished scholars to make such criticisms of the legislation many policy experts regard as the most significant in U.S. history? The answer to this question can be found in a brief review of the historical context in which the legislation emerged.

The 1935 Social Security Act, of which the Title II program was an integral part, was shaped in an era when both racism and sexism were considered a natural part of society. Racism and sexism played critical roles in shaping every facet of the U.S. life-style at that time, and a clear example of this is reflected in the racial politics that shaped the development of the Title II program.

As I have pointed out in earlier work, the interests of the African American elderly were at least partially included in the original draft of the Title II legislation submitted by the Roosevelt administration (Williams, 1986). Franklin Roosevelt initially was a strong advocate of the inclusion of a universal coverage Title II provision. He believed that all workers should have the right to a federal pension through Title II participation. However, in the face of mounting southern criticism and opposition, Roosevelt's strong advocacy of universal coverage weakened rapidly. Southerners rejected the universal coverage for three primary reasons: (1) The heavy federal administration of Title II evoked memories of Reconstruction, (2) the program had implications for treating Whites and Blacks as equals, and (3) the program was thought to have negative implications for southern control of its Black labor force.

The South made it clear that it would not tolerate any threat to its way of life. Powerful racial demagogues such as Carter Glass and Harry Byrd of Virginia; Pat Harrison, Theodore Bilbo, and James Rankin of Mississippi; "Cotton Ed" Smith and James Brynes of South Carolina; Tennessee's Joseph Byrns; Alabama's William Bankhead; Texas's Sam Rayburn; Walter F. George and Eugene Talmadge of Georgia; and North Carolina's Robert L. "Muley" Doughton and Josiah Bailey told the Roosevelt administration in no uncertain terms that they would defeat any New Deal legislation that contained the slightest hint of altering their White supremacy system (Williams, 1983, 1986). In their view, the proposed Title II program held such potential, with its universal coverage provisions and federal administration of the program.

Roosevelt, recognizing the political power of the South, decided that it was in his best interests not to insist upon universal coverage as a condition of Title II passage. To his way of thinking, it would be better to defer to southern racial sentiments than to risk certain defeat of critically needed New Deal legislation (Sitkoff, 1978; Williams, 1986).

Roosevelt's decision not to challenge southern opposition to the universal coverage provision resulted in a redrafting of Title II. The net result of this redrafting was that many of the occupation categories that had heavy numbers of African Americans, such as farmers and domestic workers, were deleted from coverage. Approximately 72% of all African Americans could not participate in the redrafted program (Williams, 1983, 1986).

The decision to capitulate to southern demands was justified by the Roosevelt administration on the following grounds. First, the New Deal legislation was considered too important to risk defeat for a stand on civil rights. This was particularly true given that many of Roosevelt's closest advisers were southerners who did not support the universal coverage provision to begin with (Sitkoff, 1978). Second, there seemed to exist within the Roosevelt administration an assumption that the need for universal coverage could be addressed in future years, when a better climate would exist. It was the hope of several members of Roosevelt's cabinet that the South would become more moderate in its racial sentiments, thus paving the way for expansion of Title II coverage. They also believed that they could sell universal coverage as a method to reduce the need for the federal government to support the welfare-related Title I Old Age Assistance Program (Witte, 1962).

The unwillingness to insist upon universal coverage combined with the assumption that the issue could be addressed in future years had an immediate effect upon African American elderly well-being. It meant that when the program became operational in 1942, the vast majority of the African American elderly found themselves in the unenviable position of not being eligible to receive Title II benefits. As observed above, over 72% of the African American labor force was excluded from Title II coverage. The Title II exclusion of Blacks was critical to the predominantly Black southern population, whose average cash income was less than $100 per year (Harris, 1982). The struggle for economical survival would continue to be an unwanted companion of the African American elderly.

Braxton (1940) has highlighted another important negative consequence of African American Title II exclusion. The exclusion forced many African American elderly to rely upon the state controlled, welfare-oriented Title I program for economic sustenance. Forced reliance upon Title I proved to be problematic for several crucial reasons. First, little thought was given to the development and implementation of the Title I program. The Roosevelt administration viewed Title I as a temporary economic support program that would "wither away" as more of the labor force gained Title II coverage (Perkins, 1946; Witte, 1962). This shortsighted view proved to be disastrous to the large proportion of African American elderly who were forced to depend upon Title I as their only means of income. These individuals found themselves living on the economic edge because Title I allowed each state to determine benefit levels.

The vast majority of the states provided only token Title I benefits to be in compliance with the federal mandate (H.R. 7260). This was true of southern states, where the vast majority of the African American population resided (Douglass, 1939). For example, Mississippi's Title I program did not set a minimum Title I benefit level, choosing instead to provide a "reasonable subsistence" benefit. The state determined what the minimal allowance was that an indigent person needed to survive. This "reasonable subsistence" amount varied from person to person and from locale to locale (Douglass, 1939). Given the token nature of many of the states' Title I programs, it should not be surprising that the programs proved to be of only meager assistance to the African American elderly.

A second detrimental consequence of African American Title II exclusion was the federal government's decision to allow the states to control Title I, a situation that resulted in many African Americans being denied access to the program due to the discriminatory practices of the various states. The federal government allowed the states to devise their own Title I eligibility standards, and states often designed criteria that eliminated certain groups that they did not look favorably upon. For example, in the Southwest and West, Title I eligibility criteria eliminated Native Americans and Hispanics (migrant workers) from program participation (Douglass, 1939).

Braxton (1940) reviewed early African American Title I participation and found that while African Americans were participating in the program in a disproportionate fashion based upon their percentage of the general population, they were underrepresented on the basis of an objective examination of their state of need. Braxton attributes this underrepresentation to the way in which the states wrote their eligibility standards. For example, most of the states required that individuals seeking Title I eligibility present proof of age and state residency. In the South, the birth certificate was the only legal document accepted as proof. This criterion proved to be highly discriminatory against African Americans. Few southern African Americans had birth certificates, because most were born at home due to southern racism, which would not allow them to use hospital facilities (Williams, 1983). Without such documentation, obtaining Title I assistance was at best difficult.

A final negative consequence of African American Title I exclusion was that it placed African Americans in the position of not being able to take advantage of future improvements in Title II benefits. For instance, in 1939, Title II was amended to provide survivors' benefits. This was a critical benefit for maintaining some semblance of family stability in the case of loss of the family's principal wage earner. African American families were denied this assistance by virtue of having their principal wage earners' occupations excluded from initial Title II coverage.

Early African American Title II experience indicates that the needs of African Americans were at best only marginally considered. The literature clearly reveals that Title I and Title II provided only meager assistance to a population in need. As we turn our attention to the contemporary African American Title II experience (1954-1987), the initial lack of inclusion of African American economic needs continues to manifest itself in the operation of Title II. The next section presents an examination of the effects of the decision to have a wage-based Title II program upon the well-being of African Americans.

The Present (1954-1987)

In 1950, Title II was amended to extend coverage to more of the nation's work force. Under the 1950 amendment, the following groups received program coverage: (1) regularly employed farm and domestic workers, (2) self-employed persons not in agriculture, (3) federal employees not under the Civil Service Retirement System, (4) people employed by U.S. firms outside of the continental United States, and (5) state and local government workers at the option of their employers. The new amendment resulted in the eligibility of more than 10 million individuals working in the listed areas to participate in the Title II program (H.R. 6000).

On September 1, 1954, President Eisenhower signed into law H.R. 9366, more commonly known as the 1954 Title II amendments. The enactment of the 1954 amendments marked the second major expansion of Title II coverage during the 1950s. The new amendments brought approximately 10 million additional persons into the program. Among those covered by the new provisions were (1) farm operators, (2) farm workers, (3) ministers, (4) the remaining domestic workers not covered by the 1950 amendments, and (5) homeworkers (Social Security Administration, 1955).

The decision to expand Title II coverage was prompted by rising costs associated with the welfare-oriented Title I program. Contrary to initial assertions made by the Roosevelt administration, the need for the Title I program did not wither away, but rather became an important income maintenance program for senior citizens not covered by Title II. The Truman and Eisenhower administrations were not pleased with the increased reliance upon Title I by growing numbers of the nation's elderly. More important, they did not like expending resources on a welfare-related program.

It became evident to both the Truman and Eisenhower administrations that if steps were not taken, the federal government would be responsible for the rapidly escalating Title I costs. The only feasible way to reduce or control the Title I program was to expand Title II coverage of the nation's work force. The 1950 and 1954 Title II amendments were designed to shift the costs of providing for the economic needs of all but the neediest senior citizens away from the federal government to workers and employers (Williams, 1986).

The decision to expand Title II coverage afforded many African Americans access to the program. In 1951, for example, the number of African American Title II applicants more than doubled that of 1950. In 1950, 319,272 African Americans applied for Title II coverage. As a direct result of the 1950 Title II amendment, 708,533 African Americans applied for coverage in 1951. The number of African American male applicants went from 157,739 in 1950 to 282,037 in 1951. The number of female applicants rose from 161,533 to 426,496 between 1950 and 1951 (Social Security Administration, 1954). A similarly dramatic increase in the number of African Americans applicants occurred after the passage of the 1954 amendments.

The 1950 and 1954 Title II amendments were important for both the short- and long-term futures of African Americans. In the short term, the amendments provided many African Americans the economic benefits afforded by the program. For example, new African American applicants and their families became eligible for survivors' benefits. This was important, as many African Americans—particularly males—worked in labor areas that put them at risk of being killed on the job or of dying prematurely from work-related causes. The survivor benefit was an invaluable source of income for a family that had lost a principal breadwinner.

A major long-term consequence of the expansion of Title II coverage was that it brought millions of previously uncovered workers into the program without a reexamination of the program's goals and objectives. Remember that the 1950 and 1954 Title II amendments came about as a result of the need to reduce Title I welfare costs. No consideration was given as to how the actual operation of Title II affected those participating in the program. The need for such an evaluation becomes apparent as one reviews the contemporary status of African Americans under Title II.

In recent years the African American community, like the general society, has experienced a gradual but steady "graying" of its population. The number of African Americans living beyond age 65 has increased each year since the turn of the century. In 1986, of the 29 million individuals age 65 or older in the United States, 2.4 million were of African American descent. This number represented 8% of the total African American population (U.S. Department of Commerce, 1987c).

The rise in the number of African American elderly is expected to continue. It is projected that by the year 2030, 15.3% of the African American community, or one of every seven African Americans, will be age 65 or older. By the year 2050 it is estimated that there will be 9.2 million elderly African Americans (U.S. Department of Commerce, 1987c).

Not only are more African Americans reaching age 65, but they are also living further beyond this important milestone age. As of the 1980 census, 18.9% of the African American elderly were aged 80 or older. By the year 2050, it is projected that 35.3% of the African American elderly population will be 80 or older (U.S. Department of Commerce, 1987c).

The increased longevity of African Americans has been a mixed blessing. For a small number of African Americans, increased longevity has allowed them to spend more time with their loved ones or to pursue personal ambitions. The vast majority of the elderly, however, are confronted with the difficult—if not impossible—task of determining how they will financially support themselves during their twilight years. This is clearly demonstrated when one reviews the financial status of elderly African Americans.

In 1985 the median annual income for an African American age 65 or older was $4,925. African American males had a median income of $6,490. African American females' annual income averaged $4,441. The annual income level of African Americans was approximately 60% that of their White counterparts (U.S. Department of Commerce, 1987a). For the year in question (1985), the Census Bureau defined poverty for an elderly individual as income that fell below $5,156. The Census Bureau also defined an aged couple as being poor if their combined income was less than $6,503. Applying the Census Bureau's poverty standards to the African American aged population, one finds that as of 1985, 31.5% of the population was mired in poverty.

The extent of aged African American poverty is further highlighted when one examines additional measures of economic well-being. One such measure is the percentage of people having incomes below $3,000, $5,000, and $10,000 per year. Slightly more than 85% of all aged African Americans have annual incomes of less than $10,000. Almost 52% of elderly African Americans have incomes of less than $5,000 per year. Finally, approximately 13% of the African American aged population have incomes of less than $3,000 per year (U.S. Department of Commerce, 1987a).

A closer analysis of aged African American annual incomes reveals the following gender differences. Approximately 7% of elderly African American males have annual incomes of less than $3,000, compared with 17% of all African Americans. Some 64.9% of all African American females have incomes of less than $5,000 per year; 32% of all aged African American males are in the same income bracket. Some 91% of aged African American females have annual incomes of less than $10,000 per year, compared with 77% of the aged African American male population (U.S. Department of Commerce, 1987a).

In 1985, the U.S. Census Bureau defined people as "economically vulnerable" if they had an annual income between the poverty level and twice the poverty level. By this definition, 72% of aged African Americans are considered to be economically vulnerable. Statistics reveal that 88% of aged African American females were economically vulnerable in 1985 (U.S. Department of Commerce, 1987a).

The Title I and II programs play a vital role in providing aged African Americans with a source of income. In 1984, for example, 87% of elderly African Americans received some portion of their income from these programs. Titles I and II provided three-fourths or more of total income for 49% of aged African Americans. For 53% of the impoverished elderly, Titles I and II were the sole income source (Social Security Administration, 1984).

While access barriers to Titles I and II were eliminated by the 1950 and 1954 amendments, elderly African Americans' well-being is still negatively affected by the Roosevelt administration's decision to make Title II a wage-related program (H.R. 7020). This decision was based upon two factors: (1) the political climate of the era, and (2) Roosevelt's desire to create a program that would resist political tampering in future years. Each factor will be briefly elaborated upon below.

It has already been noted that Roosevelt faced many powerful obstacles in his attempt to secure passage of the Social Security Act. One the most important barriers to the passage of the act was the public perception that social security would lessen people's motivation to fend for themselves. Consider Senator A. Harry Moore's critical comments regarding the proposed legislation: "The Social Security Act would take all the romance out of life. We might as well take a child from the nursery, give him a nurse, and protect him from every experience that life affords" (Leuchtenburg, 1963).

Roosevelt, recognizing the political climate surrounding his proposed legislation, took steps to blunt criticism. He decided to have workers and employers contribute equally to the financing and operation of programs such as Title II. In addition, he downplayed the welfare-oriented Title I program by suggesting that the program would "wither away" as the total labor force gained Title II coverage (Perkins, 1946). These actions were taken to promote the perception that Title II was not a "giveaway" program and was consistent with current U.S. values.

Roosevelt's desire to create a program that could withstand future political tampering was an even greater motivation factor for him than his desire to conform to existing social and political values. Roosevelt reasoned that if he made Title II a wage-related program and promoted its insurance aspects, workers would perceive that they had earned the rights to their benefits. Furthermore, Roosevelt believed that people would take political and social action to influence those in power not to tamper with this "perceived right to a pension." Altmeyer (1968) makes this point:

> At a meeting during the early days of the committee, he [Roosevelt] told Miss Perkins, Dr. Witte, and me that he opposed the Townsend Plan or any other plan supported by general revenues to finance assistance to people already old and without means. The President's desire to place chief reliance on a system of contributory social insurance was due as much to his belief that it was a financially safe system as to his belief that it provided protection as a matter of earned right. He felt that requiring the benefits to be financed entirely by contributions furnished a built-in safeguard.

While Roosevelt's decision to make Title II a wage-related program may have been politically wise, it failed to take into consideration economic consequences for unemployed and underemployed Americans. The American worker—particularly the African American worker—continues to be negatively affected by the decision to have a wage-related program versus a need-related one. The data cited earlier outlining the current economic status of aged African Americans clearly point to several important issues that Roosevelt's decision did not address. Each issue will be elaborated upon briefly below.

The current operation of Title II does not take into consideration the historical consequences of American employment, unemployment, and underemployment. The economic status of aged African Americans clearly reflects this history. When examining, for example, the census data regarding African American employment since 1948, one finds a consistent pattern of African Americans heavily employed in low-paying occupations. For example, as late as the 1960s, African Americans were heavily employed in such occupations as domestic work and unskilled labor (U.S. Department of Commerce, 1987c).

The concentration of African Americans in menial, low-paying jobs has serious implications for the wage-related Title II system. Since Title II pegs benefit levels to contributions, the implications of employment in low-paid covered positions become obvious. First, if an individual is not able to contribute sufficiently during his or her working years, that person is doomed to be poor during his or her retirement years. The plight of African American females makes this point painfully clear. Recall that almost 65% of aged African American females have incomes of less than $5,000 per year. It is clear that a reevaluation of Title II operation is in order to address the problems described.

Second, the current Title II system fails to consider the unemployment history of most Americans. This is particularly true in regard to African Americans. Census data from 1980 reveal that since 1948, African Americans have had an unemployment rate twice that of their White counterparts. The higher unemployment rate of African Americans makes it more difficult for them to make regular contributions, and this ultimately translates into lower benefits during old age. Lower benefit levels generally mean living in poverty for the vast majority of African Americans.

Third, the Title II system requires that an individual accumulate a certain number of calendar quarters worked in a covered occupation to be eligible for program benefits. African Americans face a more difficult time meeting the criteria due to their higher unemployment rates. Each time a person is laid off or displaced from a job, his or her ability to meet the calendar quarter standards is impaired.

Consider the situation of those African Americans who became eligible for Title II benefits in 1988. Because of exclusionary tactics faced by many Blacks in their younger years of life, they were denied the opportunity for many contribution years, and, consequently, their retirement benefits are accordingly limited. This situation was further exacerbated by their working in fields that regularly laid off their work forces during slow economic periods, such as steelwork. Each unemployment period delays the workers' ability to accumulate the required number of calendar quarters necessary to qualify for Title II benefits.

Fourth, serious questions have been raised by African American scholars, such as Davis (1977), concerning whether the Title II system actually functions to lower the living standard of both working and retired African Americans. Davis argues that working African Americans are forced to take resources that they could use to meet their present-day needs to make contributions to a retirement system that they are not able to take full advantage of in old age. Consider, for example, the plight of most African American males. With a median life expectancy of 64.5 years, most African American males receive little if any direct benefit from participating in the current retirement system.

Fifth, the decision to have a wage-related Title II system has resulted in more aged African Americans having to work during their retirement years. In 1985, for example, slightly more than 24% of aged African American males between 65 and 69 years old were employed. African American females in the same age bracket had a 17.1% employment rate (U.S. Department of Commerce, 1987c). Many of these employed persons are not working for a sense of fulfillment, but out of necessity.

Given the high percentage of aged African Americans living in poverty, it may seem surprising that a higher proportion of them are not employed. There may be three reasons that account for the low percentage of aged African American employment. These reasons may serve as starting points for further investigation.

First, one must consider the health status of the population in question. Data indicate that many African Americans enter their retirement years in poorer health than do other groups. This poorer health status seems to be a direct result of receiving poor health care during their younger years, and is reflected in increased morbidity and disability rates. Given this situation, many aged African Americans—particularly those of lower socioeconomic status—are not in a condition to work even if they wish to do so (see also Reed, this volume; Watson, this volume).

Second, aged African Americans face continued discrimination in the labor market. They face both racial and age discrimination. African American females are also at risk due to gender discrimination. Employment discrimination is something that is encountered by all segments of the aged African American community. Even when individuals wish to work during their retirement years, often there is no employment available to them.

Finally, the current wage-based Title II program has resulted in more elderly African Americans depending upon the welfare-oriented Title I program. Roosevelt—in thinking that the need for Title I would wither away as more people gained Title II coverage—failed to take into consideration the factors outlined thus far. This in turn led to the development of a poorly thought-out Title I program.

African American Title I participation has had a negative effect upon this group's social and economic well-being. From a social perspective, Title I participation means being stigmatized as a "welfare recipient." This label often results in the rest of society looking down upon the person as being inadequate in meeting his or her own retirement needs.

From an economic perspective, those elderly African Americans dependent upon Title I are at the mercy of the rest of society for their economic survival. Society, depending upon the political, social, and economic climate, has demonstrated that it can be inconsiderate when it comes to meeting the needs of the less fortunate. While some members of society often voice their concern for the less fortunate, those same members have been slow to support their concerns with appropriate legislative enactments or policies. As a result, not only does the African American elderly suffer, but so do a significant number of children, adults, and older adults who are denied access to an adequate living standard in our affluent society.

In summary, the economic plight of aged African Americans remains critical under the present Title II system. The income maintenance system fails to take into account the employment, unemployment, and underemployment history of the population in question. As a result, we find that the vast majority of elderly African Americans are living below or near the poverty level. It is clear that the decision to make Title II wage based was not in the best interest of aged African Americans, and this disadvantage is likely to continue in the near future.

Future of African Americans Under Title II

What are the economic prospects of future aged African Americans under Title II? The answer to this question lies in gaining an understanding of how African Americans are situated in the labor force. Since Title II is a wage-related program, a look at the types of jobs held by African Americans provides a projection of how they will fare in retirement.

The 1980 census highlighted the African American labor force's concentration in three principal areas: (1) operators, fabricators, and laborers (27%); (2) technical, sales, and administrative support (24%); and (3) service occupations (23%). Some 13% of the African American labor force hold professional and managerial jobs; 9% work in occupations pertaining to "precision, production, craft and repair." Finally, 2% are employed in farming, forestry, or fishing (U.S. Department of Commerce, 1987b).

A closer analysis of the African American work force reveals several interesting occupational distributions. For example, 19.2% of African Americans holding professional or managerial jobs, almost one out of every five, are employed as social workers. African Americans constitute 3% of the nation's doctors, lawyers, and engineers; 44% of the nation's domestics and personal cleaners; and one-third (33%) of the country's maids, housemen, and garbage collectors (U.S. Department of Commerce, 1987b).

The economic consequences of African Americans' employment patterns are reflected in their per capita income. In 1985, the median per capita income of the African American community was $6,840. The median family income was $16,786. This compared to median per capita and median family incomes for Whites of $11,671 and $29,152, respectively. African American per capita income was only 58.6% of White Americans' income. African American median family income was approximately 57.6% that of White families (Swinton, 1987).

The present constellation of the African American work force, combined with the low median per capita and family incomes, suggests that many African Americans will continue to be disadvantaged economically under Title II. Recent economic and social trends point to the fact that the situation for African Americans may become progressively worse if steps are not taken to address the economic needs of aged Americans. Elaboration upon these trends should provide clarification.

It has been well documented by Neisbitt (1984) and others that the world is going through a restructuring process. Industrialized countries, such as the United States, are rapidly becoming information-based societies. Labor-intensive industrial jobs are being assumed by developing Third World countries.

The world restructuring process is most harmful to the African American community. The restructuring becomes problematic precisely because African Americans are heavily employed in occupations that are being eliminated by the movement toward an information-based society. Demand for manual and semiskilled labor is diminishing, while demand for high-technology skills is increasing. This transformation into an information society will mean that many industrial U.S. workers will find themselves unemployed or forced to seek employment in the growing service sector of the economy. Many of the jobs in the service sector pay low wages. Often they are minimum-wage jobs with little potential for career advancement or growth. Most of the employment created during Ronald Reagan's tenure as president falls in this sector.

The implications of the above discussion should begin to crystallize for the reader. For a small minority of the African American work force, the transformation of the United States into an information society will provide opportunities to prosper and grow. This is particularly true for those African Americans whose skills and training allow them to assume high-paying skilled, managerial, and professional jobs. For these individuals, preparing for their twilight years will be less difficult, as they will be in the position to make sufficient Title II contributions to ensure a decent old-age standard of living. These individuals will also be in a position to take advantage of federal programs such as Individual Retirement Accounts to save additional dollars to supplement Title II benefits.

The prospects for the vast majority of African American workers do not appear so bright, however. Many African Americans will be forced to seek employment in the service sector, and this will have dramatic effects upon their abilities to prepare for old-age retirement. Even if they are lucky enough to secure long-term employment with no layoff periods, their level of Title II contributions will be minimal given the average low pay of service sector occupations. This will translate to benefits conducive to an impoverished old age, and the necessity to rely upon society for assistance.

The future fortunes of African Americans under Title II were also affected by a number of changes to the program made during President Reagan's first term in office. While a number of changes were made, for illustrative purposes, discussion will be limited to only one change: the change in age eligibility.

In 1983, the age of eligibility was changed to 70. This change is designed to be phased in over time. It is to be fully operational by the year 2015. This change could negatively affect the well-being of African Americans, particularly males. African American males, in 1987, had a life expectancy of 64.5 years. How long will it take before African American male life expectancy meets or exceeds the eligibility age? African American males could find themselves in the same position they are in today—making contributions to a program from which, statistically, they have little chance of benefiting. This is just one example of how African American well-being will suffer under the new Title II amendments.

In summary, between 1950 and 1988 African Americans gained increased access to Title II. In fact, only a few occupations are not covered by the program. Increased coverage, however, should not be confused with the issue of effective benefit levels. While more African Americans receive Title II benefits than ever before in the program's history, increased numbers also live near or at the poverty level.

It appears that the economic plight of elderly African Americans will not improve in the near future. In fact, their plight may become worse if trends predicted by Neisbitt and others come to pass. This will result in possible increased dependency upon family, civic, and government institutions for support. This is a scenario exactly opposite to that envisioned by the creators of Title II.

Conclusions and Implications

The time is long overdue for a comprehensive review of the Title II program. It is clear from the experience of elderly African Americans that the program is not achieving the purposes set forth by its designers in 1935. Too many of our senior citizens find themselves living their remaining years in or near poverty. This is clearly not what the members of Roosevelt's Committee on Economic Security had in mind when they developed and implemented Title II.

The Title II experience of African Americans calls into question many of the basic premises of the program. For example, can we still realistically consider Title II a "supplemental" income program when for many of the nation's elderly population the program provides most if not all of their financial resources? As was noted above, 93% of the country's seniors receive Title II benefits. The time has come for lawmakers and policy experts to come to grips with the imperative need to reevaluate the role Title II should play in the struggle to ensure a decent standard of living for all senior citizens.

The reconsideration of the "supplemental" Title II role opens many exciting possibilities for meeting the economic needs of the nation's elderly. Perhaps consideration can be given to devising a new program in which no senior citizen's income would fall below the poverty level. The costs for such a program could be paid by taking existing Title II revenues and developing a more equitable benefit structure. Such a program may be controversial, but it would benefit the elderly who are struggling to survive.

The African American Title II experience also raises the issue of equity versus equality. The current system promotes equality in the sense that individuals receive benefits in proportion to their ability to make contributions during their working years. Such an approach does not take into consideration a multitude of factors that may hamper an individual's making regular contributions, such as not being regularly employed or working for low wages.

In promoting equality, Title II actually perpetuates inequality. The "haves" of society continue to benefit during their aged years, while the "have-nots" continue to suffer economically during their remaining years. It seems that the time is long overdue for strong consideration to be given to an attempt to incorporate equity into the nation's retirement program. A way must be devised to take into consideration factors that affect a person's ability to make Title II contributions when determining benefit levels. The twin concepts of equality and equity must be balanced if we are to enjoy an effective Title II system.

Ultimately, the nation must determine what standard of living it wishes for its elderly citizens. Do we want to set a standard of living for our elderly such that none will fall below poverty? Do we wish to maintain the existing system? Do we wish to modify the existing system? These are but a few of the many options before us. The path we take in addressing the economic plight of the elderly will make a statement not only about how we view our responsibilities to our elders but about us as a society.

References

Altmeyer, A. J. 1968. *The Formative Years of Social Security.* Madison: University of Wisconsin Press.

Braxton, B. 1939. "Broadening Our Social Security Law." *Opportunity* 17:372-74.

———. 1940. "Will the Wagner Bill Benefit Us?" *Opportunity* 18:101-3.

Davis, F. 1977. *Burden-Benefit: The Case of Poor Blacks.* Washington, DC: Howard University, Institute for Urban Affairs and Research.

Douglass, P. 1939. *Social Security in the United States: An Analysis and Appraisal of the Federal Social Security Act.* New York: McGraw-Hill.

Harris, W. 1982. *The Harder We Run: Black Workers Since the Civil War.* London: Oxford University Press.

Harrison, Bonita. 1936. "Social Security: What Does It Mean for the Negro." *Opportunity* 9:10-15.

Neisbitt, J. 1984. *Megatrends: Ten New Directions Transforming Our Lives.* New York: Warner.

Leuchtenburg, W. E. 1963. *Franklin D. Roosevelt and the New Deal 1932.* New York: Harper & Row.

Perkins, Francis. 1946. *The Roosevelt I Knew.* New York: Viking.

Sitkoff, Harvard. 1978. *A New Deal for Blacks: The Emergence of Civil Rights as a National Issue: The Depression Era.* London: Oxford University Press.

Social Security Administration. 1954. *Social Security Applicants.* Washington, DC: Government Printing Office.

———. 1955. *Social Security Applicants.* Washington, DC: Government Printing Office.

———. 1984. *Applicants for Account Numbers.* Washington, DC: Government Printing Office.

——— 1986. *Social Security Bulletin, Annual Statistical Supplement.* Washington, DC: Government Printing Office.

Swinton, D. 1987. "Economic Status of Blacks, 1986." Pp. 49-73 in *State of Black America,* edited by J. Dewart. New York: National Urban League.

U.S. Department of Commerce, Bureau of the Census. 1987a. *The Social and Economic Status of the Black Population in the United States: An Historical Overview 1790-1978.* Washington, DC: Government Printing Office.

———. 1987b. *Summary Characteristics of the Black Population for States and Selected Counties and Places: 1980.* Washington, DC: Government Printing Office.

———. 1987c. *Demographic and Socio-Economic Aspects of Aging in the U.S.* Special Reports. Washington, DC: Government Printing Office.

U.S. House of Representatives, Select Committee on Aging. 1987. "U.S. National Black Caucus on Aging: Testimony." Washington, DC: Government Printing Office.

Williams, M. 1983. "The Impact of Racial Prejudice upon the Formulation of the Social Security Act." M.A. thesis, University of Pittsburgh.

———. 1984. "The Effects of Social Security's Title I and II Program Amendment Changes upon the Social/Economic Well-Being of Elderly Black Americans, 1935-1972." Ph.D. dissertation, University of Pittsburgh.

———. 1986. "The Role of Racism in Shaping the 1935 Social Security Act." *Journal of Applied Social Sciences* 31-47.

Witte, E. 1962. *Development of the Social Security Act.* Madison: University of Wisconsin Press.

8

Targeting Benefits
for the Black Elderly

The Older Americans Act

JOHN H. SKINNER

The subject of targeting, while not solely germane to programs on aging, is particularly characteristic of those funded under the Older Americans Act (OAA) of 1965. The OAA was born a child of the "Great Society" at the same time Medicare and Medicaid were established, when high hopes were held that government could identify, crystallize, and solve most social problems. Like so many of these programs, the OAA was not sufficiently funded to expedite its lofty aims. Targeting, as a public policy device, is important to the Black elderly because it is a mechanism that governs the way in which specific proportions of OAA funds will be allocated.

This chapter examines the role of targeting and other resource optimization strategies under the OAA that affect the Black elderly. The Older Americans Act is briefly reviewed to provide the historical context in which targeting operates. Targeting is then discussed as a public policy strategy that has serious implications for Black and minority elderly persons. Current targeting approaches are described, and their effectiveness is evaluated. This is followed by a discussion of the possible factors that contribute to the success or failure of current targeting strategies. The chapter concludes with a review of some additional approaches that can complement or replace existing funds distribution schemes. These new approaches are need driven and offer an alternative to the less efficient approaches of using age, sex, and race or minority status as factors in funding formulas. A need-driven methodology emphasizes functional characteristics rather than culturally inflammatory predisposing factors such as race or minority status.

History of the Older Americans Act

The passing of the OAA in 1965 was the culmination of many years of activity in the field of aging. One of the earliest activities was the convening of the National Conference on the Aging in 1950 in Washington, D.C. In January 1951, the Federal Committee on Aging and Geriatrics was established, with the intent of coordinating and reinforcing existing federal activities related to aging. Connecticut was the first state to establish a commission on aging, which was called the Connecticut State Commission on the Care and Treatment of the Chronically Ill, Aged, and Infirm. The first National Conference of State Commissions on Aging was convened in September 1952 in Washington, D.C. (U.S. Department of Health, Education and Welfare, 1970).

In 1956 the Special Staff on Aging in the Office of the Secretary of Health, Education and Welfare was given responsibility for support of the functions of the Federal Committee on Aging and Geriatrics (Ficke, 1985a). In April of that year the Federal Council on Aging was established within the U.S. Department of Health, Education and Welfare. This council was to replace the earlier Federal Committee on Aging and Geriatrics. By 1960, every state had established at least one official unit to address issues related to aging; however, some were created only to qualify for funds to plan for the first White House Conference on Aging (WHCoA). The first WHCoA was held in 1961 and produced various recommendations about the federal role in research, demonstrations, training, and organizational leadership.

By 1963, President John F. Kennedy recommended that Congress develop a five-year program of funding to state and local agencies and voluntary organizations for projects to aid older people. The OAA was finally passed and signed by President Johnson on July 14, 1965, as Public Law 89-73. The OAA incorporated many of the recommendations coming out of the 1961 WHCoA.

While the passing of the Social Security Act in 1935 was probably the major landmark in social legislation directly affecting the income security of older persons, the passing of the OAA was probably the most significant legislation affecting public advocacy and social programs for the aged. The OAA established the Administration on Aging (AoA) to administer the majority of the provisions of the act.

The objectives of the OAA are so global and far reaching that they extend beyond the legislative authority of the AoA and its yearly appropriations. Since its creation, the OAA has gone through at least four periods of development (Ficke, 1985a). The earliest period, from 1965 to 1972, was concerned with the creation of the necessary components of the act. The second period, 1973-1978, addressed issues of expansion of program provisions. The third period, 1978-1983, focused more on internal coordination during a period of minimal funding growth. The fourth period, starting in 1984 and continuing to the present, appears to be focused on expanding the scope of policy areas addressed by agencies authorized under the OAA.

The OAA has undergone a number of changes over the years. These changes have been in the form of amendments that have been introduced during the reauthorization of the act. At present, the act consists of seven titles that set forth the mission, authority, and programs of the OAA. The first title of the act establishes the goals of the OAA. Title II provides for the establishment of the Administration on Aging and outlines its functions. The second title also establishes the position of commissioner on aging and the Federal Council on Aging. Title III of the OAA provides the authority to develop programs for the elderly. It is under this title that authority is given to the AoA to provide grants to states to plan and administer community programs for older Americans. Title III also provides specific instructions on how federal funds shall be allotted to states. It is here that the requirements for state plans and area plans are established as well as "authority for development of programs to assist older persons (especially those with the greatest economic or social needs) through grants to states, which in turn award funds to Area Agencies on Aging" (Ficke, 1985b, p. 43).

Title IV authorizes the development of discretionary grants and contracts for programs in training, research, and demonstrations. These programs fund directly state and local agencies, Area Agencies on Aging (AAAs), institutions of higher education, public or nonprofit agencies, organizations, or institutions. Title V provides authority to develop community service employment programs. Title VI specifically provides programs for native Americans, and Title VII establishes training and health education programs in multipurpose senior centers.

From the very beginning of its existence, the OAA presented a practical dilemma that made its administration problematic. That dilemma was how to make an underfunded program as effective as possible, and at the same time maintain the support and interest of all the elderly in the United States (Fisk, 1987). On the one hand, the act established universal eligibility for all elderly persons in the United States; on the other hand, the authority given to the AoA and its level of funding resulted in the ability to serve only a portion of the elderly population. Estes (1980) has indicated that in its infancy the OAA viewed the problems of the elderly as social isolation and lack of social activity. Little attention was paid to the differences in disability, poverty, and illness among the elderly.

While the funding for the OAA grew very rapidly in its early years, starting at $6.5 million in 1965 and growing to $908.5 million in 1980, recent years have seen a leveling off in funds. These funds, even at their highest, have been grossly inadequate to address the concept of universal eligibility. The per capita amount represented by OAA funding for the elderly is less than $5.00 per older person. The only way to utilize funds of the act effectively is to focus, or target, them in a manner that assures that services are used appropriately. The Congress tried to accomplish this in two ways: first, by establishing priority services for which a percentage of service funds to states was allotted, and second, by requiring, in later amendments, that states and AAAs assure that attention would be given to serving those in "greatest social and economic need."

The OAA was established to decentralize decision making about service delivery to the state and local levels. As such, the AoA has the responsibility of working closely with state agencies to assure that a comprehensive service plan is established and to provide each state with funds according to a legislatively mandated formula. States are, in turn, required to establish service plans with substate area agencies and devise formulas for the distribution of funds to those agencies. To a great extent the formulas have been left to the discretion of the local areas, subject to state approval and federal review of state plans.

The subjects of funds allocation, distribution, and targeting are of recurring interest to students of services to the elderly. These topics continue to be timely because they directly and indirectly influence who gets service, which services are offered, and how much service will be provided. Ficke (1985a) states that "one of the greatest needs in the field of aging, in the entire spectrum of human services, if you will, is a philosophy, a system of thought, a rational way of thinking about the means and processes of allocating public resources" (p. 1). This chapter contributes to the debate on the subject of resource allocation and targeting.

What Is Targeting?

The practices of resource allocation and resource targeting are not new. Most people and organizations do them on an ongoing basis. However, when resource allocation and targeting become public policy issues, they take on much more formal meaning and scrutiny. Over the last decade, concerns about increasing deficits, budget balances, and spending on domestic programs have led to greater interest in finding better ways to use available resources. A natural result has been a reexamination of methods of resource allocation and targeting.

The concepts of resource allocation and resource targeting, while similar, have very different connotations. They are both resource utilization approaches, but they produce different outcomes. Resource allocation is a policy or strategy of distributing resources according to some plan or formula to assure equity. The equity generally results in some proportionate allotment of resources. On the other hand, resource targeting is a policy or strategy of narrowing or focusing resources according to some plan or formula where the focus or target of the resources may be a group, condition, or status that is deemed to require special attention. These two resource distribution strategies, allocation and targeting, are common to publicly funded programs. They are different but complementary approaches that involve issues of equity, efficiency, and effectiveness. The two approaches are complementary because resource allocation is a systemwide distribution policy and resource targeting is a subsystem-specific policy of matching resources to needs. These two elements clearly complement each other.

Resource allocation is the primary purview of the federal government. Targeting concerns, at the federal level, are primarily limited to policy guidance to states. At the state level, resource allocation is still the primary concern, although more attention is given to targeting. Area Agencies on Aging are about equally concerned with allocation and targeting issues. The AAAs are the pivotal point in the shift from allocation to targeting concerns. Service providers are more concerned with issues of targeting than with the allocation of funds. Finally, the case manager or service supervisor is the one who makes the primary targeting decisions about who should receive which service, when, and for how long.

Critical decisions about the use of scarce resources are being made at all of these levels. At the highest levels, budgetary decisions are made by the Congress and the executive branch of government about the funds appropriated for aging service programs. The Congress, moreover, mandates specific formulas for the allocation of budgeted resources to the states. These allocation formulas must be administered by federal agencies to state agencies. Title III of the OAA contains specific language directing the Administration on Aging to allot funds to states, as well as directing states in their methods of distributing funds to AAAs. The AAAs must make additional decisions about which services and service providers they will support. Finally, service providers are faced with the ultimate decisions about which services to deliver to whom.

The 1987 amendments to the OAA give special attention to focusing on special elderly populations. The amendments provide new Parts D and E under Title III to fund services expressly for the frail elderly and to target services for those in greatest economic or social need. Part D supports nonmedical in-home services for the frail elderly. Part E supports transportation, outreach, targeting, long-term care ombudsman services, and other services where there is unmet need. The services supported under Part D are affected by a funding trigger that provides that new authorizations may not be appropriated unless the total amount of all OAA funds exceeds the 1978 appropriations level by at least 5% over the previous year. While this provision was intended to protect existing OAA programs, it also forestalls the possible implementation of these new parts of the act. The 1987 amendments also require that data be collected and analyses conducted on the effectiveness of state and area agency targeting. Of particular interest to the Black elderly is the fact that state plans must now identify the number of low-income and minority older persons in the state or planning and service area. Each state must describe the methods used to meet the needs of these groups in the previous year. Service providers are now required to specify how they will address the needs of low-income persons and minorities and must attempt to provide services to these groups in at least the same proportion as they are represented in the population of the area.

While decisions about the appropriation, distribution, and targeting of resources are similar, they are very different in terms of the amount of autonomy that rests in the decision making. Clearly, Congress acts with some degree of autonomy in determining the budget for an agency and the allotment formula for the distribution of those funds. However, these decisions occur in a political legislative context and are subject to the pressures, constraints, and trade-offs of the political process. The decision about how federal dollars are allocated to states is very circumscribed for the AoA. It must follow a very detailed formula for allotment described in the OAA that is primarily based on the population of people over 60 years of age in each state.

At the state level there is somewhat more flexibility. States must designate planning and service areas. They have the ability to determine, within broad parameters, what factors will be used in the designation, subject to review and concurrence of AoA. States also have the responsibility to develop formulas for the distribution of funds to the area agencies. It is with these formulas that states have the ability to include or omit factors that influence the way funds are distributed.

Although states must give assurances that "preferences will be given to providing services to older individuals with the greatest economic or social needs" (Gelfand, 1984), the major mechanism available to affect those preferences is through the distribution of funds to AAAs and the review and approval of AAA plans. It is at the state level that the Black elderly and other minorities may be defined as being in the greatest economic or social need. The public has an opportunity to comment on state plans, which include targeting formulas.

What is commonly called targeting at the state level consists of including certain factors in allocation formulas that affect the way funds are distributed. The law requires that the formulas consider the geographic distribution of persons over 60 years of age and that special attention be given to low-income minority individuals. While these factors vary from state to state, they tend to include factors for the proportions of the poor, minorities (particularly the proportion of Black elderly), and the old-old (persons over 75 or 85 years of age). The factors used in these formulas represent population characteristics and result in the redistribution of funds according to their combined effects; however, these characteristics do not necessarily represent the distribution of underlying need. Even though these factors can have an effect on how much an AAA gets for its programs, many states have not examined the effects of different formulas on that distribution of funds (Cutler and Harris, 1983).

Area agencies have the ability to select service providers and, within limits, to determine where services will be delivered and which services they will support. At this level the issue of managing scarce resources shifts from the equitable distribution of resources to the effective use of resources. As such, the emphasis switches from allocation to targeting of resources, where the service provider and the case manager make the ultimate service targeting decisions. When faced with limited resources, these professionals must determine (1) the kind and level of need, (2) which services to render, (3) which persons need which services, (4) how long the services should be provided, and (5) what combinations of services will do the most for the client.

For services funded under the OAA, the federal allocation of resources follows a plan that is intended to ensure the equitable distribution of funds among states in proportion to the sizes of their elderly populations. Because targeting is a resource-optimization strategy, it focuses resources on subgroups. For the most part, targeting in aging programs has been directed at defined (although often vaguely defined) groups of people believed to be in need or "at risk." This rather unsophisticated approach of targeting at-risk groups has led to the identification of such groups as the Black elderly, minorities, the frail elderly, and those in "greatest economic and social need" (Cuellar and Weeks, 1980; Guttmann, 1980). This approach of declaring group eligibility offers only a gross proxy of the actual incidence of need in a group. To clarify, persons over 85 years of age are more likely to be in need of long-term care service, but, at the same time, not all persons over 85 years of age are in need of long-term care services. This approach provides only superficial estimates.

One problem with declaring group eligibility is that the terms of group membership are not clear. A major problem in using race, sex, and ethnicity as indicators or predisposing variables is that they, as proxies of need, are constant and do not reflect varying states of need. Another is that persons in these groups do not have the same needs, and many may not require services. Determining need on the basis of group characteristics creates the possibility of dedicating more resources to one group than are required to meet that group's needs while not providing enough resources to meet the needs of other groups. True indicators of need must be transitional and sensitive to changes in the levels of need. They must be able to determine when an individual or group of individuals is or is not in a state of need. They must be able to detect changes in the need state of individuals and populations. The current methods of using targeting formulas are both ineffective and inefficient. The concept of targeting is useful, but the methods of its application need rethinking.

How Well Does Targeting Work?

Unfortunately, the techniques for targeting have generally been a failure. A report by the National Association of Area Agencies on Aging (1986) asserts that the project was conceived and proposed in response to many critical studies and reports regarding the lack of participation by minorities in OAA programs. One report particularly critical of these programs is the U.S. Commission on Civil Rights (1982) report, *Minority Elderly Services: New Programs, Old Problems.* This report criticizes the Administration on Aging, the state units on aging, and the Area Agencies on Aging in their (1) hiring practices, (2) lack of affirmative action, and (3) underrepresentation of minority participants in their programs. Another report cited by Ficke (1985b) was conducted by the Connecticut State Unit on Aging and found that large proportions of minorities used at least one service supported by the Older Americans Act, but those proportions were still lower than expected for the amount of need in those groups.

Probably one of the most important actions to affect the future of targeting and funds allocation under the OAA is the suit filed by the AAA serving Dade and Monroe counties against the State of Florida (Aldrich, 1987). Filed in the U.S. District Court for Southern Florida, the lawsuit, *Meek v. Martinez*, alleges that the intrastate funding formula did not comply with stipulations of the OAA and related regulations. The essential aspect of the suit is the assertion that the formula applied systematically excludes minorities. The Florida formula considers three factors that relate to the proportion of persons who are (1) poor and 60 years old or older, (2) living alone and 65 years old or older, and (3) 75 years of age and over. By omitting a factor on the proportion of Black aged and other minorities, Florida minimizes the representation of these groups in consideration of funds distribution. Mayas et al. (1981), using aggregated census data at the federal, regional, and state levels, found that nutrition sites funded with OAA funds were generally geographically located in areas representative of targeted populations in those areas. This use of aggregated data at the regional and state levels masks the true variation that may exist at local levels. Area agencies are responsible for coordinating service delivery at the local substate level and nutrition sites generally serve an even more circumscribed area. The National Association of Area Agencies on Aging (1986) states:

> The literature on minority service utilization clearly shows that older minorities have not received an adequate share of Title III services for which they are eligible. It also points out that minorities tend to be underrepresented in the Network on Aging not only as service recipients, but as professional employees and service providers. (p. 6)

Holmes et al. (1979) found that minorities were overrepresented in their use of community-based services in long-term care. Of course, these figures are misleading because they do not reflect participation levels in the communities where the sites are located. Krain and Trevino-Richard (1985) studied elderly Black and White participation in senior programs in Arkansas. They found that Blacks had participation rates that were higher than those of Whites, but Blacks were also more likely to need community services. The U.S. Commission on Civil Rights (1982) reports that analysis based on national statistics on the proportions of minorities

> ignores the fact that a much higher proportion of older Black persons are poorer than older Whites. For example, although only about 8.1 percent of all older persons (65 years of age and older) in the United States were Black, approximately 16.5 percent of those older persons in poverty were Black. Only 11 percent of those served in the nutrition programs in 1977 were Black.

Another study, by Guttmann (1980), examined the equitable share of benefits going to the four legislatively defined minority groups. This study revealed that nonminority elderly use significantly more public benefits than older Hispanics and Asians. However, older Blacks use somewhat more services than nonminority elderly persons. The subject of equity of access to public services has also been studied by Cuellar and Weeks (1980), who arrive at the general conclusion that minority elderly persons are not receiving an equitable share of public benefits relative to their needs. They also report that the inability to pay for medical care is the most important reason for minorities not using this kind of care. The problem of ability to pay is particularly difficult for Black elderly persons. The next most pressing problem in fully utilizing medical benefits is difficulty with transportation.

Why Is Targeting Not Working?

Several authors have posed solutions to the problems of equity and utilization of services by those who are in "greatest economic and social need" (Cuellar and Weeks, 1980; Guttmann, 1980; U.S. Commission on Civil Rights, 1982). Most of these solutions address structural changes in the operation of service programs. They address issues like locating programs in geographical areas with high concentrations of groups in need. They also address the need for better recruitment of minorities on the staffs of program providers and of more outreach to inform minorities and others of the availability of services (Skinner, 1986).

There is considerable tension associated with the issue of targeting. This tension is created by the need, on the one hand, to appeal to the concepts of universal eligibility and thus foster a large political base of support for OAA programs and, on the other hand, the need to find the most effective and efficient ways of utilizing scarce resources. If one is trying to promote a program and garner popular support, one might lean on the side of minimizing the targeting aspects of the act. If one is concerned about optimizing resources, one would place greater emphasis on the targeting provisions of the act. Unfortunately, decisions that deemphasize targeting generally minimize services to Blacks and other minorities.

Gibson (1986) has indicated that the well-being of Blacks is jeopardized by placing them in competition with other rapidly growing population subgroups, and expanding numbers of elderly Whites, for the nation's available economic and social resources. To a great extent, the solution to effective targeting may rest as much on political equations that balance the growing competition for access to public resources as on formulas that focus on subgroups of the population. However, a truly "need-based" targeting system may minimize the necessity for political manipulation of these formulas.

The use of functional status may be more effective than the use of demographic characteristics such as race, sex, and age. When examining a population of elderly, no single demographic indicator or any combination of indicators can adequately represent the needs for which they may be intended. If increased age is considered to be an indicator of vulnerability, not all persons in this category will possess functional status problems. A similar condition will occur with other demographic characteristics such as race or sex.

Most targeting formulas incorporate at least one of the six demographic variables of age (65+ and 85+), sex (male or female), race (White, Black, or other), and income (poverty). These formulas generally use the proportion of persons in the geographic area possessing a combination of attributes used in determining how funds will be allocated to an area. To the extent that the factors used are intended to indicate underlying need, their effectiveness should be judged by the degree to which they represent need in that population. Conversely, to the extent that they fail to reflect the underlying need, they may also be considered to be ineffective. Targeting on functional status needs is more effective than using demographic characteristics such as race, sex, age, and income.

To base targeting on age alone or in any combination with other demographic indicators is misleading and inappropriate. Because targeting formulas utilize aggregate data on demographic characteristics, the net result is an erroneous estimate and inappropriate emphasis given to factors that do not truly represent need.

Patterns of Need

Targeting formulas have been found to be ineffective in assuring that services are targeted to those in greatest economic and social need. Part of the problem lies in the level of aggregation of the data used in the formulas. No one indicator provides a complete estimate of the level of need. When those indicators are added to a formula, the combined effect is further misapportioned resources. But even if targeting formulas were effective in assuring that funds were allocated to geographic areas containing persons in the greatest economic and social need, there would still be a targeting issue of assuring that those funds were channeled to services and benefits for the target group. Targeting formulas serve only to direct or redirect funds proportionately to geographic areas with high concentrations of the target groups of concern. Clearly, any change in targeting formulas can have a dramatic impact on the funds that are ultimately distributed to local service areas.

Ensuring that funds are allotted to a specific geographic area provides no assurance that those in need will get the service or benefits they need. At the level of the program provider, the ultimate decision of who gets what service is often left to circumstance. Without an aid in targeting on those persons needing specific services and determining which services are most effective for which needs patterns, local service providers are left with little guidance in targeting. One method of targeting used at the service delivery level is case management. This approach is usually based on some form of case assessment to determine the level of need of the client. Based on the findings of the case assessment, an assessment team or case manager decides on the most appropriate services required by the client.

Unfortunately, case management teams have little guidance on which services to provide for which needs. They have no information on the effectiveness of these services for different needs patterns. As a matter of fact, the entire social program delivery field has very little knowledge of how specific services affect specific needs patterns. In the absence of empirical data, the case management team must make its best clinical judgment, a judgment that is often made in something of a vacuum.

An Alternative Approach

In earlier work, Skinner (1981) identified and tested a conceptual systems model for targeting resources for the elderly. This model proposes a causal scheme that describes the role of functional disability, income, social support, and the physical environment in influencing the delivery of services to the community based elderly:

> It must be determined as precisely as possible, who among the elderly require assistance in order to maintain independent functioning in their homes and their communities. The information available is sufficient to permit the designation of need indicators, which provide clear policy options in defining a target population. The definition of the target population also helps clarify the scope and scale of the problem and permits the improved design of a comprehensive service system and provides a rational continuum of care with a realistic projection of its cost. (p. 98)

The same article also describes a prioritization process that could be helpful in targeting resources. This system is based on determining three levels of priority for each of three primary indicators of need: disability, the availability of significant others, and income. By combining priorities, four levels of combined priority needs may be identified. Resources can then be targeted using these levels of need, thus producing a need-driven service delivery system.

An expansion on this earlier work introduces the concept of end-product-oriented targeting (Skinner, 1985). This new approach is based on the assumption that targeting of services at the point of delivery would be more effective if services that were known to have an impact on need status were matched with persons possessing specific needs patterns. The study consisted of a secondary analysis of the U.S. General Accounting Office *Study of the Well Being of Older People in Cleveland, Ohio* (1977). This data set was particularly useful for the study because it contained information on functional status and service utilization collected at two points in time over a one-year interval.

The end-product-oriented targeting approach is based on the idea that six measures of functional status can be combined and patterns of need can be empirically determined. The method used to determine the needs patterns is to convert each need measure into a bivariate measure of need and no need. By combining these bivariate measures into all possible combinations, 25 usable patterns are identified representing 96% of all persons having needs. This project then studied the effects of service delivery on functional need measures, over a one-year interval, while controlling for persons with the same needs patterns. This analysis provides insights into which services appear to make a difference in functioning for each group of persons with a particular pattern of needs.

The aim of this research was to determine the differential effects of services on functional status measures for persons with different needs. This research has policy implications for service agencies looking for ways of targeting resources to assure that funds dedicated to services are best spent. The research resulted in a guide for agencies that could assist them in making the hard resource allocation decisions of which services to give to which persons or groups or people. The study also found that some services are effective for selective need patterns.

The end-product-oriented targeting study provides important insights into a method of targeting based on matching need patterns to services with proven effectiveness. However, this study was limited because it used data that were collected only in Cleveland, Ohio; the services identified were generic and did not fully represent services being offered by the Aging Network; and the data were not collected as part of a controlled comparison design. The next logical step in testing this approach is through a demonstration of its capabilities in a service delivery setting. Such a demonstration would include an evaluation of the effectiveness of the approach through a controlled experimental design.

Conclusion

This chapter has sought to address the issue of resource utilization by examining the strategies of resource allocation and targeting. A review of the experience of the Aging Network with targeting strategies has revealed that there is considerable room for improvement. To a great extent, the failure results as much from the formulation of the methods of distributing funds as from the ways these procedures are implemented. This chapter has also introduced some new approaches in the search for better ways to assure that the old, the frail, and the poor are given attention in the use of any funds. The primary difference in the new approaches discussed in this chapter is that they are based on the matching of assessed need with services that have empirical efficacy. We are going to continue to have few financial resources for the foreseeable future, with a need to target those resources most effectively. It is hoped that this chapter has helped to clarify the subject and that it has provided the seed for the development of new methods for solving these problems in the future.

The OAA is not unlike most publicly funded social programs—it has been sold as a panacea for all and funded as a balm for a few. Attempts have been made to rectify the dilemma of appearing to be the solution to the problems of all older Americans while acknowledging that resources permit it merely to placate the needs of the many while, at the same time, ineffectively meeting the needs of the most needy. The Congress has attempted to assure that attention is given to the needy through the requirement of expending proportions of funded dollars for priority services and the use of formulas to assure the distribution of funds to targeted populations. These have been shown to be inadequate to address the specific aims of targeting and to direct funds in ways that enhance neither the cause of targeting nor the universal eligibility strategy.

The reauthorization of the OAA in 1987 reflects the continuing concern and debate over the targeting and universal eligibility strategy. Donna McDowell (1987), testifying for the National Association of State Units on Aging, asked the House Subcommittee on Human Resources of the Education and Labor Committee to reaffirm that the OAA was intended for all older Americans, regardless of income, ethnic origin, or disability. The National Governors' Association has called for maintenance of the current emphasis on interstate and intrastate formulas (Diprete, 1987). Support for the continuation of targeting was also rendered by the American Association of Retired Persons (Denning, 1987).

The Administration on Aging has indicated its commitment to targeting. It has proposed that the funding formula to states should use the population that is 65 years of age, instead of the present requirement of using the population 60 years old and older. Both houses in Congress have supported and strengthened the targeting provisions of the OAA with specific attention to minorities.

With the increased interest of the Congress in assuring greater attention to minorities and the Black elderly, the 1987 amendments to the OAA are a positive step toward improving the condition and access to services of these vulnerable populations. However, these changes relate mainly to the planning process and the distribution of funds to the states. To the extent that both states and AAAs now have legislative mandates requiring that they pay attention to the economic and social needs of low-income minorities, one would expect more services to be rendered to those groups. Yet, these legislative mandates fall short of helping AAAs and service providers in making the difficult decisions about which services to provide to which individuals. The end-product-oriented targeting approach offers systematic methods that augment funds distribution strategies. These new approaches, when combined with existing distribution strategies, will assure that the limited resources available under the OAA are used most efficaciously.

References

Aldrich, N., ed. 1987. "Florida Lawsuit Challenges Intrastate Funding Formula." *Older Americans Report* 11(35, September 4):1.

Chatters, L. M., R. J. Taylor, and J. S. Jackson. 1985. "Size and Composition of the Informal Helper Networks of Elderly Blacks." *Journal of Gerontology* 40:605-14.

Cuellar, J. B. and J. Weeks. 1980. *Minority Elderly Americans: A Prototype for Area Agencies on Aging: Executive Summary.* San Diego: Allied Home Health Association.

Cutler, N. E. and C. S. Harris. 1983. *Approaches to Best Practices in the Use of Interstate Funding Formulas for Targeting Services to Older Americans.* Final Report. Washington, DC: Bureau of Social Science Research.

Denning, J. T. 1987. Testimony on behalf of the American Association of Retired Persons regarding reauthorization of the Older Americans Act. U.S. House Committee on Education and Labor, Subcommittee on Human Resources.

Diprete, E. D. 1987. Statement of the Honorable Edward D. Diprete, governor of Rhode Island, on behalf of the National Governors' Association. U.S. Senate Committee on Labor and Human Resources, Subcommittee on Aging, March 31.

Estes, C. L. 1980. *The Aging Enterprise.* San Francisco: Jossey-Bass.

Ficke, S. C., ed. 1985a. *An Orientation to the Older Americans Act.* Revised ed. Washington, DC: National Association of State Units on Aging.

———, ed. 1985b. *Allocating Resources for the Aged: Strategies for State Leaders.* Washington, DC: National Association of State Units on Aging.

Fisk, C. F. 1987. Statement by Carol Fraser Fisk, commissioner on aging, Administration on Aging, before the Senate Labor and Human Resources, Subcommittee on Aging.

Gelfand, D. (1984). *The aging network: Programs and services.* New York: Springer.

Gibson, R. C. 1986. *Blacks in an Aging Society.* New York: Carnegie Corporation.

Guttmann, D. 1980. *Perspective on Equitable Share in Public Benefits by Minority Elderly: Executive Summary.* Washington, DC: Catholic University of America.

Holmes D., M. Holmes, L. Steindach, T. Hausner, & B. Rocheleau. (1979). The use of community-based services in long term care by older minority persons. *The Gerontologist, 4,* 389-397.

Krain, M. A. and T. L. Trevino-Richard. 1985. *Differential Participation of Blacks and Whites in Area Agency on Aging Services to the Elderly: Final Report.* Little Rock: University of Arkansas, University Studies Program.

Lawrence Johnson & Associates. 1981. *Location of Nutrition Sites Relative to Concentration of Low Income and Minority Elderly.* Washington, DC: Author.

Mahoney, K. J. 1984. "A Negotiated Approach for Allocating Block." Paper presented at the 36th Annual Meeting of Gerontological Society of America, Washington, DC.

Mayas, J. B., D. E. Goldenberg, and M. A. Collins. 1981. *Location of Nutrition Site Relative to Concentration of Low Income and Minority Elderly: Draft Final Report.* Washington, DC: Lawrence Johnson & Associates.

McDowell, D. 1987. Statement of National Association of State Units on Aging on reauthorization of the Older Americans Act. U.S. House Committee of Education and Labor, Subcommittee on Human Resources.

National Association of Area Agencies on Aging. 1986. *Targeting Resources to the Minority Elderly.* Washington, DC: National Association of Area Agencies on Aging.

Skinner, J. H. 1981. "Targeting Resources for Long-Term Care." In *Allocating Health for the Aged and Disabled,* edited by R. Morris. Lexington, MA: Lexington.

———. 1985. *End Product Oriented Targeting: The Relationship of Needs Patterns and Services to Outcomes.* Dallas: University of Texas, Southwest Long Term Care Gerontology Center: Project Share.

———, ed. 1986. *Mental Health: The Response to Community Needs of Special Populations.* Canton, MA: Prodist.

Taylor, R. J. 1985. "The Extended Family as a Source of Support to Elderly Blacks."
    Gerontologist 25:488-95.

U.S. Commission on Civil Rights. 1982. *Minority Elderly Services: New Programs, Old
    Problems.* Part I. Washington, DC: Author.

U.S. Department of Health, Education and Welfare. 1970. *Older Americans Act of 1965,
    as Amended: Text and History.* Washington, DC: Author.

U.S. General Accounting Office. 1977. *Study of the Well Being of Older People in
    Cleveland, Ohio.* Washington, DC: Government Printing Office.

U.S. House of Representatives, Select Committee on Aging. 1985. *Older Americans Act:
    A Staff Summary.* Washington, DC: Government Printing Office.

U.S. Senate, Special Committee on Aging. 1987. *Older Americans Act Amendments of
    1987: A Summary of Provisions.* Public Law 100-175. Washington, DC: Government
    Printing Office.

Yordi, C. L. and J. Waldman. 1985. "A Consolidated Model of Long-Term Care: Service
    Utilization and Cost Impacts." *The Gerontologist* 25:389-97.

9

Health Care Needs and Services

WORNIE L. REED

Health and medical care are two key concerns of elderly persons in general and the Black elderly in particular. Old age is generally accompanied by deteriorating health and an increasing need for medical care. These attributes of old age are especially problematic for the Black elderly, as they suffer disadvantages in both health status and health care. In this chapter I will examine health status and access to medical care services among the Black elderly. A need-based measure of access to medical care is used to assess whether the Black elderly have equity of access to medical care in comparison to Whites. The access measure is examined across Black subgroups in an effort to determine which subgroups underutilize medical care services and under what conditions. Specifically, the effects of factors enabling access as well as those inhibiting access (barriers) to medical care services are evaluated.

Health Status

The Black elderly are at greater risk than the White elderly for both morbidity and mortality. Blacks are in poorer health than Whites and

AUTHOR'S NOTE: This chapter is a revised version of a paper presented at "Understanding and Serving Black Aged: A Community Conference and Forum," sponsored by Cleveland State University and the Cleveland Clinic Foundation and cofunded by the Cleveland Foundation, Cleveland State University, Cleveland, Ohio, February 26-27, 1987. This research was partially supported by the National Center for Health Services Research, U.S. Department of Health and Human Services, Grant No. HS03125.

they also die more readily. For the 15 leading causes of death, 50% more Blacks of all ages die more readily than Whites (U.S. Department of Health and Human Services, 1985a). Although the death rate alone is not a comprehensive measure of health status, it is a reliable single indicator of health conditions in a population.

Table 9.1 shows that in the period 1979-1981, Blacks between the ages of 65 and 84 died more readily than Whites of the same ages. (By the age of 85, the Black-White mortality crossover rate has taken effect; Manton, 1982.) For several of the leading causes of death—including cardiovascular disease, accidents, diabetes, and homicide—the Black elderly are at greater risk than the White elderly (see Table 9.2).

Mortality statistics, however, while useful, are indicative of only a fraction of the morbidity in a population. Consequently, morbidity and disability measures are used in addition to mortality measures to describe the health status of a population. Among the major chronic diseases, the Black elderly are more at risk than the White elderly for hypertension, diseases of the circulatory system, diabetes, and arthritis. As shown in Table 9.3, this is true for both males and females.

To complete this brief comparison of the health status of the Black elderly to the White elderly, we will use the health status measure of days of disability. *Days of disability* refers to both temporary and long-term reduction of a person's activity due to acute or chronic conditions (restricted-activity days, bed-disability days, work-loss days, and school-loss days). Since the first two types—restricted activity and bed disability—are more applicable to elderly populations, they are used for this comparison. A day of restricted activity is one during which a person reduces his or her normal activity for all or most of the day because of an illness or injury. A restricted-activity day may also be a day of bed disability if the person stays in bed for more than half of the daylight hours.

Among persons 65 years of age and older, Black males have 60% more restricted-activity days than White males, and Black females have one-third more restricted-activity days than White females (see Table 9.4). The racial gaps are even wider for bed-disability days, as older Black males have 1.5 times as much bed disability and older Black females have 42% more bed disability than their White counterparts. However measured, the Black elderly continue to be at greater risk than the White elderly.

Table 9.1 Relative Risk of Mortality for Blacks Compared with Whites, All Causes of Death, 1979-1981

	Blacks	
Age	*Male*	*Female*
65-74	1.27	1.47
75-84	1.04	1.15
85+	0.84	0.82

SOURCE: U.S. Department of Health and Human Services (1985a, Table 4).

Table 9.2 Relative Risk of Mortality for Blacks Compared with Whites, Selected Causes of Death by Age and Gender, 1979-1981

	Blacks		
	65-74	*75-84*	*85+*
Cardiovascular disease			
male	1.06	0.92	0.76
female	1.51	1.08	0.77
Malignant neoplasms			
male	1.32	1.14	1.00
female	1.09	1.02	0.91
Cerebrovascular disease			
male	1.96	1.24	0.83
female	2.09	1.25	0.80
Accidents			
male	1.77	1.41	0.90
female	1.58	1.39	0.97
Diabetes mellitus			
male	1.68	1.42	0.95
female	2.55	1.81	1.42
Chronic liver disease			
male	0.91	0.61	0.68
female	0.96	0.66	0.43
Homicide			
male	4.91	4.38	2.68
female	3.44	2.03	2.12
Suicide			
male	0.34	0.23	0.35
female	0.24	0.24	—

SOURCE: U.S. Department of Health and Human Services (1985a, Table 5).
NOTE: "Relative risk of mortality" is the ratio of the Black death rate to the White rate; it indicates the proportional risk to Blacks relative to Whites.

Table 9.3 Relative Risk of Morbidity for Blacks Compared with Whites, Selected Conditions by Age and Gender, 1978-1980

	Ages	Males	Females
Hypertension			
	65-69	2.53	2.31
	70+	2.39	2.22
Diseases of circulatory system			
	65-69	1.40	1.68
	70+	1.33	1.62
Diabetes			
	65-69	2.30	2.87
	70+	1.85	2.22
Arthritis			
	65-69	1.57	1.40
	70+	1.71	1.54
Nervous and mental disorders			
	65-69	1.19	0.91
	70+	1.19	1.10

SOURCE: U.S. Department of Health and Human Services (1985a, Table 6).

Table 9.4 Days of Restricted Activity and Bed Disability per Person per Year, by Race and Sex for Persons 65 Years and Over: United States, 1980

Types of Disability Day by Sex	White	Black
Restricted ativity		
male	33.1	52.8
female	41.2	54.7
Bed disability		
male	10.3	25.3
female	14.8	21.1

SOURCE: Wilder (1983, Table 5, p. 24).

Variations in Health Status
Among the Black Elderly

We compare the health status of older Blacks to older Whites to indicate the racial distribution of health conditions; however, Blacks are not monolithic in terms of health. In Tables 9.1, 9.2, and 9.3, there are indications of age differentials among Blacks for risk of mortality and morbidity. In general, the risks for Blacks in comparison to Whites decrease with age. Table 9.4 shows some small sex differen-

Table 9.5 Functional Health Status by Sex and Income Among Blacks over 65 Years of Age

| Characteristic | N | Health Scale Score | |
		Worst (%)	Best (%)
Sex*			
male	183	33.3	66.7
female	262	46.6	53.4
Family income*			
low	296	45.9	54.1
high	131	28.2	71.8

SOURCE: Reed (1984).
*Significant at $p < .05$.

tials among Blacks for disability days: Females have slightly more restricted-activity days but fewer days spent in bed.

Table 9.5 shows another functional measure of health by sex and income. The measure used in this table is a dichotomized Guttman Health Scale for the Aged. The scale was constructed from six questions concerning respondents' abilities to perform activities. The undichotomized health scale score, which ranged from 0 to 6, describes where an individual is located on the continuum of functional health. For this table, the responses were divided in half—0 to 3 is "worst" and 4 or more is "best." Older Black females have poorer scores on this health measure and, as would be expected, those with low income have poorer health.

Access to Medical Care

Utilization of Medical Services

Since the Black elderly are in poorer health than the White elderly, they should require more medical services. One of the more frequently used measures of the use of medical services is the number of visits made to a physician during the period of one year. Table 9.6 shows that the Black elderly do not have significantly more physician visits than the White elderly, as may be warranted by their greater proportion of health problems.

Table 9.6 Number of Physician Visits per Person per Year by Race, Sex, and Age for Persons 65 Years and Over: United States, 1980

Sex and Age	Total	Race Black	White
Both sexes			
65-74	6.4	6.3	6.9
75 years and over	6.5	6.5	6.1
Male			
65-74	5.5	5.5	5.1
75 years and over	6.7	5.6	8.0
Female			
65-74	7.0	6.9	8.2
75 years and over	6.4	6.4	5.0

SOURCE: Collins (1983, Table 6, p. 34)

A problem of access to medical care is suggested by the data in Table 9.7. While income is not a factor in affecting physician visits of the White elderly, it is a factor for the Black elderly: The higher the income, the lower the physician visits. While the White elderly tend to have slight increases in the number of physician visits as income increases, the Black elderly have the opposite effect. Perhaps the eligibility for Medicaid at the lower income level results in more visits by the Black elderly at that income level, and the noneligibility for Medicaid at the somewhat higher income levels mitigates against what might be a greater—and more appropriate—number of physician visits at those income levels.

Use of Services Relative to Need

Although, as shown above, gross utilization of medical services by Blacks sometimes exceeds that of Whites, Blacks still do not have equity of access. "Equity of access is best considered in the context of whether people actually *in need* of medical care receive it or not" (Andersen, 1978, p. 458). Non-Whites are in poorer health than Whites, and consequently would be *expected* to have more physician visits. However, when utilization is compared to need, non-Whites obtain needed care less readily than do Whites (Aday and Andersen, 1975; Health Resources Administration, 1977). This fact, coupled with data presented by Taylor et al. (1975) showing that persons 55 years of age and over obtain care less often than necessary, strongly suggests that

Table 9.7 Number of Physician Visits per Year, by Race and Family Income for Persons 65 years and Over: United States, 1980

		Race	
Family Income and Age	Total	White	Black
All incomes	6.4	6.4	6.6
Less than $5,000	6.7	6.4	8.2
$5,000-$9,999	6.1	6.1	6.0
$10,000-$9,999	6.7	6.7	5.3
$15,000-$24,999	6.6	6.8	5.1*
$25,000 or more	6.9	6.9	4.0*

SOURCE: Collins (1983, Table 7, p. 40).
*Figure does not meet standards of reliablity or precision (more than 30% relative standard error).

older Black persons obtain medical care less readily than required. In fact, Aday and Andersen (1975), in an analysis of equity of access for residence-race-age groups, found that poor, urban, non-White persons 75 years of age and over have less utilization of services by need than any other residence-race-age group in the United States.

Other studies related specifically to the Black elderly have found that they consistently underutilize community resources (see Bell et al., 1976). This is not surprising, since racial and ethnic differences in help-seeking behavior have been shown in numerous studies (McKinlay, 1972, 1973). Thus we have the question of whether the Black elderly have equity of access to medical services.

A recent study of the Black urban elderly sought to answer this question (Reed, 1984). The normed measure of access to medical care used in this study is based on a list of general symptoms of illness. Included in this list are coughs, weakness, excessive fatigue, headaches, rashes, diarrhea, shortness of breath, aching joints, backaches, weight loss, heart pains, and infected eyes or ears. This checklist of symptoms is used to develop a Symptoms-Response Ratio. For each reported symptom, the respondent was asked whether a physician was seen in response to the symptom. The severity of each symptom was determined for each of five different age groups (1-5, 6-15, 16-44, 45-64, 65 and over) by a panel of 40 physicians (Taylor et al., 1975). The physicians estimated what proportion of individuals in each age group would need to see a physician for the symptom. Thus these estimates suggest how often care *should* be sought, and this can be compared to how often care *was* sought.

A summary measure of access combines the physicians' judgments and the actual population response. The computational formula is $(A - E)/E$, where A equals the actual number of visits in response to symptoms for a population segment and E represents the physicians' estimates of the number of visits that should have occurred. A minus score means fewer persons sought care than the physicians judged necessary. A plus score indicates that a greater proportion sought care than the physicians thought necessary.

The Symptoms-Response Ratio, as described above, was used as a measure of the utilization of services relative to need. The ratio for the entire sample is -13, which indicates that the total sample saw a physician less often than medically determined norms suggest they should. Table 9.8 shows the Symptoms-Response Ratio by race, age, and sex. Elderly Whites and the young-old sought care at medically appropriate rates; however, elderly Blacks, the old-old, and males sought care significantly less often than medical norms suggest. Note that the race effect still obtains with age and sex controlled. And although females sought care in response to symptoms much more readily than did males, their responses were also inadequate.

Symptoms Response by Factors by Race

Health. The effect of health status on symptoms response differed by race (see Table 9.9). Among individuals who judged themselves to be in poor health, Blacks used services appropriately and Whites over-utilized services relative to appropriateness. Blacks with no disabling condition underutilized services, while Whites with bed-disability days overutilized; and as measured by the Health Scale, Whites in the worst condition underutilized and Blacks in better condition underutilized. In general, Blacks in the better health categories tended to underutilize services, and no Black health status group overutilized services.

Social structure. In terms of marital status and living arrangement, no White subgroup underutilized services. Among Blacks, only those divorced or separated or living alone did *not* underutilize. There were also significant differences between Blacks and Whites on the effects of socioeconomic status. Only the Black elderly with post-high school education used services approaching suggested rates, while the distribution of White responses by education resembled that of the total population. Income did not have an effect on Blacks or Whites; however, the meaning of the income level did have some effect: When

(text continues on page 196)

Table 9.8 Adjusted Symptoms-Response Ratio by Race, Age, and Sex

Characteristics	N	Actual Number of Visits for Symptoms (A)	Estimated Number of Visits for Symptoms (E)	Discrepancy Between Estimated and Actual Number Visits (A − E)	Symptoms-Response Ratio $\frac{(A-E)}{E} \times (100)$
Race					
White	839	1,278	1,309	−31	−2
Black	502	574	787	−213	−26*
Age					
65-75	879	1,267	1,289	−22	−1
over 75	462	586	807	−221	−27*
Sex					
male	455	433	575	−142	−25*
female	886	1,419	1,521	−102	−7*
Total	1,341	1,852	2,096	−275	−13*

SOURCE: Reed (1984).
NOTE: Ratio for age is adjusted for sex, ratio for sex is adjusted for age, and ratio for race is adjusted for age and sex.
*$p \leq .05$.

Table 9.9 Symptoms-Response Ratio by Race by Selected Factors

Characteristics Ratio	Total		White		Black	
	N	Ratio	N	Ratio	N	Ratio
Health, self-evaluation[a]						
good	579	-16*	415	-40*	163	-42*
fair	467	4	270	0	198	-49*
poor	293	10*	154	15*	141	1
Disability level[a]						
none	1,004	-21*	607	-4	396	-44*
limited activity	115	-17*	80	-29*	35	6
some bed days	639	11*	152	12*	70	7
Health scale[a]						
0-2 (worst)	152	-17*	91	-31*	61	4
3	307	-13*	172	-4*	135	-25*
4	664	-10*	428	7	236	-40*
5-6 (best)	218	-10	149	-1	69	-27*
Marital status[a]						
married	400	-14*	241	-5	158	-29*
divorced/separated	105	22*	47	39*	58	6
widowed	773	-11*	501	1	272	-32*
never married	63	-45*	49	47*	14	-32
Live alone[a]						
no	704	-22*	379	-6	325	-39*
yes	636	-1	460	0	176	-2
Education						
less than high school	804	-17*	474	-8*	330	-29*
some high school	251	0	168	9	83	-15
high school graduate	161	-20*	105	-13*	56	-31*
post-high school study	123	15*	92	19*	31	-7

Self-care belief						
high	374	-18*	251	-6	123	-36*
medium	520	-14*	319	-10*	201	-20*
low	447	-3	269	10*	178	-33*
Medical efficacy belief						
high	525	-11*	392	-13*	133	-5
medium	459	-5	267	16*	192	-42*
low	357	-22*	180	-15*	177	-28*
Professional trust						
high	451	-3	257	6	194	-16*
medium	501	-7*	312	16*	119	-43*
low	388	-25*	270	-29*	119	-17*
Medical distrust						
high	418	-10*	239	5	179	-26*
medium	492	-8*	321	0	170	-26*
low	431	-18*	279	-13*	152	-30*
Attitude: own aging						
high	312	2	198	14*	114	-19*
medium	530	-18*	346	10*	184	-31*
low	499	-28*	295	-23*	204	-34*
Lonely dissatisfaction						
high	241	-11*	241	-6	91	-23*
medium	308	5	308	-18*	127	-15*
low	792	-22*	792	-11*	284	-41*
Agency personnel unresponsive						
yes	209	-14*	111	-16*	98	-11
don't know	468	-37*	385	-15*	83	-18*
no	820	-27*	333	-18*	286	-34*

(continued)

Table 9.9 Continued

Characteristics Ratio	Total		White		Black	
	N	Ratio	N	Ratio	N	Ratio
Agency personnel know needs[a]						
yes	727	−6*	390	4	336	−22*
don't know	420	−17*	358	−14*	62	−39*
no	149	−17*	82	10	68	−32*
Family income[a]						
low	492	−14*	243	−5	249	−24*
medium	495	−6	320	5	174	−26*
high	273	−12*	216	7	57	−55*
Income problem[a]						
none	833	−21*	602	−16*	232	−34*
somewhat	322	9*	163	1	159	−24*
very important	179	10*	68	60*	111	−22*
Transportation						
none	1,058	−10*	884	0	378	−28*
somewhat	204	−23*	309	−20	89	−27*
very important	79	7	116	30*	34	−21*
Relative network size						
none	280	−2	135	21*	145	−26*
one	582	−15*	346	−8	236	−26*
two or more	479	−14*	358	−9*	121	−31*
Amount of relative consulting/support[a]						
low	440	−14*	253	−1	187	−31*
medium	381	−37*	244	−30*	137	−49*
high	520	−9*	342	15*	178	−3

Amount of relative visits[a]						
low	282	-2	135	-21*	147	-24*
medium	622	-18*	391	-9*	230	-33*
high	437	-11*	313	-7	124	-19*
Amount of relative contact[a]						
low	449	-21*	311	-14*	138	-38*
medium	420	-38*	282	-14*	138	-16*
high	472	-40*	246	-27*	226	-28*
Social group member[a]						
yes	288	-17*	223	-13*	65	-41*
no	1,037	-10*	609	1	428	-26*
Heard of local citizen center						
yes	1,205	-19*	759	-9*	446	-36*
no	132	41*	79	-38*	53	47*
Friends of network size[a]						
none	921	-12*	602	-4*	319	29*
one	263	8	156	20*	107	-8*
two or more	157	-37*	81	-28*	76	-45*
Amount of friends consulting/support[a]						
low	935	-12*	609	-5	327	-29*
high	405	-12*	230	3	175	-25*
Amount of friends visits[a]						
high	921	-12*	602	-4	319	-29*
low	420	-11*	237	1	183	-25*

SOURCE: Reed (1984)

a. Black-White frequency differences significant at $p < .05$.

*Ratios significant at $p < .05$.

income is *not* a problem, Whites underutilized; when income *is* a problem, Whites overutilized.

Attitudes/beliefs. Negative medical care orientations are associated with more inappropriate responses to symptoms of illness among the White elderly: Those with medium or high self-care orientations, low belief in medical efficacy, high medical distrust, and low trust in professionals seek care less often than they should. These tendencies are not quite as evident among the Black elderly.

Transportation. Transportation is not a factor for Blacks or Whites. The response ratio of neither group is affected significantly by whether transportation is a problem.

Informal support system. Blacks are affected significantly only by the amount of consulting/support received from relatives. The White elderly overutilize when there are no relatives in their social network, when they have a high amount of consulting/support from relatives, and when the amount of relative visiting is low. Whites and Blacks tend to underutilize to a greater-than-average degree when their friends network size is two or more. The other friends network factors have no significant effects on utilization of either Whites or Blacks.

Summary. Access was examined against a set of factors representing potential barriers and facilitators to medical care services. In addition to such factors as age, sex, race, and transportation situation, four sets of factors were examined for their influence on access: (1) health, (2) social structure, (3) attitudes/beliefs, and (4) social network.

The sample as a whole has less-than-adequate use of medical services relative to need. And significantly, some of those who have poorer health—Blacks and the old-old—also have more inappropriate access to care. *Appropriateness*, of course, refers to the use of services relative to need. The importance of taking the approach used here is illustrated by the situation of the Black elderly. Blacks have more physician visits than Whites, but they have fewer visits than Whites in comparison to need.

Health status is related to access to medical care in that persons in the worst health status underutilize services and those in the best health status overutilize. Social structure is related to access as follows. Those who live alone or have high levels of education utilize medical services appropriately, but income has no effect. Several measures of attitudes and health care beliefs were examined, and some are correlated with the level of access. Specifically, negative health orientations act as inhibitors to utilization. Individuals with high self-care orientations, low belief in medical efficacy, high medical distrust, and low trust in professionals have more inappropriate rates of use.

The nature of an individual's social network is a factor in his or her use of medical services. The stronger the social network, the less readily the individual will seek physician services for illness. This finding supports the "strong tie" network hypothesis, which holds that great social cohesion impedes the process of formal care-seeking behavior.

Variations in Access Among the Black Elderly

When compared with medical norms, the level of use of medical care services by the Black elderly is lower than it should be. However, there are variations in patterns of access among the Black elderly. Some factors are associated with appropriate use of medical services (see Table 9.9). For example, health status is a significant factor. Older Blacks who judge themselves to be in poor health, those who have restricted activity, and those who exemplify the worst health status on the functional Health Scale Score utilize medical care services appropriately.

It appears that the Black elderly are reluctant or hesitant users of medical care. As shown above, Blacks in this sample tend to use medical care services less often than deemed appropriate. Bell et al. (1976) have proposed that Blacks have fewer felt needs. Since Blacks are more dissatisfied with their places of medical care and with the care they receive (Aday and Andersen, 1975), use of such services apparently does not readily occur unless there is a serious, high level of need.

Blacks vary by social structure, medical care orientations, and social support structures, each of which is a factor in access to medical services. Persons who live alone or who have high levels of education (social structure) seek care appropriately, as do those with high attitudes on medical efficacy (attitudes/belief) or high relative consulting (informal support system). On the other hand, in contrast to the White elderly, no factor causes the Black elderly to overutilize.

Obviously, positive medical orientations are associated with greater tendencies to use medical care services, and if an elderly Black person's social support network is one that provides consultations on matters of health, it may encourage the appropriate seeking of medical care.

Other Problems of Access

Although in 1981 the median income of elderly persons was high enough to keep most of that group's members above the poverty level, many lived below the poverty level. And when those at the "near-poor" level are considered, some 30% live in poverty or near poverty (Huttman, 1985). Among the Black elderly, over one-third live *below* the poverty level.

What this means is that, despite Medicare, a large segment of the elderly do not have access to medical care or have no means to pay for it. Furthermore, it cannot be assumed that Medicaid finances health care services for all the poor. Many elderly persons do not qualify for Medicaid because of various state eligibility policies. For example, owning a home makes one ineligible for Medicaid. As a result of the restrictions on Medicaid coverage, about 60% of the poor (of all ages) are not covered by Medicaid (Davis and Rowland, 1983).

During recent years, Medicare premiums, deductibles, copayments, and other fees to be paid by patients have increased. Ceilings have been imposed on what doctors and hospitals can charge the government under Medicare, but in many cases excess charges have been passed on to the patient, or services have been reduced. Today, nationwide, Medicare pays for about 45% of the total health care costs of older citizens, and Medicaid pays about 12%. The rest is paid out of pocket, either directly or through private insurance plans; those who cannot afford care may not go to the doctor or purchase prescribed medicines.

It is the near-poor elderly who bear the brunt of out-of-pocket costs, as the elderly who were between 151% and 200% of the poverty level in 1980 paid more out-of-pocket medical expenses ($391.85) than any other poverty-level group.

With the rapid rise in health care costs, Medicare protection is gradually being eroded. In 1980, older Americans (65 and over) paid, on the average, $327 out of their pockets for health care services. This figure, which includes insurance costs, means that the elderly pay 18.5% of their medical care costs.

Medicare neither provides comprehensive coverage for all health care services nor completely pays for those services it does cover. Cost-sharing mechanisms, such as coinsurance and deductibles, reduce the benefit levels such that only 74% of the total costs incurred for hospital care and 55% of costs for physician services are paid by Medicare. Supplementary or "gap" insurance provides some financial relief for persons who can afford it; however, only one-third of the Black elderly who do not qualify for Medicaid have such insurance, compared with two-thirds of the White elderly.

When Blacks do utilize available services, their care tends to be episodic and to lack continuity. While crude overall utilization statistics reveal few racial disparities, there are marked differences in the location, source, and quality of care for Black health care seekers (Link et al., 1982). Recent data indicate an average annual rate of office visits to physicians for coronary heart disease in non-Whites that is about half that for Whites (42/1,000 versus 80/1,000) (Aday and Andersen, 1984). Office visits of all kinds by Black patients were most likely to be to general and family practitioners (46.6%); 10.7% of visits were to internists and 0.8% to cardiovascular disease (CVD) specialists. Black patients are much less likely than White patients to see CVD specialists, which "probably has an adverse effect on the exposure of Black patients with CHD to accurate diagnosis and appropriate treatment" (U.S. Department of Health and Human Services, 1985b, p. 50). Visits to physicians in hospital clinics and emergency rooms constitute 11.2% of physician visits by Whites and 25.6% of physician visits by Blacks. In contrast, 69% of all visits by Whites were to physicians' offices, compared with 58% of visits by Blacks (13% versus 5%). Non-Whites (68%) are less likely to have regular family doctors for their health care, compared with Whites (78%).

Blacks and other minorities are overrepresented among families who report a need for medical care but fail to obtain it (Shorr and Nutting, 1977), or are refused for financial reasons. Himmelstein et al. (1984) show that members of minority groups admitted to public hospital emergency rooms for evaluation are sometimes transferred to other facilities, despite the risk of life-threatening arrhythmias, because of their inability to pay for medical care. "Patient dumping" for economic reasons appears widespread and disproportionately affects Blacks (Thurow, 1984; Schieff, 1985). With the increased corporatization of medical care and the emerging dominance of the for-profit motive in health care, these trends, already disproportionately affecting Blacks, are likely to worsen.

Not only does race affect *whether, when, how often,* and *where* utilization of medical care occurs, it also profoundly influences *what* services are received, assuming that contact with the system is made. For example, National Center for Health Statistics (NCHS) data indicate that the rate of cardiac catheterization among Blacks (1.15/1,000) was only 60% of that reported for Whites (1.93/1,000 population) (Feller, 1983). Blacks diagnosed with coronary heart disease are less likely to undergo ECG than other races (2.7% versus 3.3%). In 1982, only 4,000 out of 170,000 coronary bypass procedures were performed on Black patients (Feller, 1983). Oberman and Cutter (1984), studying a patient population in Birmingham, Alabama, found that Whites were disproportionately represented among 6,594 patients undergoing coronary arteriography, and White patients were two to three times more likely to undergo coronary artery bypass surgery than Blacks, even when disease severity was similar. This social disparity confirms earlier results from Baltimore (Watkins et al., 1983). Even Blacks admitted to the trial of the effectiveness of coronary artery bypass surgery (which required randomization) were significantly less likely to undergo the procedure, despite similar clinical and angiographic characteristics (Maynard et al., 1986).

Discussion and Conclusion

In this chapter I have examined the health status and access to medical care of the Black elderly. We have seen that the Black elderly are at greater risk than the White elderly for acute as well as chronic diseases, but that is just the beginning of their problems. The Black elderly do not have equity of access to medical care services for their health conditions.

Although the Black elderly have as many or more visits to physicians as the White elderly, it would appear that because they have more health problems they actually require more medical care. When this proposition is examined with a normed measure of the use of services relative to need, the Black elderly are revealed as underutilizers of medical care.

The consequence of underutilization of medical care services is undoubtedly poorer health. Although the poorer health status of Blacks in comparison to Whites is a function of the social differences in their social and physical environments as well as other social structural factors, it is generally assumed that inadequate access to medical care plays some part in the greater severity of morbidity and excess mortality among Blacks, especially in the instances of chronic diseases.

It appears that there are two primary considerations to the underutilization of medical care by the Black elderly. On the one hand, there is a general tendency to underutilize, a tendency that may be a function of the Black elderly's experiences with medical care services. Blacks tend to use public facilities and hospitals more readily than Whites, and the concomitant result is a greater dissatisfaction with the care they receive. In addition, many of the Black elderly do not have supplementary insurance to pay for visits to other places of care.

Individual attitudes and orientations among the Black elderly affect their use of medical care services; however, such behaviors and attitudes occur within the context of the structure of medical care service opportunities and the Black elderly's experiences with these services. In comparison to Whites, the Black elderly tend to be without regular sources of care, and they tend to be less likely to have regular family physicians. Their regular places of care are more often hospital and other clinics. The result of their experiences with such irregular sources of care is that Blacks are less satisfied with their care, which undoubtedly adversely affects utilization.

In addition to influencing the medical care-seeking behavior of Blacks indirectly through the development of negative attitudes toward medical care, social structural factors also have direct effects. Perhaps the most critical of these is the barrier of lack of financial resources. Since Medicare provides for only one-half to three-fourths of the costs of medical care, many elderly must depend upon Medicaid to pay the other costs. Yet, many of the near-poor elderly do not qualify for Medicaid. So nearly 20% of the elderly's medical care costs must be paid out of pocket or by supplementary insurance. However, only one-third of the Black elderly have such insurance, compared to two-thirds of the White elderly. Consequently, many of the Black elderly do not have any insurance in addition to Medicare.

One approach to increasing the appropriate use of medical care services of the Black elderly would be to change the behavior of individuals so they might tend to seek required medical care more readily. However, a structural view of the underutilization of medical services by the Black elderly requires examinations of the structure and process of the provision of medical care (see Reissman, 1986). In this view, even after gaining access to services, the poor—including a significant portion of the Black elderly—have multiple negative experiences with organizational systems such as medical care services. It suggests the need for changes in health professionals and in the organization of care. In addition, it makes the assumption that positive experiences will result in behavior change. Changes in the provision of care may be as minor as setting office hours to be more convenient to patients, or they may be as major as changing the location of medical offices or restructuring the provision of care—home visits instead of office visits.

This structural approach, which addresses the problem of negative individual experiences with medical care, should be gained through an attempt to address the issue of equity of access to care. Many public health analysts have called for well-specified, targeted initiatives to address "pockets of inequity." However, broader-based efforts must also be attempted. For example, there have been calls for increased emphasis on state-level approaches to solving health policy problems, including the establishment of programs to finance health services for near-poor individuals who are unable to qualify for Medicaid. Proposals include providing direct insurance to individuals as well as financial support to local hospitals. One hopes that such strategies as these do not detract from the effort to develop a national health plan that is more comprehensive than the current provisions of Medicare and Medicaid.

References

Aday, L. and R. Andersen. 1975. *Development of Indices of Access to Medical Care.* Ann Arbor, MI: Health Administration Press.

———. 1984. "The National Profile of Access to Medical Care: Where Do We Stand?" *American Journal of Public Health* 74(12):1331-39.

Aday, L., R. Andersen, and G. Fleming. 1976. *Health Care in the U.S.* Beverly Hills, CA: Sage.

Andersen, R. 1978. "Health Status Indices and Access to Medical Care." *American Journal of Public Health* 68(5):458-62.

Bell, D., P. Kassachau, and G. Zellman. 1976. *Delivering Services to Elderly Members of Minority Groups: A Critical Review of the Literature.* Santa Monica, CA: RAND Corporation.

Bott, E. 1967. *Family and Social Network.* London: Tavistock.

Collins, J. G. 1983. *Physician Visits, Volume and Interval Since Last Visit, United States, 1980.* National Center for Health Statistics, Series 10, No. 144. DHHS Publication No. (PHS) 83-1572. Washington, DC: Government Printing Office.

Crandall, R. C. 1980. *Gerontology: A Behavioral Science Approach.* Reading, MA: Addison-Wesley.

Davis, K. and D. Rowland. 1983. "Uninsured and Underserved: Inequities in Health Care in the United States." *Millbank Memorial Fund Quarterly* 53(Fall):449-88.

Feller, B. 1983. "Americans Needing Help to Function at Home." Advance Data from Vital and Health Services, National Center for Health Statistics. Washington, DC: Government Printing Office.

Health Resources Administration. 1977. *Health of the Disadvantaged.* Chartbook. DHEW Publication No. (HRA) 77-628. Washington, DC: U.S. Department of Health, Education and Welfare, Public Health Service, Office of Health Resources Opportunity.

Himmelstein, D. U., S. Woolhandler, M. Harnly, M. Bader, R. Silber, H. D. Backer, and A. A. Jones. 1984. "Patient Transfers: Medical Practice as Social Triage." *American Journal of Public Health* 74(5):494-97.

Huttman, E. D. 1985. *Social Service for the Elderly.* New York: Free Press.

Jackson, J. S., J. D. Bacon, and J. Peterson. 1977. "Life Satisfaction Among Black Urban Elderly." *Journal of Aging and Human Development* 8(2):169-79.

Link, C. R., S. H. Long, and R. F. Settle. 1982. "Access to Medical Care Under Medicaid: Differentials by Race." *Journal of Health Politics and Law* 7(2):345-65.

Lopata, H. 1975. "Support Systems of Elderly Urbanites: Chicago of the 1970's." *Gerontologist* 15:35-41.

Manton, K. G. 1982. "Differential Life Expectancy: Possible Explorations During the Later Ages." Pp. 63-68 in *Minority Aging: Sociological and Social Psychological Issues,* edited by R. C. Manuel. Westport, CT: Greenwood.

Maynard, C., L. D. Fisher, E. L. Alderman, I. Ringqvist, M. G. Bourassa, G. C. Kaiser, and M. J. Gillespie. 1986. "Institutional Differences in Therapeutic Decision Making in the Coronary Artery Surgery Study (CASS): The Role of Organizational Factors." *Medical Decision Making* 6:127-35.

McKinlay, J. B. 1972. "Some Approaches and Problems in the Study of the Use Services: An Overview." *Journal of Health and Social Behavior* 13(2, June):115-52.

———. 1973. "Social Networks, Lay Consultation and Help-Seeking Behavior." *Social Forces* 51(3, March):275-91.

McKinlay, J. B. and D. B. Dutton. 1974. "Social-Psychological Factors Affecting Health Service Utilization." Pp. 251-303 in *Consumer Incentives for Health Care,* edited by S. J. Mushkin. New York: Prodist.

Oberman, A. and G. Cutter. 1984. "Issues in the Natural History and Treatment of Coronary Heart Disease in Black Populations: Surgical Treatment." *American Heart Journal* 108:688-94.

Reed, W. L. 1984. *Access to Services by the Urban Elderly.* NTIS Publication No. PB84-245364. Baltimore: Institute for Urban Research.

Reeder, S., A. C. Marcus, and T. E. Seeman. 1979. "The Influence of Social Networks on the Use of Health Services." Paper presented at the annual meeting of the American Sociological Association, August 27-31, Boston.

Reissman, C. H. 1986. Improving Health Experiences of Low Income Patients. Pp. 399-412 in *The Sociology of Health and Illness: Critical Perspective,* edited by P. Conrad and R. Hern. New York: St. Martin's.

Schieff, G. 1985. "The 'Dumping' Problem: No Insurance; No Admission." *New England Journal of Medicine* 312(23):1522.

Shorr, G. I. and P. A. Nutting. 1977. "A Population-Based Assessment of the Continuity of Ambulatory Care." *Medical Care* 15(6):455-64.

Stirner, R. W. 1978. "The Transportation Needs of the Elderly in a Large Urban Environment." *Gerontologist* 18(2):207.

Suchman, E. A. 1964. "Socio-Medical Variations Among Ethnic Groups." *American Journal of Sociology* 70(November):319-31.

———. 1965. "Social Patterns of Illness and Medical Care." *Journal of Health and Human Behavior* 6(Spring):2-16.

Taylor, D. G., L. A. Aday, and R. Andersen. 1975. "A Social Indicator of Access to Medical Care." *Journal of Health and Social Behavior* 16:38-49.

Thurow, L. C. 1984. "Learning to Say 'No.'" *New England Journal of Medicine* 311:1569-72.

Watkins, L., Jr., K. Gardner, V. Gott, and T. J. Gardner. 1983. "Coronary Heart Disease and Bypass Surgery in Urban Blacks." *Research on Aging* 75(4):381-83.

U.S. Department of Health and Human Services. 1985a. *Report of the Secretary's Task Force on Black and Minority Health.* Vol. 2, *Crosscutting issues in Minority Health.* Washington, DC: Government Printing Office.

U.S. Department of Health and Human Services. 1985b. *Report of the Secretary's Task Force on Black and Minority Health.* Vol. 4, *Cardiovascular and Cerebrovascular Diseases.* Washington, DC: Government Printing Office.

Wilder, C. S. 1983. *Disability Days: United States, 1980.* National Center for Health Statistics, Vital and Health Statistics Series 10, No. 143, DHHS Publication No. (PHS) 83-1571. Washington, DC: Government Printing Office.

10

The Health of
the Black Aged Female

MARY McKINNEY EDMONDS

This chapter focuses on the conditions of older Black women in the context of their sociohistorical experiences, their present health status, and their coping strategies, in order to ascertain how these influence their health and illness behavior. Much attention has been focused on the health status of the elderly in the United States, for many reasons. Their status has economic, social, health care, and political implications. Assessment of health status gives us one basis for understanding some interactions between health and the aging process. Hickey (1980) indicates that understanding why and how people perform in a certain way in the face of aging and the accompanying chronic conditions is perhaps more important, on societal and epidemiological levels, than knowing other types of more investigated behaviors. For example, it is useful to understand the coping processes that occur as physical functioning declines. We know that there are individuals whose functional behavior exceeds their physical and organic states and vice versa. The question of interest, then, is one posed by Hickey: "Why do some people function successfully in the presence of significant chronic disabilities and limitations while others, in the same condition, give up?" (p. 82). Of interest in this chapter is the health of the aged Black female in the United States.

Why study aged Black females? The problem of myths is nowhere more apparent than on the topic of the aging of minority women. "Not enough is known about the process of Blacks growing old in America as compared to what is known about growing old, in general, in America and in the world" (Beard, 1978, p. 105). There is a paucity of studies comparing Blacks to Blacks on any dimension. This has led to an erroneous assumption of homogeneity in the Black population. Beard (1978), in her study of the health status of economically successful aged Blacks, notes that Blacks are not all alike even in the same social class: "Although there are behavioral similarities between many, there are also variations that appear in association within their environment" (p. 110).

Black women have been subjected to discriminatory practice throughout their lives. They have had to develop coping strategies to maintain equilibrium in social and economic situations. In addition, they have faced the stigma of sexism and now ageism. *Triple jeopardy* is a term attached to the Black aged female, because she finds herself subjected to the negative stereotypes of ageism, sexism, and racism. In studying the constraints these stereotypes impose on older Black women, Gatz et al. (1982) found some positive outcomes. They were looking at the "role of restricted opportunity in shaping competence patterns":

> The older Black women nominated as competent scored highest of all groups on the BAPS [Behavioral Attributes of Psychosocial Competence Scale] suggesting that in this group successful adaptation has required particularly strong active planful coping skill. . . . less concern with social approval seemed adaptive. Indeed it makes sense that a group who is more negatively valued by the social structure might respond by becoming strong believers in self-reliance, be initiating, show persistent effort, and learn from one's successes and failures without blaming oneself or becoming too concerned about others' judgement. (p. 11)

The health care needs of Black aged women can be better understood if more is known about (1) their unique characteristics, (2) their own self-perceptions of their health status, (3) factors that account for their health care utilization patterns, and (4) the consequences of their illness behavior. A better understanding of these factors should provide health care planners and providers with directions for more appropriate strategies to facilitate more effective utilization of health care services by aged Black women. Additionally, such insights could provide directions for policy formulation and decision making to counter and reverse the alarming mortality and morbidity figures for Blacks.

Importance of Studying Aged Black Women

Understanding the aged Black woman is critical in gaining insights into the racial mortality crossover phenomenon, which suggests that, should Black aged females reach age 85, they will most likely outlive their White counterparts. This has been called "racial crossover in life expectancy." Prevailing theories range from "survival of the fittest" to the genetic inheritance theory (Manton, 1982; Manton et al., 1979; Manton and Stallard, 1981; Nam et al., 1982).

> The most appealing hypothesis is that socioeconomic conditions favoring one group result in lower death rates at younger ages which permit many to survive to older ages who are not physically and/or physiologically strong. The less-advantaged group, it can be further supposed, has higher death rates at the younger ages, and those who survive those early years are physically and/or physiologically more fit to continue on to older ages, even to overcome persistent socioeconomic disadvantage. Such an explanatory model, in effect, regards biological and social factors as being in interaction. (Nam et al., 1982, p. 308)

This certainly adequately portrays the aged Black women in the United States today. Continuing research is needed, however, to determine why the aged Black female is the "survivor" of the nation. Studying the survivors among the Black aged is important. In spite of this encouraging trend, the data on the plight of Blacks in the area of health is not encouraging. According to recent reports, there was continuing disparity in the burden of death and illness experienced by Blacks, compared with our nation's population as a whole (U.S. Department of Health and Human Services, 1985).

The U.S. Department of Health and Human Services Task Force on Black and Minority Health (1985) has indicated that heart disease and stroke, homicides and accidents, cancer, infant mortality, cirrhosis, and diabetes are 80% higher among Blacks than among Whites. Another alarming finding in the task force's report is the fact that Blacks tend to give less credence to warning signs, get fewer screening tests, and are diagnosed at later stages of cancer than are their nonminority counterparts:

For a variety of reasons, elderly Blacks more than Whites tend to put off seeking medical care, and are also less likely to have a regular source of medical care. There are proportionately fewer doctors clinics and other health care providers in Black neighborhoods, and many inner-city hospitals are either closing or moving to the suburbs.

The National Center on the Black Aged (1978) provides important data on the availability and quality of health care services in the areas where many older Black women live:

The patient-to-doctor ratio is twice or more as high in poverty neighborhoods (where many Black elderly live) as in nonpoverty areas. Moreover, the doctors that are most readily available to the Black elderly tend to be generalists rather than specialists, much older than average, many from medical schools that no longer exist and lacking in board certification. It is, thus, not surprising that not only do elderly Blacks receive less health care—an estimated 4 percent are said to have unmet health care needs—but indications are that what they do receive is less effective. (p. 3).

Furthermore, there are wide variations in Medicare provisions and use of services based on income, race, and geographic location. Mechanic (1978) indicates that both the amount and quality of medical facilities and resources are distributed in such a way as to favor the more affluent elderly. He also suggests that patterns of health care utilization behaviors that were formed prior to the enactment of Medicare and Medicaid may continue to inhibit some poor persons from obtaining necessary services that are consumed routinely by those more affluent. These concerns are indeed applicable for older Black women, who are disproportionately represented among the nation's poor.

According to the U.S. Department of Health and Human Services Task Force on Black and Minority Health (1985), there are four social characteristics that have significant influence on minority health: demographic profile, nutritional and dietary practices, environmental and occupational exposures, and stress and coping patterns. The task force's report notes that Blacks are more likely to be city dwellers, and thus exposed to greater amounts of pollution, traffic, substandard housing, and crime. In the workplace, they are more likely to be in more hazardous occupations than Whites, with greater exposure to toxic substances and physical damage.

Haynes (1975, p. 12) has documented the fact that Blacks enter the health care delivery system later than their White counterparts, are sicker on entry, and stay longer. Compared with the population as a whole, Blacks consider themselves ill only when their illnesses have progressed to higher levels of severity. Racial prejudice, lack of education, suspicion of and alienation from bureaucratic organizations, lack of access to facilities, and unrealistic perceptions of health status may explain this behavior. Additional reasons for the lateness of help seeking for Blacks are finances, child-care problems, fear of hospitals, possibility of becoming a guinea pig, and fear of death (White, 1979).

By living longer, aged Black women are subjected to more chronic as well as acute conditions, which indicates a greater need for services. Blount (1986) focused on the health status and service needs of aged Black women specifically in his presentation at the Hearing on Health Care Problems of the Black Aged before the Select Committee on Aging of the U.S. House of Representatives (Ninety-ninth Congress). He cited four physical and social factors that could lead to premature dependency and need for services: social isolation, uncorrected sensory impairment, poor nutrition, and overmedication. Blount noted that although aged Black women generally have more social support systems, their poverty denies them needed resources. Describing elderly Black women in Detroit, he stated that they have higher incidence of cancer, hypertension, heart disease, diabetes, and stroke. Obesity and uncorrected sensory impairment reduce their quality of life.

According to the National Center for Health Statistics (1981), the utilization rates for elderly Black women indicate that ambulatory visits to physicians are less frequent than those for White women. Therefore, screening procedures are not as prevalent. The use of hospitals is lower, suggesting that elderly Black women delay seeking health services until later stages of illness. Elderly Black women have higher hospital fatality rates than their White counterparts, which might support the finding that their conditions are more serious and are at later stages when they are admitted. Further, according to the National Center for Health Statistics (1981), fewer reside in nursing homes; they are more likely to be cared for in an extended family situation.

The Sociohistorical Context

In order to understand how older Black women perceive their social world and how they respond when faced with health problems, it is necessary to place them within their sociohistorical context. The characteristics and health behaviors of older Black women have been shaped by racial, cultural, and sociohistorical experiences. From the sociohistorical perspective, the aged Black female's grandparents were slaves.

Women age 65 and older were born prior to 1923. What did their formative years and adult life experiences look like? From the emancipation to World War I, approximately 90% of all Blacks lived in the rural South. Many of those who did not remain in the South have since migrated to three major areas of the country—the urban South and the urban North and West—looking for a better life. They were concentrated in the inner-city ghettos. Very few moved from the South to the rural North. The first out-migration of Blacks from the South began around 1915 as a result of the agricultural depression. They gravitated to the urban North to take menial jobs during World War I. Even in those jobs they were the last hired and the first fired (Billingsley, 1968).

Rodgers-Rose (1980) gives a graphic description of the economic conditions under which the present aged females existed in their earlier years. By 1910, 90% of all Black females who worked were working in agriculture, as servants, or in laundries. There were approximately 2,013,981 Black female workers, of whom 1,828,109, or 91%, were in the above-mentioned fields. On the professional level, there were 22,450 teachers (1% of the working population), 2 Black female lawyers, and 333 Black female physicians. The occupations open to Black women were very restricted. There were many in lower classes, particularly in the South, who did not receive much education because at an early age they were forced to work the land with their sharecropper parents. If schooling did occur, it was under adverse or segregated circumstances. Racial and social class differences determined the age at which an individual assumed the duties and obligations of womanhood (Rodgers-Rose, 1980). Older Black women entered the work world earlier than normally would have been expected.

> Becoming a woman in the low income Black community is somewhat different from the routes followed by the middle class girl. The poor Black girl reaches her status of womanhood at an earlier age because of the different prescriptions and expectations of her culture. (Ladner, 1971, p. 11)

One source of stress for these women was underemployment. Although education was identified as a vehicle for upward mobility among Black women, the rewards were negligible. In fact, education caused frustration and dissatisfaction when college-educated Black women could find work only as domestics and trained nurses were forced to work in someone's home as an aide or companion. This underemployment gave rise to additional stress identified as "status inconsistency" by Lenski (1969):

> A body of theory and research has developed which suggests that pronounced status inconsistencies of certain kinds tend to be a source of stress and give rise to distinctive reactions which are not predictable simply from a knowledge of the rank of the individual in each of the respective status systems. (p. 204)

Kasl and Cobb (1971) term this phenomenon "status incongruence." They report that in their study, individuals whose education was greater than what was needed for their occupations showed poorer mental health than those with other paired combinations. It is evident from the above discussion that there are many antecedents to and influences on the formation of perceptions.

Black women have encountered over their life spans various experiences concerning health knowledge, health delivery, and quality of life. The majority lived in their formative years in the segregated, rural South, which affected their health knowledge, their perceptions of health care, and their assumptions about quality of life.

Elderly Black women have seen tremendous changes in sanitation and nutrition. They lived through the influenza epidemics of 1918-1919. They survived World Wars I and II. They experienced the Depression and the polio epidemics of the 1940s and 1950s. They lived through the Korean War. They observed and were affected by the devastating effects of tuberculosis and its eventual cure; they witnessed malaria, syphilis, diphtheria, and typhoid fever. They rejoiced with the discovery of penicillin for human use in the 1940s and the Salk and Sabin polio vaccines of the early 1960s. They observed the changing medical treatment for the same diseases and experienced exposure to nuclear, industrial, and other environmental hazards. History has taken its toll on them. Poverty has been an unwelcome guest. But they survived. They survived acute infectious diseases, trauma, and inadequate nutrition. Their bodies were left with the same chronic illnesses as those of their White counterparts. But given the scenario of their experience with southern segregated health care systems, they may not have received the same benefits of medical breakthroughs as others (Edmonds, 1982).

Perceptions of Health Status

Perceptions of health status influence health service utilization. To understand the manner in which the Black woman responds to and copes with her living situation, it is necessary to know how she perceives and defines significant events in her life. One major concern to her, as to most people, is her health and especially her ability to maintain herself in activities of daily living. Additionally, folk beliefs about health and illness may have varying effects on how an individual reacts to signs and symptoms of poor health (U.S. Department of Health and Human Services, 1985). The Ohio Governor's Task Force report suggests that fatalism has been an important factor explaining the attitude of the minority community toward health care (State of Ohio, 1987). This fatalism may invade other areas of life. For example, Celie in *The Color Purple* (Walker, 1982) displays such fatalism when, asked why she took the abuse from Mister, she remarks, "This life soon be over I say. Heaven lasts always" (p. 47).

How one perceives a phenomenon will influence how one is likely to react to it. W. I. Thomas's (1928) famous quote "If men define situations as real, they are real in their consequences" (p. 584) has great meaning for a study dealing with how women perceive and define their social world as it relates to health. It is assumed that the social world into which an individual is socialized makes him or her perceive the world and life chances in a particular way. Cantril (1968) points out that "perceptions are purposeful and derived from group loyalties and social norms" (p. 9). What are social perceptions for some are not necessary social perceptions for others. According to Lazarus (1966), the manner in which an event is experienced and the meaning attached to it determine the degree of threat that is perceptually and cognitively appraised. Social psychologists such as Bruner (1958) have examined the effects of perceptual selectivity on social behavior and on the cultural patterning of perception. Knutson (1965) asserts that it does not matter if an event or experience is accurate or how it is defined by others: "Even a person with a chronic pain may not perceive himself as needing treatment if he has learned to accept his condition as 'normal' for himself or if others in his group have a condition similar to his own" (p. 160). Insidious changes may go unnoticed because they are not considered threatening. Zola (1964) underscores the discrepancy between the high prevalence of clinical illness and the low acknowledgment rate. He suggests that a selective process is operating that determines what gets counted and what is not tabulated as illness. He suggests the importance of value orientation, which determines when an individual's "limits of tolerance of his symptoms" are reached.

There is a great deal of evidence for sociocultural and socioeconomic influences on health and illness behavior (Becker et al., 1974; Bullough, 1972; Coburn and Pope, 1974; Langlie, 1977; Rosengren, 1964; Zola, 1964). Zborowski (1958), in a study of the effect of instantaneous pain on four ethnocultural groups, found that differences in pain response were influenced by socioeconomic background, education, and degree of religiosity. Berkanovic and Reeder (1973) note that people from different cultures order their priorities differently. They further show that willingness to gamble with one's health may be culturally determined.

Based on the reviewed evidence, it is apparent that perceptions play a significant role in how individuals rate their health status. Self-rated health status may influence whether access to health care is deemed necessary. Maddox and Douglas (1973) note that (1) there is a persistent, positive congruence of self- and physician's ratings of health, and (2) whenever there is an incongruity between the two types of ratings, the tendency is for individuals to overestimate rather than underestimate their health.

The overestimation of health status may account for late entry into the health care system (Edmonds, 1982; Jackson and Gurin, 1987). In a study of a population with high incidence of arthritis, cancer, hypertension, diabetes, liver and kidney problems, strokes, and cardiovascular conditions, Jackson and Gurin (1987) found a high rate of satisfaction with one's health and an indication that health services were easy to obtain. Overestimation of one's health status and satisfaction with the health care delivery system could have several explanations in a population where mortality and morbidity are so high.

One plausible explanation may be a limited awareness of signs and symptoms of disease. However, in earlier work it was found that although the Black women studied had little basic medical knowledge, they had a great deal of experiential health information (Edmonds, 1982). These women had lived through influenza epidemics, observed "sugar" diabetes, and were susceptible to tuberculosis and sickle cell anemia. However, they also lived in a culture that considered some vicissitudes as "the cross one must bear" or where medical attention, while possibly accessible, was not always adequate. Also, many were reared in a health care system that was segregated and highly inadequate.

Another explanation could be that overestimation of health status, with its negative consequences, may serve as a coping mechanism. Pearlin and Schooler (1978) note that people are actively responsive to threats. They delineate three protective behaviors or coping responses that can mediate such stressors: (1) elimination or modification of the conditions causing the problems, (2) development of perceptual control of problematic meanings so as to neutralize them, and (3) containment of the emotional consequences or problems within manageable limits.

Although the elimination or modification of problematic conditions would appear to be the most appropriate and realistic approach, the individual often lacks the power to do this. Historically, the Black aged female has been in a power-dependent position and, therefore, has not been able to accrue the resources needed to modify or eliminate the racist, sexist, and, more recently, ageist conditions imposed upon her.

The second and third coping responses identified by Pearlin and Schooler are of interest in explaining why people may differentially perceive their health status. One way to control the meaning of stress is to ignore noxious stimuli selectively by turning attention to more gratifying endeavors. The third is a coping management strategy to assist people in accommodating existing stress without being over-whelmed by it. Some of the coping mechanisms mentioned by Pearlin and Schooler (1978) include "denial, passive acceptance, withdrawal, [which] are elements of magical thinking, a helpfulness bordering on blind faith, and belief that the avoidance of worry and tension is the same as problem solving" (p. 8).

Sick Role and Health Beliefs

A third explanation for the overestimation of health status may be found in the literature on sick role theory and health belief models. According to Parsons (1958), the following elements characterize sick role behavior: (1) The individual is not responsible for the condition; (2) the individual is exempt from normal tasks and social roles; (3) there is a recognition that sickness is undesirable and there is a responsibility to get well; and (4) there is a duty to seek help and comply with remedies to get well.

Mechanic (1978) identifies determinants of an individual's willingness or lack of willingness to seek medical help. Three of them are (1) the extent to which symptoms disrupt family, work, and other social activities; (2) available information, knowledge, and cultural assumptions; and (3) other needs competing with the illness response, which play roles in determining illness behaviors of aging Black women. People tend to take the sick role under at least three different circumstances:

> First one may enact the role of the sick because of being physically incapable of doing anything else. . . . Second, one may play the sick role because it is perceived as personally obligatory as a consequence of interaction with significant other persons whose demeanor suggests that one "ought to" act sick. . . . Third, one may behave as if one were ill because the round of life in which one engages defines "illness" as being more reasonable and satisfying than some other form of conduct. (Rosengren, 1964, p. 339)

Siegler and Osmond (1979) note that there are some consequences resulting from denial of or failure to occupy the sick role:

> One, it may result in a prolongation of the illness or even death. Two, it may result in the deterioration of some vital social relationships. Three, the person who fails to occupy or appropriately maintain the sick role may become impaired or disabled. (p. 163)

Older Black women, most of whom are in the lower class, have not been able to afford to take the sick role. In the world of work, structures are in place to legitimate the sick role, such as sick pay for documented illness and prepaid health insurance plans. Because of discriminatory practices resulting in economic inequities, older Black workers have usually not been employed in occupations that enjoyed fringe benefits. When they did not work, they did not get paid. Being the main support of themselves and their families forced many Black women to work regardless of their health status. Black women needed to perceive themselves as healthy as long as they could possibly do so. Such behavior is not without ramifications, and may explain some of the dismal mortality and morbidity data for Blacks.

It is plausible to accept the health belief paradigm (Becker et al., 1974), which stipulates that the perceived susceptibility and seriousness of the disease are determined by many factors. Some of the personal factors include age, sex, and race. Other factors include peer and reference group influences, perceived benefits, and perceived barriers.

Some aged Black women may be suspicious of the health care system and, therefore, may be reluctant to become involved and use health services.

Conclusions

There is evidence to indicate that there is considerable variation in the use of health services by aged Black women. Evidence also indicates that there is a great deal of variation in the quality of health services utilized by Black aged. A number of significant factors have been identified as determinants of the health status and health care utilization of Black aged females. Some of these are as follows:

(1) segregation experiences in the formative years, especially in the rural South, where many Blacks were reared, that led to minimal or less-than-adequate health care use and where there was an absence of preventive measures

(2) suspicion of the dominant culture and its institutions

(3) reliance on kinship and friendship networks in order to cope with health concerns

(4) preference, in some areas, for traditional medicines and for faith healing

(5) religious beliefs, some of which direct an individual to look to heaven for relief from all pain and anguish rather than to the health care system

(6) lack of understanding about the consequences of the denial of signs and symptoms of illness

(7) unwillingness to adopt the sick role, whenever possible, because of more pressing obligations

(8) lack of adequate health care information, leading to inappropriate health care practices and behaviors

(9) unrealistic perception of good health, indicated by Black women as they get older, a self-appraisal that may give a false sense of wellness, leading to inappropriate utilization of health services

(10) poverty and, therefore, lack of adequate health insurance

(11) lack of an adequate number of Black health care planners who may more adequately plan for the service needs of Black aged

(12) lack of an adequate number of Black health care practitioners whom aged Black females might better accept and trust

Recommendations and Action Plans

Two major task force reports, those of the National Task Force on Black and Minority Health (U.S. Department of Health and Human Services, 1985) and the Ohio Governor's Task Force on Black and Minority Health (State of Ohio, 1987), make similar recommendations in order to address the disproportionately high mortality and morbidity figures of Blacks and to enhance access for Blacks to health care services. The following are some recommendations for improvement based on the two task force reports:

(1) Outreach programs should be launched to disseminate information designed for specific minority groups.

(2) There is a need to increase the number of qualified applicants for medical schools and for allied health professional programs. Black physicians see the majority of Black patients, practice in primary care fields and in underserved areas, and treat a higher percentage of Medicaid patients. Therefore, attention to recruitment, retention, and graduation of minority health care practitioners is important.

(3) The Black aged population, including the Black aged female population, is not homogeneous. Therefore, health care planning should address the diverse health care needs of Black aged females. Additionally, appropriate health care information should include culturally tailored audiovisual and written materials.

(4) Health care providers need to increase their sensitivity to the needs and perceptions of Black aged females. Without appropriate sensitivity and respect, health care services will not be responsive and effective.

(5) There is a need to locate health care facilities and health care professionals in areas in closer proximity to where Black aged females reside.

(6) Financial resources must be made available to supplement what Medicare does not cover for Black aged females, since they are less likely to have additional health insurance policies.

(7) There needs to be a constant concern on the part of elected and appointed public officials to improve health care policies, including long-term care policies.

(8) Health care professional organizations, academic institutions, seniors' organizations, and health service organizations need to enhance access, availability, and quality of health care services.

In summary, the health status of aged Black women has been affected by lifelong experiences of disadvantage and discrimination. Therefore, health care planners and providers need to be more sensitive in order to allay the suspicions of Black women and encourage service use on their part. The consequences of inadequate financial resources, housing, nutrition, education, and life-style have converged to exacerbate the health problems of the aged in general and of Black aged women in particular.

A national agenda to address the health care needs of all Americans, including the specific health concerns of older Black women, is called for. Quality health care services need to be seen as a priority service available to all members of our affluent society.

References

Beard, V. H. 1978. "Health Status of a Successful Black Aged Population Related to Life Satisfaction and Self Concept." In *Health and the Black Aged: A Research Symposium,* edited by W. H. Watson et al. Washington, DC: National Center on Black Aged.

Becker, M., R. Drachman, and J. Kirscht. 1974. "A New Approach to Explaining Sick Role Behavior in Low-Income Populations." *American Journal of Public Health* 64:205-16.

Berkanovic, E. and L. G. Reeder. 1973. "Ethnic, Economic and Social Psychological Factors in the Source of Medical Care." *Social Problems* 21(2):246-59.

Billingsley, A. 1968. *Black Families in White America.* Englewood Cliffs, NJ: Prentice-Hall.

Blount, Stephen B. 1986. *Health Care Problems of the Black Aged.* Select Committee on Aging, House of Representatives 99th Congress Comm. Publication No. 99-592. Washington, DC: Government Printing Office.

Bruner, J. 1958. "Social Psychology and Perception." Pp. 85-94 in *Readings in Social Psychology,* edited by E. Maccoby et al. New York: Holt.

Bullough, B. 1972. "Poverty, Ethnic Identity and Preventive Health Care." *Journal of Health and Social Behavior* 13:347-59.

Cantril, H. 1968. "The Nature of Social Perception." Pp. 3-9 in *Social Perception,* edited by H. Loch and H. C. Smith. Princeton, NJ: Van Nostrand.

Coburn, D. and C. R. Pope. 1974. "Socioeconomic Status and Preventive Health Behavior." *Journal of Health and Social Behavior* 15:67-78.

Edmonds, M. M. 1982. "Social Class and the Functional Health Status of the Aged Black Female." Ph.D. dissertation, Case Western Reserve University, Cleveland, OH.

Gatz, M., E. I. Gease, and J. A. Moran. 1982. "Psychosocial Competence Characteristics of Black and White Women: The Constraining Effects of 'Triple Jeopardy.'" *Black Scholar* 13(1):5-12.

Haynes, A. M. 1975. "The Gap in Health Status Between Black and White Americans." Pp. 2-30 in *Textbook of Black Related Diseases,* edited by R. A. Williams. New York: McGraw-Hill.

Hickey, T. 1980. *Health and Aging.* Monterey, CA: Brooks/Cole.

Jackson, S. and G. Gurin. 1987. *National Survey of Black Americans, 1979-1980*. ICRSR-8512. Ann Arbor: University of Michigan.

Kasl, S. K. and S. Cobb. 1971. "Physical and Mental Correlates of Status Incongruence." *Social Psychiatry* 6:1-10.

Knutson, A. L. 1965. *The Individual, Society and Health Behavior*. New York: Russell Sage.

Ladner, Joyce A. 1971. *Tomorrow's Tomorrow: The Black Woman*. Garden City, NY: Doubleday.

Langlie, J. K. 1977. "Social Networks, Health Beliefs and Preventive Health Behavior." *Journal of Health and Social Behavior* 18:244-60.

Lazarus, R. 1966. *Psychological Stress and Coping Process*. New York: McGraw-Hill.

Lenski, G. E. 1969. "Status Consistency and Inconsistency." Pp. 204-6 in *Structural Social Inequality: A Reader in Comparative Social Stratification*, edited by C. S. Heller. London: Macmillan.

Maddox, G. L. and E. B. Douglas. 1973. "Self-Assessment of Health: A Longitudinal Study of Elderly Subjects." *Journal of Health and Social Behavior* 14:87-93.

Manton, K. G. 1982. "Temporal and Age Variation of United States Black/White Cause Specific Mortality Differentials: A Study of the Recent Changes in the Relative Health Status of the United States Black Population." *Gerontologist* 22:170-79.

Manton, K. G., S. S. Poss, and S. Wing. 1979. "The Black/White Mortality Crossover: Investigation from the Perspective of the Components of Aging." *Gerontologist* 19:291-300.

Manton, K. G. and E. Stallard 1981. "Methods for Evaluating the Heterogeneity of Aging Processes in Human Populations Using Vital Statistics Data: Explaining the Black/White Mortality Crossover by a Model of Mortality Selection." *Human Biology* 53:47-67.

Mechanic, D. 1978. *Medical Sociology*. New York: Free Press.

Nam, C. B., N. L. Weatherby, and K. A. Ockay. 1982. "Causes of Death Which Contribute to the Mortality Crossover Effect." *Social Biology* 25:306-14.

National Center on Black Aged. 1978. "The Plight of the Black Elderly: A Briefing Paper." Washington, DC: Author.

National Center for Health Statistics. 1981. *Use of Services by Women 65 Years of Age and Over*. DHHS Publication No. (PHS) 81-1720. Public Health Service. Washington, DC: Government Printing Office.

Parsons, T. 1958. "Definitions of Health and Illness in the Light of American Values and Social Structure." Pp. 165-87 in *Patients, Physicians and Illness*, edited by E. G. Jaco. New York: Free Press.

Pearlin, L. and C. Schooler. 1978. "The Structure of Aging." *Journal of Health and Social Behavior* 19:2-21.

Rodgers-Rose, L. F. 1980. "The Black Woman: A Historical Overview." In *The Black Woman*, edited by L. F. Rodgers-Rose. Beverly Hills, CA: Sage.

Rosengren, W. R. 1964. "Social Class and Becoming Ill." Pp. 333-40 in *Blue Collar World: Studies of the American Worker*, edited by A. B. Shostak and W. Gomberg. Englewood Cliffs, NJ: Prentice-Hall.

Siegler, M. and H. Osmond. 1979. "The Sick Role Revisited." Pp. 146-66 in *Health, Illness and Medicine: A Reader in Medical Sociology*, edited by G. Albrecht and P. C. Higgins. Chicago: Rand McNally College.

State of Ohio. 1987. *The Ohio Governor's Task Force on Black and Minority Health: Final Report.* Columbus: Author.

Thomas, W. I. 1928. *The Child in America.* New York: Knopf.

U.S. Department of Health and Human Services, Task Force on Black and Minority Health. 1985. *Report of the Secretary's Task Force on Black and Minority Health.* Margaret M. Heckler, Secretary. Washington, DC: Author.

Walker, A. 1982. *The Color Purple.* New York: Washington Square.

White, E. H. 1979. "Giving Health Care to Minority Patients." *Nursing Clinics of North America* 12:27-40.

Zborowski, Mark. 1958. "Cultural Components in Response to Pain." Pp. 256-68 in *Patients, Physicians and Illness,* edited by E. G. Jaco. Glencoe, IL: Free Press.

Zola, I. K. 1964. "Illness Behavior of the Working Class: Implications and Recommendations." Pp. 350-61 in *Blue Collar World: Studies of the American Worker,* edited by A. B. Shostak and W. Gomberg. Englewood Cliffs, NJ: Prentice-Hall.

11

Diversity in
Black Family Caregiving

CHARLES M. BARRESI
GEETA MENON

By the middle 1980s, about 8% of the Black population of the United States was made up of individuals 65 years of age or older. Of that group, approximately 8% were 85 or over. Further, the Black elderly made up 8% of the total elderly population in our society. In 1985, the U.S. Bureau of the Census predicted that by the year 2000, the Black aged population will reach 4 million, a rate of growth that will exceed that of the White aged population by 26% (U.S. Department of Commerce, 1986). These demographic trends have significant implications for social gerontologists and other professionals concerned with the elderly. It is becoming increasingly evident that social services and policies geared toward enhancing the well-being of our aging population will need to consider this growing minority group, their needs and resources, in understanding and coping with the phenomenon of social aging.

An essential source of emotional and general well-being of the elderly can be traced to their informal support networks (relatives, friends, and neighbors). Informal supports are supplemented by the formal support networks provided by the institutional structure of public and private agencies. However, a major source of support for Black elderly is provided by the family.

Much of what has been written about the Black family has assumed that there is only one family form, with little or no variation. This assumption could not be further from the truth. In fact, there is much diversity based on socioeconomic status, region, urban-rural location, family size and type, and other characteristics. This chapter reviews the current literature concerning the diversity of caregiving networks within the Black American family, and examines the patterns and impact this diversity has on the elderly in these families.

A more realistic picture of caregiving behavior among Black Americans will enable social scientists, service professionals, and other interested persons to examine weaknesses and strengths of the Black elderly's informal networks with greater accuracy. Such insights will provide a background for the formulation of more effective research, practice, and policy decisions regarding elderly Blacks.

Theoretical Explanations

Explanations that have been postulated by social scientists to explain caregiving patterns among Black Americans can be grouped into three general categories: family type (extended networks), socioeconomic factors, and cultural factors. Family type explanations state that most caregiving is provided by immediate and nonimmediate family members (Billingsley, 1968; Cantor, 1979; Chatters et al., 1986; Dilworth-Anderson, 1981; Gibson, 1982; Taylor, 1985; Taylor and Chatters, 1986; Jackson, 1971; Mutran, 1985). Closely related to this view is one that identifies major sources of care and support as emanating from nonkin members such as friends, neighbors, and church members (Chatters et al., 1986; Harper, 1982; Tate, 1981; Taylor and Chatters, 1986).

Socioeconomic status explanations suggest that caregiving patterns among Black Americans are predominantly influenced by their socioeconomic conditions (Mitchell and Register, 1984; Mutran, 1985; Sokolovsky, 1985). This perspective also suggests that Black Americans are more inclined to belong to extended family networks because of need and economic necessity.

The cultural explanation suggests that caregiving behaviors among Black Americans are a consequence of socialization (Anderson and Allen, 1984; Chatters et al., 1986; Gibson, 1982; Harper, 1982; Mutran, 1985; Taylor, 1985). This view supports the notion that Black Americans are socialized or inculcated with attitudes that encourage providing respect and assistance to elderly family members. As a consequence of this cultural trait, Black elderly tend to receive care from their family informal networks.

Further insight into the patterns of caregiving behaviors among the Black elderly is provided by the hierarchical-compensatory model of social support (Cantor, 1979; Taylor, 1985; Taylor and Chatters, 1986). Elderly Blacks tend to prefer to receive assistance, care, and support from a daughter, followed by a son, spouse, sister, brother, friend, neighbor, and, finally, parents. Thus caregiving among Black Americans tends to be more acceptable from immediate family members and other relatives. If this source of help is not available, then assistance from nonkin members (neighbors, friends, and church members) is preferred. Given the unavailability of informal supports, formal supports are sought (Chatters et al., 1986; Taylor, 1985; Taylor and Chatters, 1986).

An extension of the hierarchical-compensatory model suggests that among Black Americans kin and nonkin support networks seem more applicable when the elderly are in crisis or emergency situations (Taylor and Chatters, 1986). However, in noncrisis situations sources of support and caregiving tend to overlap. This perspective suggests that kin networks tend to provide long-term, instrumental, and infrequent care based on obligatory relationships. On the other hand, nonkin networks tend to provide socioemotional support and care for short-term needs. This care tends to be based on discretionary friendships and often is ongoing and frequent. It has also been suggested that care provided by discretionary relationships typically enhances the elderly's sense of well-being and emotional satisfaction more than care based on obligatory relationships (Taylor and Chatters, 1986).

Family Types and Support Networks

Billingsley (1968) has proposed that Black American families can be categorized as nuclear, extended, or augmented family types. Nuclear families are described as incipient (husband and wife), simple (husband, wife, and children), and attenuated (single parent with children). The extended family is described as incipient (husband, wife, and relatives) or attenuated (single parent, children, and relatives). Billingsley defines the augmented family as unrelated individuals living together.

This model was later modified to include the following additional or modified family types: single-person households, attenuated nuclear families made up of an elderly parent and grown-up children, nuclear families without children, extended families consisting of a couple-headed household with an elderly parent and grandchildren, and augmented families with an elderly household head and nonrelatives (Billingsley and McCarley, 1986; Cantor, 1979). The inclusion of these latter types seems to represent a more realistic picture of the Black family structure. Another modification of Billingsley's Black family typology characterizes the Black extended family structure as consisting of nuclear core and nonnuclear core components (Dressler et al., 1985).

It has been found that Black elderly living in extended and augmented family types are more likely to engage in caregiving behaviors (receiving and providing) than are those in nuclear family types and living alone (Cantor, 1979). A logical explanation for this phenomenon is the influence of physical proximity of family members. Due to the nature of the extended family structure, the Black elderly are more likely to engage in mutual assistance behaviors with their kin family members.

The tendency for Black Americans to belong to extended family structures is also influenced by other factors, such as low levels of education, income, occupational status, absence of children, couple-headed households, residing in the South, being female and over 45 years old, and the willingness to take care of young children (Anderson and Allen, 1984; Mitchell and Register, 1984). These factors seem to imply that the socioeconomic factor could be a viable reason Black Americans tend to belong to extended family types.

It is evident that the Black elderly tend to receive relatively high levels of care and support through their informal networks. This may be partly explained by the fact that many Black elderly reside either in extended family structures or in close proximity to them, so that care and support are readily available (Taylor, 1985, 1986). Another factor that may influence support levels for Black elderly is the tendency for them to act as surrogate parents, thus increasing the likelihood of having family members present to provide care (Mitchell and Register, 1984).

Such factors have led some researchers to conclude that cultural values that encourage positive attitudes and feelings of filial responsibility toward elderly family members are the main reasons for extensive caregiving sources for the Black elderly. However, this view has undergone some changes. The notion that filial responsibility is a more pervasive value among Black Americans than among other groups has not been supported by research (Hanson et al., 1983; Seelbach, 1980). The explanation that filial responsibility has become increasingly impractical in today's changing societal conditions may be a feasible conclusion. A more popular explanation for the pervasiveness of extended family households among Blacks would be that of economic necessity.

Caregiving Patterns Among Black Americans

Caregiving includes those activities that help to satisfy the instrumental and expressive needs of the care recipient. Instrumental needs of Black elderly are often related to their economic needs and the material aspects of their physical and social lives. Provisions for instrumental needs are often conceptualized and measured by financial assistance, assistance in maintaining the physical environment, and transportation. Expressive needs relate to the elderly's psychic security (sense of belonging, self-worth, self-awareness, and dignity), companionship, and the generation and prolongation of love (Billingsley, 1968). Caregiving patterns among Black Americans tend to be more often characterized as a mutual exchange of instrumental and expressive assistance between adult children and their elderly parents (Cantor, 1979; Jackson, 1971; Taylor and Chatters, 1986).

Instrumental assistance and supports that elderly receive from adult children are gifts (nonmonetary), aid in time of illness, shopping, fixing things around the house, financial aid, keeping house, transportation, meal preparation, taking the elder along on vacation, and assistance with church attendance. Typical instrumental assistance provided by elderly parents to adult children tends to be child care, crisis assistance, financial assistance, transportation, help with household tasks, gifts, aid in time of illness, fixing things around the house, and housekeeping activities (Cantor, 1979; Jackson, 1971; Taylor and Chatters, 1986).

Expressive and affective assistance consists of elements such as advice and encouragement, companionship, prayer, advice on jobs, advice on business and purchases, and moral support (Cantor, 1979; Jackson, 1971; Taylor and Chatters, 1986). Research indicates that expressive/affective assistance is often mutually exchanged between Black adult children and elderly parents. However, expressive caregiving patterns among Black Americans require more in-depth investigation and understanding. Closely related to this is the Black elderly's perceptions about family closeness. It has been found that Black elderly express high levels of affective feelings about being close to their family members (Cantor, 1979; Chatters et al., 1985; Jackson, 1971; Tate, 1981; Taylor, 1986).

In general, previous research suggests that instrumental assistance is more often provided by family members, whereas expressive aid is supplied by nonkin networks such as friends, neighbors, and church members. Although these two types of caregiving behaviors have been discussed separately, they are in reality interrelated. It is often the interaction of instrumental and expressive support mutually exchanged between the elderly and their informal support systems that influences the elderly Black person's sense of general well-being (Dilworth-Anderson, 1981; Cantor, 1979; Jackson, 1971).

The major source of caregiving for elderly Blacks are their kin and nonkin networks (informal support systems). Kin supports include immediate family (siblings and other relatives); nonkin networks, comprising friends (confidants), neighbors, and church members, also provide significant caregiving support (Chatters et al., 1985; Gibson, 1982; Jackson, 1971; Peoples, 1984; Rubenstein, 1971; Tate, 1981; Taylor, 1986; Taylor and Chatters, 1986). In the absence of close kin helpers, Black elderly turn to nonkin and formal sources of assistance in an application of the "principle of substitution" (Chatters et al., 1986). In addition, there is some indication that membership and participation in social organizations and the church form another source of support for elderly Blacks (Clemente et al., 1975; Lambing, 1972).

Quantity and Frequency of Caregiving

Elderly Blacks, in general, tend to report relatively high levels of interaction and contact with their informal networks (Chatters et al., 1985; Dilworth-Anderson, 1981; Tate, 1981; Taylor, 1985; Taylor and Chatters, 1986). They also tend to experience high degrees of familial affection and high levels of satisfaction with family life (Taylor, 1985). Frequency and size of support networks for elderly Blacks are influenced by factors such as residential proximity of family members, family affection (closeness and satisfaction), presence of children in the household, being female, living in southern regions, age, marital status (widowed, never married), health status, and respect for youth and older persons (Chatters et al., 1985; Mutran, 1985; Taylor, 1985). In general, giving help in Black families is influenced by levels of education and income, marital status, health, and number of children at home.

Social class appears to be another factor that affects caregiving behaviors between Black adult children and elderly parents. It has been suggested that caregiving, when considering social class status, tends to be based on the intensity of need of the care receiver and the capability of the caregiver to provide care (Mitchell and Register, 1984; Mutran, 1985; Sokolovsky, 1985). Jackson (1971) has reported that adult children from elderly parents of upper-class backgrounds usually provide and receive more instrumental assistance than those from lower classes. It has also been found that expressive assistance is more frequently exchanged between adult children and elderly parents who come from upper classes. The occupational status of elderly Blacks prior to retirement is another determinant of the amount and frequency of social participation and interaction among elderly Blacks. Elderly Blacks from higher occupational status backgrounds (professionals) are more likely to attend family reunions, to hold memberships in social associations, and to be active in church-related activities (Lambing, 1972).

Quality of Caregiving Behaviors of Black Elderly

Research data suggest that Black elderly report relatively high levels of satisfaction with the care they receive from their informal supports (Chatters et al., 1985; Rubenstein, 1971; Tate, 1981). They are not isolated and do not necessarily experience low levels of morale. Further, they generally perceive that they have adequate support helpers in times of need. Elderly Blacks often express feelings of closeness to family, friends, and church members. They are also confident that in times of need they can count on assistance from family members (kin networks) and friends (nonkin networks) (Chatters et al., 1985; Tate, 1981; Taylor, 1985, 1986; Taylor and Chatters, 1986). Evidence that Black elderly are more willing to take young children into their homes (Mitchell and Register, 1984), have high levels of social participation in voluntary social organizations (Clemente et al., 1975), and have large pools of informal support networks (Chatters et al., 1986) reflects relatively high levels of quality of life and well-being among Black elderly.

In a related study, Gibson (1982) found that Black elderly are more flexible and tend to utilize multiple sources of support. This finding provides evidence regarding levels of adaptation and adjustment to aging among the Black elderly. It has also been suggested that Black elderly who are ill and isolated usually have higher levels of life satisfaction than their White counterparts in similar situations. Some suggest that this is because they generally have better coping mechanisms under adverse circumstances because of their historical backgrounds of discrimination and deprivation (Billingsley, 1968; McCaslin and Calvert, 1975).

A popular notion among social scientists suggests that the Black extended family structure, with its cultural emphasis on filial responsibility and respect for and assistance to elderly family members, reflects one of the assets of ethnicity (Billingsley, 1968; Mutran, 1985; Taylor, 1985). Recently there has been an increasing skepticism concerning the notion of ethnicity being a resource of the well-being of the Black elderly. This has come about because of social and economic conditions, historical patterns of exclusion of Blacks from major social institutions of the society, and government cutbacks of social services and facilities that tend to affect Blacks adversely (Hanson et al., 1983; Sokolovsky, 1985).

Other evidence suggests that the quality of caregiving behaviors provided for Black elderly is influenced by factors such as income, perceived health status, attitude toward present life situation, presence of voluntary relationships (confidants), combinations of instrumental assistance from nonkin members, being female, and living in southern regions (Tate, 1981; Taylor and Chatters, 1986). It has been found, contrary to expectations, that the majority of Black Americans display low levels of both filial responsibility expectations and realizations (Hanson et al., 1983; Seelbach, 1980). This finding does not differ from that for Whites in the sample, and seems to suggest that Black Americans are realistic about their capacities to provide and receive care. A possible implication of this on the quality of caregiving provided to Black elderly could be that when care is provided, it is done on a sincere and honest basis, without regard for possible returns on the part of the caregiver.

Assistance and Caregiving Needs

It is evident that the major sources of caregiving support for Black elderly are their informal support networks. Both kin and nonkin networks provide for most of the Black elderly's physical, psychological, and emotional needs. It is also apparent that the utilization of formal supports among Black elderly tends to be minimal and dissatisfying. Further, research studies of caregiving behaviors and patterns reveal that there is a relatively high extent of mutual exchange of assistance between the elderly and kin networks. This suggests the presence of interdependence between these two groups.

Patterns of caregiving among the Black elderly may have developed, in part, because of the necessity on the part of a significant number of older Black individuals and families to rely on informal assistance. The proportion of elderly Blacks in poverty has increased since 1978, and the gap between Black and White elderly has also increased considerably. Blacks in poverty outnumber Whites three to one. There are four Blacks for every one White among the very poor (annual income of less than $3,000). The Black elderly poor constitute 42.6% of all elderly poor in our society (Pilisuk and Mitchell, 1983-1984).

Half the elderly Blacks in poverty are isolated and tend to live alone. Half of all elderly Blacks survive on incomes that are below 125% of the poverty line. Generally, this is because Black males tend to be in low and less diverse earning capacity situations, are frequently unemployed, and hold low-status jobs with lower pay, fewer benefits, and greater risk of accidents and physically disabling problems than other jobs. Blacks, in general, are less likely than other groups to receive income from assets, interest or rent, and pensions. This results in the majority of Black elderly relying on social security, supplemental security income, public assistance, unemployment benefits, and workers' compensation. Black elderly women are in worse positions than men. Over 50% of elderly female Blacks are in poverty, and this figure rises to 80% if those near the poverty level are included (Pilisuk and Mitchell, 1983-1984).

In terms of residence, 50% of Blacks live in substandard housing; this figure rises to 85% when those in rural areas are included. In general, a significant number of rural elderly Blacks tend to have inadequate health, housing, and transport conveniences, and smaller shares of Medicare, Medicaid, social security, and supplemental medical insurance. It is also reported that 9 out of 20 Black elderly are rural residents.

Black elderly are also likely to experience poor health conditions. More than 50% of Blacks have poor health characterized by chronic illness that affects employment. Blacks spend less on health care, visit doctors less often, and receive less preventive care than their counterparts. They are also more likely to be unhappy and thus susceptible to mental health problems (Pilisuk and Mitchell, 1983-1984).

When considering income, residential, and health conditions of Black elderly, institutional forces in our society tend to work adversely for them. Age-specific programs that have been developed to assist the elderly, such as social security and Medicare, have become increasingly inadequate for the Black elderly. Recent cutbacks in social service programs, increasing bureaucratization, and cost containment procedures have to some extent disadvantaged the Black elderly, more so than their White counterparts.

Based on the above conditions, caregiving behaviors and patterns of the Black elderly can be more realistically evaluated. Although the informal support systems (kin and nonkin networks) provide for most of the Black elderly's caregiving needs, the literature indicates that certain factors tend to have significant influence on this phenomenon. Sex, region, health status, marital status, presence of children, and residential proximity are some of the factors that determine caregiving behaviors of the Black elderly. Being female, living in the South, having health problems, the presence of children in the household, the availability of helpers, and being widowed are some of the prominent factors that increase caregiving behaviors for Black elderly.

Sex, health problems, region, presence of children (hence more responsibilities), and marital status can influence need. It has also been found that socioeconomic status has an effect on the amount and type of assistance received from family and other informal sources. All the factors that predict the extent of caregiving the Black elderly receive from their informal support networks suggest that caregiving patterns are predominantly based on the needs of the elderly and the capacity of caregivers realistically to provide care.

The cultural/ethnicity explanation for caregiving behaviors of Black elderly could be feasible. However, most arguments for this perspective have been descriptive. To be accepted scientifically, this perspective needs to be investigated scientifically. A possible reason for this lack of scientific information could be the difficulty of operationalizing abstract concepts related to the cultural perspective, such as culture and filial feelings.

It is also evident that, until very recently, scientific research specifically designed to examine various aspects of the Black American has been minimal. Most research that provides information about Black Americans has been derived from research designs that pertain more often to the White American population. Such research fails to consider the unique conditions and characteristics of Black American people (Staples, 1971). Although social scientists have attempted to rectify this problem, the scientific literature on Black Americans is in its early stages.

It is apparent that the theories regarding Black family caregiving patterns reviewed above do not provide an adequate framework to allow a realistic understanding of the issue. The major problem with such theories is that they tend to be static; they do not account for the many dynamic aspects of the caregiving process. A more feasible theoretical explanation would be the "convoy of social support" model (Antonucci, 1985; Kahn, 1979; Kahn and Antonucci, 1980). This model utilizes social networks as the structures within which support is given, received, and exchanged. It describes the dynamic process of social networks over the life course.

The term *convoy* suggests the idea that the individual, from birth, engages in interpersonal relationships that provide a convoy of supports over the life course. As the individual matures and develops, his or her convoy also tends to develop and change. With new experiences, life events, and changes, certain supports are eliminated and new supports are formed. Hence an individual's convoy of supports, at any point in time, needs to be understood in terms of its present as well as its past structure. The use of the convoy model allows a support network to be understood from a longitudinal perspective in evaluating its adequacy and outcomes.

From this view, the convoy model of social support emphasizes the dynamic and cumulative aspect of social interactions over time. The main determinants of this model are personal characteristics, situational characteristics, network/convoy structure and functions, adequacy, and outcomes (Antonucci, 1985).

Because of the detail contained in this model, it would be useful for investigating the support networks of elderly Black Americans. It would provide a more substantial understanding of the kinds of caregiving patterns and behaviors involving elderly Blacks than the theories mentioned previously. A further value of such research would be the capacity to identify the weakness and strength of the cumulative convoy of supports among this group. Such an insight would be valuable for practitioners and planners, who would be able to use the information in terms of formulating effective and creative intervention strategies geared toward enhancing the quality of life and well-being of Black elderly persons.

Conclusion

It is not likely that the socioeconomic conditions of the Black elderly will undergo any radical changes in the next few decades. Structural forces and institutions will require major transformations before the conditions of Black elderly improve. It is thus more pragmatic to plan and formulate realistic policies that will facilitate and reinforce the existing resources of the Black elderly when considering their quality of life and general well-being.

Although there was a reduction in federal funding for social programs in the 1980s, a review of programs for the aged indicates that there are a number of sources of formal support for Black elderly. They are entitled to a variety of programs, such as multipurpose senior centers, housing, in-home services, adult day care, long-term care residence, crime and legal assistance programs, health and mental health services, and transportation, to name a few. These programs coincide with the needs that many Black elderly exhibit. However, research reviewed in this chapter suggests that elderly Blacks do not often use formal sources of support. It would be useful, therefore, for helping professionals to appraise and evaluate the reasons for this phenomenon. This should be done at the local community level in order to provide a realistic understanding about the kinds of obstacles that prevent elderly Blacks from utilizing services and facilities to which they are entitled.

A possible explanation for this underutilization of services could be associated with a lack of information and adequate and effective referral procedures. It would seem that efforts to establish programs that would enhance these processes would lead to greater use of formal services by Black elderly. Assistance from the community through neighborhood, school, and church organizations could be mobilized to help in this activity. The use of local leadership to transmit information about services and facilities that are available for the well-being of Black elderly could also serve to legitimate these formal sources of support and make them more desirable to those who are eligible but are not currently users.

The problem of accessibility could be another possible explanation for the underutilization of services and facilities. *Sozialstationen,* an interesting concept in use in West Germany, seems to suggest an innovative and creative way in which social services and facilities can be provided for the aged (Grunow, 1980). Basic services such as nursing care, personal aides, and homemaker services are provided at public housing sites for the elderly. This not only furnishes needed assistance to the elderly where they live, it also allows them more independence from informal caregivers and reduces their burden. At the same time, it helps postpone institutionalization. With local community, state, and federal support, a decentralized program of care such as this could be an effective way of providing services and facilities that Black elderly require. A program of this type would also reduce the stress that primary caregivers tend to experience.

Another innovation that could be tried is the warden system used in Great Britain. A warden or "friendly visitor" is assigned to a block of dwelling units to look in on the occupants each day and help them (Heumann, 1980). The warden is typically a middle-aged woman who acts much the same as an interested neighbor would. She arranges formal services, accompanies elderly on medical and agency visits, and in general sees to their well-being. In short, the British warden system is a formal substitute for caregiving that would be provided by family or other informal caregivers, if they were available. More important, the warden, as a member of the formal service system, has the knowledge and experience to direct elderly to needed services and the time to see that they receive them.

While both of the foreign programs mentioned above are associated with elderly in public housing, it would be easy to modify their basic structure to include other community aged. It is also essential to modify existing programs for the elderly in order to increase their accessibility for elderly Blacks, and to enhance elderly Blacks' willingness to utilize formal support networks effectively. The uniqueness of the Black American historical experience and the structural forces that have to some extent been responsible for the problems of elderly Blacks need to be examined more conscientiously. It is evident that with the changing socioeconomic conditions of our contemporary society, the problems and needs of the elderly are more effectively handled through a combination of formal and informal networks.

The informal support networks, both kin and nonkin, of the Black elderly tend to be willing but increasingly unable to provide for the needs of their elderly members. Policies and programs geared toward enhancing the quality of life and unique needs of Black elderly, who are expected to constitute a relatively large sector of the elderly population in the coming years, need to consider this fact.

Present and future social service programs need to take into account the diverse and changing role of informal support networks and the quantity and quality of care that is provided through them. Future programs must not be based on the assumption of homogeneity in regard to caregiving among Black families. Recognition must be given to the diversity of such informal caregiving and the impact that such diversity has on the total experience of care received by Black elderly.

References

Anderson, K. L. and W. R. Allen. 1984. "Correlates of Extended Household Structure." *Phylon* 45:144-57.

Antonucci, T. C. 1985. "Personal Characteristics, Social Support, and Social Behavior." Pp. 94-128 in *Handbook of Aging and the Social Sciences,* edited by R. Binstock and E. Shanas. 2nd ed. New York: Van Nostrand Reinhold.

Billingsley, A. 1968. *Black Families in White America.* Englewood Cliffs, NJ: Prentice-Hall.

Billingsley, A. and L. McCarley. 1986. "Afro-American Families and the Elderly." Paper presented at the Conference on Mental Health and the Black Elderly, Atlanta University, March 14.

Cantor, M. H. 1979. "Social and Family Relationships of Black Aged Women in New York City." *Journal of Minority Aging* 4:50-61.

Chatters, L. M., R. T. Taylor, and J. S. Jackson. 1985. "Size and Composition of the Informal Helper Networks of Elderly Blacks." *Journal of Gerontology* 40:605-14.

———. 1986. "Aged Blacks' Choices for an Informal Helper Network." *Journal of Gerontology* 41:94-100.

Clemente, F., P. A. Rexroad, and C. Hirsch. 1975. "The Participation of the Black Aged in Voluntary Associations." *Journal of Gerontology* 30:469-72.

Dilworth-Anderson, P. 1981. "Family Closeness Between Aged Blacks and Their Adult Children." *Journal of Minority Aging* 6:56-66.

Dressler, W., S. H. Hoeppner, and B. J. Pitts. 1985. "Household Structure in a Southern Black Community." *American Anthropologist* 87:853-62.

Gibson, R. C. 1982. "Blacks at Middle and Late Life: Resources and Coping." *Annals of the American Academy of Political and Social Science* 464:79-90.

Grunow, D. 1980. "*Sozialstationen*: A New Model for Home Delivery of Care and Service." *Gerontologist* 20:308-17.

Hanson, S. L., W. J. Sauer, and W. C. Seelbach. 1983. "Racial and Cohort Variations in Filial Responsibility Norms." *Gerontologist* 23:626-31.

Harper, B. C. 1982. "Some Snapshots of Death and Dying Among Ethnic Minorities." Pp. 131-34 in *Minority Aging: Sociological and Psychological Issues,* edited by R. C. Manuel. Westport, CT: Greenwood.

Heumann, L. F. 1980. "Sheltered Housing for the Elderly: The Role of the British Warden." *Gerontologist* 20:318-30.

Jackson, J. J. 1971. "Sex and Social Class Variations in Black Aged Parent-Child Relationships." *Aging and Human Development* 2:96-107.

Kahn, R. L. 1979. "Aging and Social Support." Pp. 77-91 in *Aging from Birth to Death,* edited by M. W. Riley. Boulder, CO: Westview.

Kahn, R. L. and T. C. Antonucci. 1980. "Convoys over the Life Course: Attachments, Roles and Social Support." Pp. 254-83 in *Life-Span Development and Behavior,* edited by P. B. Baltes and O. G. Brim. New York: Academic Press.

Lambing, M. L. B. 1972. "Social Class Living Patterns of Retired Negroes." *Gerontologist* 12:258-88.

McCaslin, R. and W. R. Calvert. 1975. "Social Indicators in Black and White: Some Ethnic Considerations in Delivery of Service to the Elderly." *Journal of Gerontology* 30:60-66.

Mitchell, J. and J. C. Register. 1984. "An Exploration of Family Interaction with the Elderly by Race, Socioeconomic Status, and Residence." *Gerontologist* 24:48-54.

Mutran, E. 1985. "Intergenerational Family Support Among Blacks and Whites: Response to Culture or Socioeconomic Differences." *Journal of Gerontology* 40:382-89.

Peoples, B. Y. C. 1984. "An Exploratory Study of Noninstitutionalized Black Urban Elderly Living in Age-Homogeneous Apartments in Detroit, Michigan and Their Informal Social Support Systems." Ph.D. dissertation, Iowa State University.

Pilisuk, M. and J. Mitchell. 1983-1984. "Black Elderly: Viability During a Time of Cutbacks." *International Quarterly of Community Health Education* 4:213-30.

Rubenstein, D. I. 1971. "An Examination of Social Participation Found Among a National Sample of White and Black Elderly." *Aging and Human Development* 2:172-88.

Seelbach, W. C. 1980. "Filial Responsibility Among Aged Parents: A Racial Comparison." *Journal of Minority Aging* 5:286-92.

Sokolovsky, J. 1985. "Ethnicity, Culture and Aging: Do Differences Really Make a Difference?" *Journal of Applied Gerontology* 4:6-17.

Staples, R. 1971. "Towards a Sociology of the Black Family: A Theoretical and Methodological Assessment." *Journal of Marriage and the Family* 33:119-38.

Tate, N. P. 1981. "Social Interactional Patterns and Life Satisfaction of a Group of Elderly Black Widows." Ph.D. dissertation, Brandeis University.

Taylor, R. J. 1985. "The Extended Family as a Source of Support to Elderly Blacks." *Gerontologist* 25:488-95.

———. 1986. "Receipt of Support from Family Among Black Americans: Demographic and Familial Differences." *Journal of Marriage and the Family* 48:67-77.

Taylor, R. J. and L. M. Chatters. 1986. "Patterns of Informal Support to Elderly Black Adults: Family, Friends, and Church Members." *Social Work* 31:432-38.

U.S. Department of Commerce, Bureau of the Census. 1986. *Estimates of the Population of the U.S. by Age, Sex and Race: 1980 to 1985.* Washington, DC: Government Printing Office.

12

Clinical Social Work Practice with Black Elderly and Their Family Caregivers

CHERYL STEWART GERACE
LINDA S. NOELKER

During the 1960s and 1970s there was a great deal written about social work practice with the Black client. Those decades provided the ambience for clinicians and researchers alike to explore issues related to human behavior, race and ethnicity, and worker-client relationships. According to Manuel (1982), the 1970s clearly mark the "coming of age" in which Black elderly became a focus of investigation and minority aging was recognized as a special area of study within gerontology. This was evidenced by special issues of professional journals devoted to Black elderly, the initiation of new journals on Black and minority aged, the formation of the National Caucus on the Black Aged, and the inclusion of special sessions on Black aged in the 1971 White House Conference on Aging.

Throughout this period the foci were on poverty, health care, social support, and improving the quality of life among minority aged. However, very little was written about clinical social work practice with Black elderly clients and their family caregivers. The scant attention

AUTHORS' NOTE: This chapter is a revised version of a paper presented at "Understanding and Serving Black Aged: A Community Conference and Forum," sponsored by Cleveland State University and the Cleveland Clinic Foundation and cofunded by the Cleveland Foundation, Cleveland State University, Cleveland, Ohio, February 26-27, 1987.

paid this area persists today and points to the continued need to develop approaches for assessing, counseling, and problem solving with this client system. In an effort to meet this need, a primary purpose of our chapter is to adapt existing models for clinical social work practice with Black or minority clients to working with Black elderly clients and their family caregivers.

In accordance with the principles of social work education and the profession's code of ethics, a key premise underlying our work is the culture and cultural values as well as the ethnic identity of any client system as central concerns in rendering service (Compton and Galway, 1979; Hepworth and Larsen, 1982; Lum, 1986). These include a respect for human rights and the dignity and uniqueness of the individual, as well as adherence to the values of social responsibility and social equality.

According to Lum (1986), social workers have an ethical responsibility to promote nondiscrimination, equal opportunity, and respect for cultural diversity. These responsibilities should guide and direct all social work activities with distinct ethnic/cultural group members. Additionally, it is the social work educator's responsibility to provide and the practitioner's responsibility to obtain the appropriate knowledge and skills required to work effectively with culturally distinct clients. Such skills include gaining insight into one's own attitudes toward particular groups, acquiring an understanding of client groups, and becoming aware of the needs of ethnic groups in the community. Lum further suggests that social work values must encompass both client rights and the collective values of the minority group. Among African Americans retaining a southern cultural orientation, this collective value system emphasizes family unity, the leadership of older generations, kinship responsibilities, and the prominence of religious institutions and spirituality. Moreover, the collective value system of a culturally distinct group should serve as a guiding factor in social work practice rather than the more commonly used Euro-American value system.

Lum's recommendations take on added significance as the U.S. population ages and the number of Black elderly aged 75 and over increases disproportionately compared with the number of White aged (U.S. Senate, 1986). Accordingly, the first objective of this chapter is to identify aspects of Black culture and aging that should structure social work practice with Black elderly and their families. Although culturally sensitive treatment programs and the ethnic-sensitive model have been delineated previously (Devore, 1983; Devore and Schlesinger, 1987; Jones, 1983; Lum, 1986; Ziter, 1987), our work focuses on the special considerations that should be given to the joint effects of aging and Black culture on social work practice.

Our second purpose is to use case material from clients served by the Benjamin Rose Institute's Community Services Division to illustrate the application of these practice principles to different types of elderly Black clients whose informal support systems vary in their structure and functioning. Third, we will draw on clinical research, using data from the institute's Client Information System, to identify differences in the Black aged's family networks and their implications for social work services.

The Black Elderly Client System: A Practice Approach

When considering a practice approach relevant to working with Black aged and their families, we support the opinion that practitioners need to understand Black culture so that misdiagnosis of client problems and inappropriate treatment do not result (Downing and Copeland, 1981; Jones, 1979; Lightfoot, 1982). Because culture influences values, norms, communication patterns, and behavior, knowledge about a client's culture is essential in order for service providers to identify the normal from the aberrant and to have insight into the client's goals and expectations for the service, the service provider, and the agency. If the practitioner neglects to assess clients within the framework of their culture and its relationship to the dominant culture, errors in the assessment of client needs and functioning are likely to occur.

Keeping these points in mind, the ethnic-sensitive model of practice (Devore and Schlesinger, 1987) and the ethnic minority social work practice model (Lum, 1986) can be adapted to working with the Black elderly and their kin caregivers. As noted by Lum, this approach provides a framework not only for ethnic minority practice, but for further development of the social work field.

There are three major practice principles drawing on these models that should be applied when working with minority elderly; their use will enhance the performance of an on-target assessment and the development of an appropriate service plan:

(1) Be knowledgeable about and responsive to the minority culture as well as to elderly clients' cultural experiences related to their generation or cohort. Devore and Schlesinger (1987) have termed this "tuning in" or "being in tune."

(2) Understand the communication patterns and techniques in minority groups and how communication is affected by age-related changes, and adapt communication with the client accordingly.

(3) Complete a comprehensive assessment utilizing the life model or ecosystems approach and the ethnic-sensitive practice principles.

After a discussion of these principles, case illustrations will be used to demonstrate their application.

Minority Culture and Values

Regarding the first practice principle, being in tune to the Black elderly and their family caregivers gives recognition to their cultural norms, practices, traditions, and life-style. Although Black families share traits that identify them as American, their cultural roots originate in Africa. Certain cultural forms derive from African heritage, namely, the kin-centered support network and the importance of spirituality and religious practice. The Black kinship network emphasizes togetherness, cultural traditions, and the primacy of family over individual (Lum, 1986). This heritage has been somewhat diluted, however, by African Americans' assimilation into a dominant culture in which more modified kin networks, geographic and social mobility, and individuality are stressed.

The Black family system comprises kin related by blood or marriage as well as what are termed "fictive kin," who are actually close friends defined and treated as family members (Gaines, 1988-1989; Stack, 1974). While apparent nonrelatives can be included in the kinship system, blood relatives can be excluded if they do not perform their roles adequately or maintain appropriate affective ties (Aschenbrenner, 1975). Gaines also observes that the emphasis on affective ties rather than cognitive abilities within the Black kinship system may enable cognitively impaired aged to function at a level acceptable to the Black family for a longer period of time than would be tolerated by White families. This phenomenon would, consequently, influence what family members perceive as symptomatic or dysfunctional and when they would seek treatment for their cognitively impaired elderly.

The elaborated kin network has been viewed as an especially adaptive mechanism to meet the minority individual's and group's needs for assistance and support in a racist society (Jones, 1983; Stack, 1974). Cafferty and Chestang (1976), when discussing the duality of the Black experience, indicate that ethnic individuals are a part of a dominant or sustaining society and an ethnic nurturing environment. The nurturing environment includes the family, supportive institutions, values, and traditions. This environment offers emotional and concrete support that serves as a buffer against the larger society, which dominates and is often hostile toward the ethnic group.

In African American families there is a sense of mutual responsibility and sharing of material goods, households, child care, and emotional support (Stack, 1974). Within these kin networks children belong to the family and may be moved from household to household. Compared to White kin systems, Blacks more often reside in three-generation households, where grandparents have child-rearing responsibilities (Beck and Beck, 1984; Lum, 1986). However, as noted by Martin and Martin (1978), urban life for the extended family, compared to rural or small-town life, often has not been conducive to the maintenance of an extended family structure. Housing in urban areas, for example, has been too small and costly to accommodate large extended families. As a result, families, particularly children, are often separated into urban subextended families. Other factors in the urban environment that tend to erode the Black extended family are the fast pace of the city and family members' residence in different sections of the city, which diminishes family solidarity by inhibiting frequent visits. Nevertheless, Martin and Martin conclude that urban extended family members still attempt to live in close proximity.

The larger, more diverse, and assistance-oriented kinship system of African Americans may account for its primacy in meeting the elderly's needs. An additional factor is that minority aged have more limited access to high-quality formal services (Bass and Noelker, 1987; Downing and Copeland, 1981; Lockery, 1985). There are, however, segments within the Black aged population who do not have sizable or supportive kinship systems, such as the widowed and childless, males, elderly without proximate family members, or those with unstable or dysfunctional family systems (Gary and Leashore, 1982; Solomon, 1978). Special outreach efforts and more intensive research on their assistance use patterns may better enable service providers to respond to the special needs of these aged, but their familial orientations may lead them to distrust nonfamily members who offer assistance.

A second cultural form, the Black church, has traditionally been an important source of support and has provided social relationships, apart from family, for the elderly. According to Lum (1986), religion and spirituality have served to sustain Black Americans against prejudice and discrimination, helped them to cope with stress and tension, and validated their cultural heritage and the worth of Black people. The Black church has been and continues to be a powerful force promoting civil rights and political justice through the articulation of a liberation theology.

The church has also functioned as a social welfare agency, although the extensiveness of its services to members in need of assistance varies widely. Differences among Black churches in their organization and leadership affect the services they provide and, hence, influence elderly members' ability to continue this important affiliation once chronic disability occurs. According to Morrison's (1986) research on Black churches in Philadelphia, larger churches and those affiliated with predominantly White denominations are best able to provide services to incapacitated persons through church-sponsored social services or professionals within the congregation. Although clergy in smaller churches are aware of members with service needs, many are not aware of how to obtain services effectively. Even in larger churches with stronger programs, church-based services cannot meet the long-term care needs of chronically impaired members, nor can the clergy or service programs easily obtain these services from public agencies. Morrison concludes that a church's size, denomination, congregational composition, and financial resources influence the extensiveness of its services. Also, in his estimation, Black churches are best suited to meet the needs of active elderly for social and preventive services and to offer temporary assistance to infirm elderly who require limited help.

Although Black churches cannot be viewed as a source of long-term care for frail aged, their clergy can provide community social workers with important linkages to aged members. More specifically, they can serve as an information source about aged members in need of assistance, they can offer sites for group counseling or education programs, and they can help to organize advocacy efforts. Black clergy can also enhance social workers' knowledge about and sensitivity to Black cultural mistrust so that resistance to service providers can be minimized.

Workers should keep in mind, however, that some churches and their leaders may seek to be the major provider of services to aged members and to receive some compensation for these services. In these instances, they may view other service agencies as competitors. Consequently, concerted efforts have to be made by the worker to delineate the services each source is best able to provide and to develop a coordinated service plan.

Cohort Effects

In addition to the need to consider cultural influences when working with the Black client, there are cohort effects that exert influence on elderly clients' life experiences. *Cohort* is a term that refers to individuals born in the same time period, and cohort analysis has shown that there are notable differences in the childbearing, mortality, and divorce and remarriage patterns of various cohorts (Cherlin, 1983).

Cohort effects contribute to the heterogeneity found in the aged Black population, which includes the young-old (60-69) as well as 70-to 84-year-olds and the old-old (85 and over). The life experiences of successive cohorts of Black aged have been diverse and should be taken into account during the assessment process. For example, a Black person born in 1900 may have served in World War I, experienced the Harlem Renaissance, and entered old age during the civil rights movement in the 1960s. In contrast, a Black person born in 1920 may have served in a segregated unit in World War II and experienced the civil rights movement and affirmative action programs in middle age. In contrast, today's young Black Americans who are developing job or career aspirations have, for the first time, a Black presidential candidate, the Reverend Jesse Jackson, as a role model.

Elderly in different cohorts have also had different experiences with social and health care services that, in all likelihood, influence their current health care practices and receptivity to social work intervention. Black persons of more advanced aged experienced segregated health care and inadequate services perhaps until age 50 or 55. Many are thus in the habit of mistrusting Anglo health providers and rely on home remedies and health care advice from pharmacists or local community nurses (Lightfoot, 1982). Social workers and other practitioners may be viewed by such clients with suspicion or some paranoid ideation that is, in fact, based upon lifelong experiences with a hostile environment (Jones, 1979). In these instances, the social worker should beware of erroneously interpreting this response as pathological. Instead, the worker needs to ascertain whether the suspicion is specific to service providers or is typical of the client's interaction with others, such as kin, friends, and neighbors.

Gibson's (1982) research has also shown that there are differences in resources and coping patterns among successive cohorts of Black elderly. Although Black aged, regardless of cohort, seem to use more varied types of helpers and to substitute helpers more readily than White aged, the use of prayer as a coping resource in times of worry appears to have declined among middle-aged Blacks in 1976 compared with those in 1957. Her research suggests that despite their lower socioeconomic status, Black aged may be at something of an advantage in later life due to their broader base of helpers and greater adaptability in substituting helpers in their informal support networks to meet their changing assistance needs.

This population is also diverse because of differences in countries of origin, with cultural backgrounds ranging from African to Jamaican and Haitian. Furthermore, residence and migration patterns in the United States contribute to heterogeneity in the aged Black population. Lightfoot (1982) points out that there are differences in socialization patterns among Black Americans born in northern and southern regions and in rural areas, urban ghettos, and small towns. Diversity also results from the variety of religious affiliations held by Black Americans, including the Catholic, Baptist, Jehovah's Witness, and Pentecostal churches. In brief, being Black in America constitutes a wide range of cultural and generational experiences that should be considered by clinicians in the assessment and service planning process.

Effective Communication Techniques

The second principle derived from a culture-sensitive model for social work practice is that the worker should be knowledgeable about communication patterns and techniques in ethnic groups and should adapt his or her communication with clients accordingly. This is essential to the establishment of working relationships in which successful problem solving can occur. Devore and Schlesinger (1987) suggest that workers require "tuning in empathy" with minority clients. This allows workers to identify feelings accurately, to focus on verbal and nonverbal behaviors, and to elicit information in a sensitive yet organized and comprehensive manner.

In an initial contact with any client the worker should strive to convey respect, warmth, genuineness, and openness in order to develop trust. However, this approach for developing trust may be more problematic with minority clients because of the resistance displayed by the Black client system. A source for this resistance is suspicion and mistrust due to prior negative experiences with helping professionals as a result of institutional racism.

For these reasons, Lum (1986) recommends beginning with a brief, friendly conversation. The use of the term *conversation* connotes reciprocity in the exchange of information that is likely to foster further mutual discussion. The worker should initiate this conversation by proposing various general topics, such as a recent community event, the weather, or a comment regarding a picture of a loved one. It is also recommended that the worker consider professional disclosure. This entails the social worker's taking the initiative to build a relationship with the client system by disclosing an area of interest common to all involved in the helping relationship. According to Lum (1986), the worker who chooses to use self-disclosure evidences a willingness to approach the client as a human being and is less likely to rely on the professional role as a means to distance him- or herself from the client or to control the relationship. Apart from the goals of facilitating communication and humanizing the worker-client relationship, then, this approach reflects a specific perspective on the social work role useful with all clients.

The importance of self-disclosure is based on the belief that the minority client may be hesitant about receiving help because of reservations concerning the social worker. At the same time, however, a worker's disclosure must reflect sincere openness, otherwise an astute client, even if uneducated or illiterate, will correctly perceive it as manipulative.

It is not unusual for elderly clients to ask the worker personal questions regarding marital status, number of children, or family background. Contrary to what has been taught in many schools of social work, the worker will need to feel comfortable answering some personal questions in order to gain the client's trust and to establish rapport. Many clients, in turn, find they are more trusting of the clinician once they have been able to evaluate or judge his or her background. When clients seek to disclose racist experiences to the worker, it is critical that the worker not avoid or block discussion of these experiences. If the worker avoids or ignores such experiences, it conveys to the client that the worker is disinterested in or devalues a significant aspect of Black life and the client's personal experiences. Also, nonminority workers should be careful of too readily saying they understand these experiences or of being overly apologetic about the client's experiences of prejudice or discrimination.

An additional element essential to the initial contact with minority aged is demonstrating respect by using appropriate titles and surnames when addressing clients. Historically, many Black elders were addressed by their first names or slave names, which is disrespectful and demoralizing.

The worker also needs to be cognizant of functional limitations that make it difficult for some aged clients to communicate easily. Awareness of these limitations and making the appropriate adjustments when communicating with the client are also implicit signs of respect. For example, clients who have a hearing loss will be better able to carry on a conversation when the worker sits facing the client, with his or her face in the light, and looks directly at the client when speaking. The worker in such a situation should also try to minimize background noise and use a lower rather than a higher tone of voice (see Bloom et al., 1971, for additional discussion of this issue).

Nonverbal communication techniques are also helpful for elderly with sensory losses that impair communication. Concern and nurturance can be conveyed by holding hands or touching. Although sitting forward and maintaining direct eye contact indicate interest and attentiveness, it is important for the worker to know if a particular ethnic client expects younger people to lower their eyes and turn their heads to convey respect. This phenomenon is more common among older Hispanic Americans and those of African and American Indian descent. When workers are in tune with this tradition, it will assist in establishing a trusting relationship.

Finally, workers who use professional jargon or technical language and intellectualization will not further the relationship with elderly clients or their informal caregivers. Similarly, the worker should ask for clarification if clients or their caregivers use dialect or idioms unique to their culture and the worker is uncertain of the meaning. The worker's use of dialect should be carefully considered unless it is common to his or her speech and thus a natural part of his or her pattern of communication. Some nonminority practitioners attempt to use Black dialect as a means of gaining clients' acceptance, when, in fact, this often has the opposite effect.

Comprehensive Assessment

The third practice principle with Black aged and their family care-givers is to complete a comprehensive assessment with special attention to the client's major cultural forms. The assessment should be guided by the life model or ecosystems approach (Germain and Gitterman, 1980) and the two ethnic-sensitive practice principles previously discussed.

The life model approach is quite distinct from the medical model, which assumes that a client's problems are due to illness or pathology and are in need of a cure. In contrast, the life model is derived from the science of ecology, which investigates the balance between living things and their environments and ways in which this balance can be enhanced for their mutual benefit. Its application to social work practice emphasizes the client's place in a larger environment and requires consideration of both individual and situational factors. Rather than focusing on the person alone, the life model approach provides a broader view of the client's situation, the elements within it, and their reciprocal effects. Additionally, this approach requires a focus on the fit between the person's needs and abilities and the environment's resources and demands.

Use of the life model facilitates identification of transactions that constitute stress or support, the ability of the person to cope effectively with them, and, hence, areas for intervention or problem solving. Moreover, it mandates that the practitioner view the client as an active agent in the environment and a viable part of the total system. As such, the client's behavior and interactions with other elements in the system and their effects on that system require consideration in the assessment process. A comprehensive assessment of the elderly also requires information about the client's health history and current physical and mental health status. Other areas for assessment include the client's physical environment, family structure, and functioning, along with other informal supports (friends, neighbors), financial status, religious affiliation and participation, and personal history.

The application of this approach to the assessment of older clients indicates that some elements in an elderly person's ecosystem can include the family, neighborhood, church and other voluntary associations, and health care center or clinic. The worker should be sensitive to the relative salience of each of these to the older person, their supportive aspects, and the extent to which they are sources of stress in the client's life.

Devore (1983) maintains that application of the life model in the assessment of Black aged helps to sensitize the practitioner to the client's minority status and related cultural forms. However, she suggests that further development is needed to enhance its usage with aged minorities in stressful situations. For this reason, case illustrations are presented in the next section that typify several stressful situations encountered by frail Black aged, and the life model and ethnic-sensitive approaches are applied to the clients' assessment and service plan design. In the chapter's final section, clinical data are used to explore the extent to which these types of stressful situations that relate directly to characteristics of the aged's informal support network are experienced by Black elderly and their families.

Application of Practice Principle 1: Mrs. C's Lack of a Kin Network

Mrs. C, a 73-year-old widow, was referred to the agency when a government-funded demonstration program supplying her with home health services was terminated. Her numerous health problems, including high blood pressure, heart disease, stroke, and cancer, have resulted in left-side hemaplegia and confinement to a wheelchair. She has no children from any of her three marriages, few friends in the building or neighborhood, and no surviving relatives.

Early in her life, Mrs. C lived in a small Alabama town, where her family was active in the Baptist church, a vital support to Mrs. C during these years, which she characterized as ones of economic hardship and persecution by Whites. She moved to the North in her late teens and was employed as a day worker and seamstress. After a second failed marriage, a miscarriage, and the death of her third husband, Mrs. C became alcoholic. When her health deteriorated, she gave up drinking and became involved with a small, storefront Pentecostal church. Her relationship with the church has been strained in recent years because it is unable to offer the assistance Mrs. C needs with transportation, meals, and home help.

In the initial interview Mrs. C was anxious, confused, and bitter about her many losses and, most recently, the loss of government aid program. She has a history of relating poorly to most people of color when they represent the "White establishment." To Mrs. C these professionals and paraprofessionals are from institutions that practiced overt discrimination during her earlier years. In addition, she has inculcated the view that "White is right" and is antagonistic toward Black service providers, whom she regards as incompetent if they are professionals or as "lazy or shiftless" if they are paraprofessionals. These feelings not only cause greater stress in Mrs. C's life, but complicate her transactions with her Black physicians, home health aides, and social worker.

In the initial assessment, the worker reaffirms the realities of Mrs. C's experiences and focuses on her strengths in withstanding an era of hostility and now dealing with health- and age-related losses. Mrs. C's attempts to seek greater control over remaining situations in her life are viewed positively; however, the controlling behaviors she exhibits are generally maladaptive.

Subsequent counseling efforts are directed at reducing or defusing some of Mrs. C's anger so that better coping strategies and assistance sources in the community can be utilized. Additionally, the worker addresses the issue of *mutual* expectations for respect held by Mrs. C's service providers. This issue is carefully reviewed with Mrs. C's home health aides, who require ongoing support because they are often targets for her criticism.

The worker also acknowledges Mrs. C's frustration with her church and discusses the economic realities of the situation in an effort to improve her relationship with her pastor and congregation. A plan is subsequently developed by the social worker, client, and pastor so that the church provides Mrs. C with at least one hot meal a day. The pastor also agrees to try recruiting younger, able-bodied volunteers to assist its elderly congregants with transportation to church.

Application of Practice Principle 2: Mrs. P's Conflicted Kin Network

Mrs. P, an 88-year-old great-great-grandmother, lives alone in an age-segregated public housing apartment building. She suffers from a variety of ailments, including congestive heart failure, arthritis, hearing and vision losses, and some cognitive impairment enhanced by confusion and forgetfulness. A recent fall and subsequent hospitalization have resulted in her referral to the agency for evaluation of her home situation, counseling for depression, and future care planning.

The matriarch of five generations, Mrs. P had two daughters by her first marriage and a stepson from a second marriage, all of whom are deceased. The two daughters are survived by a total of eight children, two of whom give some assistance to Mrs. P. The remaining six grandchildren are nonproximate, deceased, or estranged. In essence, the family system is disorganized in its efforts at caring for Mrs. P and there is a history of unresolved conflicts and sibling rivalries.

The initial assessment is conducted in the client's apartment with Mrs. P and her two granddaughters. At the outset, Mrs. P is somewhat guarded and confused as to the purpose of the worker's visit. In an effort to convey respect and develop trust, the worker makes certain that she approaches Mrs. P first, addresses her by surname, and shakes her hand warmly. The granddaughters are seated at opposite ends of the room in a way that makes both introductions and group conversation difficult; this arrangement is indicative of the granddaughters' disagreements and divisiveness. Although both help Mrs. P with some personal care and household activities, they disagree about whether they share responsibilities equally and what the most appropriate care arrangement for Mrs. P is.

Because of her hearing and vision losses, Mrs. P has great difficulty following the conversation, especially when her granddaughters become emotional, raise the pitch and volume of their voices, and interrupt each other. This clearly exacerbates Mrs. P's feelings of losing control and that her granddaughters are plotting against her. The worker's efforts thus become focused on repeating the statements of each granddaughter to Mrs. P. and, during this process, helping to clarify each one's feelings and opinions.

At the end of the assessment interview, the family members and worker are in agreement about the primary problem: Troubled family relationships are exacerbating the burden of long-term family caregiving and undermining Mrs. P's continued residence in the community. It is also agreed that subsequent counseling sessions will be held separately with each family member.

Sessions with the granddaughters focus on Mrs. P's current functional limitations and consequent care needs. An educational approach is used to direct attention to the relationship between Mrs. P's stress, resulting from her age-related losses and health problems, and her cognitive impairments. Both typically increase an older person's anxiety, frustration, and maladaptive coping. The granddaughters are helped to understand that Mrs. P's resulting suspiciousness and accusations are not uncommon for aged in similar situations and that challenging those accusations in confrontation enforces rather than alleviates them. These educative sessions help to lessen the granddaughters' sense of isolation and to place their problems in broader perspective. Additionally, each granddaughter is encouraged to put aside concerns about past and present equity, to focus on the current family situation, and to decide what she is capable of doing and willing to do for Mrs. P. Once these decisions are made, the granddaughters' efforts can be coordinated and communicated to Mrs. P, which forestalls her accusations that one family member does more than the other.

Application of Practice Principle 3: Mr. T's Overburdened Kin Network

Mr. and Mrs. T, a married couple in their early 70s, have been confronted with Mr. T's escalating dependency and care needs resulting from Alzheimer's disease (AD). Mr. T requires assistance with all personal care activities, along with regular supervision. During Mr. T's recent hospitalization, it was suggested to Mrs. T that she begin considering nursing home placement in view of Mr. T's prognosis and growing incapacitation. Mrs. T is adamantly opposed to placing her husband in an institution and is convinced her husband would not last in a nursing home. This perspective on nursing home care is not uncommon, particularly in Black families, who tend not to use institutional care due to more limited access to quality nursing home care and culture-based values endorsing shared residence and family care. It also stems from a sense of personal powerlessness that is likely to occur from institutionalization in a "White establishment."

All three of the Ts' children live nearby and give regular assistance to the couple. Moreover, the daughters coordinate the assistance they give their parents so that the oldest daughter, a registered nurse, helps with shopping and monitoring the parents' health. The other two daughters escort their parents to medical appointments and help with household tasks, while the church delivers hot meals. Because the daughters are employed or are married with dependent children of their own, their other responsibilities compete with the demands of parent care. Their sense of frustration with their multiple roles has motivated them to seek more help for their parents.

The daughters also express concern about their mother's significant weight loss over the last two years and the deleterious effects that caregiving seems to be having on her health. They note overt signs of depression that may have been exacerbated by the couple's increased social isolation. Because of Mr. T's inappropriate behavior, friends have ceased visiting.

In the initial assessment of Mr. and Mrs. T, it is apparent that the couple feels strongly about "not getting any handouts." Their conviction that using community services reinforces the stereotype of Black families being welfare families prevented them from seeking much-needed assistance at an earlier point in Mr. T's illness. This is particularly important in cases of irreversible dementia, because early introduction of respite and in-home services facilitates the impaired person's acceptance of service providers. At this time, the person's cognitive (memory) skills are less impaired and reliance on the family caregiver is less extreme.

An ecosystem analysis of the Ts' situation indicates both stressful and supportive interactions with their kinship system. Although the family has strong and supportive family ties, stress is being generated by differences of opinion between Mrs. T and her daughters about Mr. T's care arrangement. The daughters are not only advocating formal service use at this time, but recognize that eventually Mr. T will require nursing home placement. Mrs. T, who finds both service options unacceptable, feels a greater sense of isolation due to the pressure from her daughters and the inability of her church and its members to supply sufficient assistance.

In a subsequent family conference with the couple and their daughters, the need for and benefits of additional help are explored. The daughters' feelings of being overwhelmed and their concern about their mother's health are discussed. The notion of seeking more help from the church is reviewed, and Mrs. T maintains that the pastor and missionary board "have their hands full with others." Because the worker is aware of services that this church as able to provide, she points out that the couple's needs for respite care, occasional household help, and personal care assistance for Mr. T cannot be met by this source. Because further decline in Mr. T's condition is inevitable, the family is encouraged to consider sources that can provide continuous or long-term care, specifically, in-home assistance for Mr. T and respite service for Mrs. T. The purpose and benefit of respite service provided by a home health aide are discussed, especially its potential for helping

Mrs. T conserve her caregiving resources so that they can be extended over time, which, in turn, could postpone nursing home placement. Mrs. T also contracts for weekly social work counseling sessions that focus on depression and related feelings of loss and helplessness.

Black Aged in Need of Social Work Service: Clinical Data

Since 1908 the Benjamin Rose Institute has provided social work services through its Community Services Division to elderly in the Greater Cleveland area. Currently, services are supplied by four neighborhood offices staffed with teams made up of social workers, nurses, and home health aides. The division's client population primarily includes frail aged, defined as those individuals whose physical, mental, or social limitations place them at risk and necessitate skilled and generally multidisciplinary interventions. In view of the fact that clients typically reside in the inner city, the client population also includes relatively equal numbers of Black and White aged.

Data from the Institute's computerized Client Information System (CIS) were used to explore further some issues raised by the social work literature on Black aged and case illustrations. The first issue concerns the extent to which there are significant differences in the availability, proximity, and type of informal caregivers assisting Black and White clients. The second issue relates to difficulties encountered by the kin support network and, specifically, whether there are any differences in the care-related stress effects experienced by Black and White caregivers.

The Institute's client assessment data are derived from a form that was jointly developed by research and practice staff. It was designed to yield comprehensive, standardized information about the client's sociodemographic characteristics, physical health condition, functional abilities, cognitive limitations, emotional health, informal and formal sources and types of assistance problems experienced by informal support, and type and quality of housing. The CIS data reported here are from assessment forms completed by team leaders or case managers on clients initially assessed or reevaluated from May 1986 through December 1986. This group includes 438 clients, 51% (225) of whom are Black and 49% (213) of whom are White.

Table 12.1 Sociodemographic Characteristics of Community Service Clients by Race (N = 438)

	Black (n = 225)		White (n = 213)		
	%	n	%	n	
Marital Status					
married	28	61	24	51	
widowed	54	118	47	100	
single/divorced/separated	18	41	29	61	p < .05
Over 75	70	158	74	158	n.s.
Female	76	172	78	167	n.s.
Lives alone	33	74	56	120	p < .001
No primary caregiver	6	14	16	34	p < .01
Relationship of primary caregiver to client					
spouse	18	39	17	31	
child	35	73	26	46	
other relative	29	62	22	40	
nonkin	17	37	35	62	p < .001
Primary caregiver is in the client's home	55	115	31	55	p < .001

NOTE: Chi-square tests of significance indicated that all of these differences by race were significant at the .05 level or greater, except for the percentages over and under 75 and the percentages of males and females.

As Table 12.1 shows, the Black clients more often have kin support networks. That is, 83% of the Black clients have primary caregivers who are relatives, compared with 65% of the White clients, and 55% reside with their primary caregivers, compared with only 31% of the White clients. Twice as many White clients as Black clients (35% versus 17%) have nonkin primary caregivers (e.g., friend, neighbor). This suggests that the informal support systems of the White clients may be less able or willing to supply long-term care or more personal types of care should they be required. The reason is that nuclear kin, meaning a spouse or daughter, typically serve as the major providers of ongoing, daily assistance to the more severely impaired elderly who live in the community (Brody, 1985; Cantor, 1983; Stone et al., 1987).

Despite the greater availability and proximity of nuclear kin to the Black clients, there are still 23% (51) who either do not have primary caregivers or do not have family members as their primary caregivers. Although this percentage is less than half that of White clients (46%),

Table 12.2 Care-Related Stress Effects Experienced by the Primary Kin Caregivers of Black (n = 174) and White Clients (n = 117)

Type of Stress Effects	Black		White	
	%	n	%	n
For the primary caregiver				
emotional strain	38	66	44	52
physical strain	42	73	39	45
burden of caregiving tasks	28	48	27	32
restricted social activities	22	39	21	25
For family relationships				
family conflict	16	28	18	21
difficulties in the primary				
caregiver-client relationship	16	27	18	21
inadequate support from kin	14	25	15	17

NOTE: There were 147 clients deleted from this analysis because they either did not have relatives as their primary caregivers or did not have primary caregivers.

it does indicate that a number of Black aged in the Institute's community service population are dependent on the agency for services and support generally available from kin caregivers. These interventions, which differ in both volume and type compared to clients with kin support systems, include case management, personal care and household assistance, escort to health care services, and help with finances, shopping, and laundry. Additionally, these cases require careful monitoring to ensure that changes in client status and functioning are detected immediately and care plans are adjusted accordingly.

In addition to the number of Black clients without kin support systems, the CIS data indicate there are other features of clients' kin support networks deserving of attention. As Table 12.2 shows, various types of care-related stress were reported by family members during the assessment process. However, there were no significant differences between Black and White clients in the percentages of family members reporting specific types of stress. In other words, although more Black than White clients have primary kin caregivers, the incidence of various stress effects among these caregivers does not appear to differ by culture.

The data do suggest, however, that two types of stress appear to affect family members. The first involves health deterioration, activity restrictions, and difficulties related to care tasks that directly affect the primary kin caregiver. These stress effects experienced by primary caregivers can occur in stable, functional family systems due to the extensive, long-term care of the aged. The second pertains to family conflict or relationship difficulties that result from instability or dysfunction in the kinship network. These clinical data, along with case illustrations, have been used to show that within the Black elderly client group there is diversity in the clients' support system and, consequently, in service needs. Included among these are clients without kin support systems, clients with unstable or dysfunctional kin support systems, and clients with functional, but overburdened, kin support systems.

Conclusions

The three cases and related clinical research data underscore the special stresses experienced by Black elderly who become chronically ill and functionally impaired. While a portion of this group is bereft of informal caregivers, the majority requiring assistance receive it from kin, primarily wives and daughters. At the same time, the demands of caregiving can resurrect and exacerbate long-standing problems in family relationships or exhaust the resources of well-functioning stable family networks. For these reasons the special needs and care-related burdens of family members should be a focus of social work intervention in the assessment, care planning, and counseling process. This approach can help to forestall or prevent institutional placement of the aged client, alleviate the strain of family caregivers, and improve the functioning of family support networks.

In recent years, several models have been proposed for education and counseling interventions with the elderly's family caregivers (Fiore et al., 1983; Montgomery, 1984; Silverman et al., 1981). While some have been designed specifically to meet the special needs of elderly couples involved in caregiving (Getzel, 1982; Wolinsky, 1986), others are targeted to adult children (Altschuler et al., 1985; Roberto, 1985). Moreover, because caregiver strain is notably widespread and severe in families with cognitively impaired or demented members, principles and techniques for social work intervention with these families have also been delineated (Aronson et al., 1984; Marples, 1986; Oliver and Bock, 1985).

However, attention to the special needs of Black aged and their family caregivers has been far more limited (Morycz et al., 1987; Taylor and Chatters, 1986). The purpose of our chapter, therefore, has been to enhance the ethnic sensitivity of social workers serving this population by considering how Black culture affects the stresses encountered by minority elderly and how cultural values and forms (family, church) can be used effectively to attenuate these stresses. In view of the projected growth in the minority aged population and consequent increased demands on younger family members for care, continued work is needed to refine social work practice techniques with minority elderly and their kinship networks.

References

Altschuler, J., S. Jacobs, and D. Shiode. 1985. "Psychodynamic Time-Limited Groups for Adult Children of Aging Parents." *American Journal of Orthopsychiatry* 55:397-404.

Aronson, M. K., G. Levin, and R. Lipkowitz. 1984. "A Community-Based Family/Patient Group Program for Alzheimer's Disease." *Gerontologist* 24:339-42.

Aschenbrenner, J. 1975. *Lifelines: Black Families in Chicago.* New York: Holt, Rinehart & Winston.

Bass, D. M. and L. S. Noelker. 1987. "The Influence of Family Caregivers on Elders' Use of In-Home Services: An Expanded Conceptual Framework." *Journal of Health and Social Behavior* 28:184-96.

Beck, S. H. and R. W. Beck. 1984. "The Formation of Extended Households During Middle Age." *Journal of Marriage and the Family* 46:277-87.

Bloom, M., E. Duchon, G. Frires, H. Hanson, G. Hurd, and V. South. 1971. "Interviewing the Ill Aged." *Gerontologist* 11:292-99.

Brody, E. M. 1985. "Parent Care as a Normative Family Stress." *Gerontologist* 25:19-29.

Cafferty, P. S. I. and L. Chestang, eds. 1976. *The Diverse Society: Implications for Social Policy.* New York: National Association of Social Workers.

Cantor, M. H. 1983. "Strain Among Caregivers: A Study of Experience in the United States." *Gerontologist* 23:597-604.

Cherlin, A. 1983. "A Sense of History: Recent Research on Aging and the Family." Pp. 5-23 in *Aging in Society: Selected Reviews of Recent Research,* edited by M. W. Riley et al. Hillsdale, NJ: Lawrence Erlbaum.

Compton, B. and B. Galway, eds. 1979. *Social Work Processes.* 3rd ed. Homewood, IL: Dorsey.

Devore, W. 1983. "Ethnic Reality: The Life Model and Work with Black Families." *Social Casework* 9(November):525-31.

Devore, W. and E. G. Schlesinger. 1987. *Ethnic-Sensitive Social Work Practice.* 2nd ed St. Louis: C. V. Mosby.

Downing, R. A. and E. J. Copeland. 1981. "Services for the Black Elderly: National or Local Problems?" *Journal of Gerontological Social Work* 2:289-303.

Fiore, J., J. Becker, and D. B. Coppel. 1983. "Social Network Interactions: A Buffer on Stress." *American Journal of Community Psychology* 11:423-39.

Gaines, A. D. 1988-1989. "Alzheimer's Disease in the Context of Black (Southern) Culture." *Health Matrix* 6(4, Winter):33-38.

Gary, L. E. and B. R. Leashore. 1982. "High-Risk Status of Black Men." *Social Work* 27(January):54-58.

Germain, C. B. and A. Gitterman. 1980. *The Life Model of Social Work Practice.* New York: Columbia University Press.

Getzel, G. S. 1982. "Helping Elderly Couples in Crisis." *Social Casework* 63:515-21.

Gibson, R. C. 1982. "Blacks at Middle and Late Life: Resources and Coping." *Annals of the American Academy of Political and Social Science* 464:79-90.

Hepworth, D. H. and J. Larsen. 1982. *Direct Social Work Practice: Theory and Skills.* Homewood, IL: Dorsey.

Jones, D. L. 1979. "African-American Clients: Clinical Practice Issues." *Social Work* 24(March):112-18.

———. 1983. "Increasing Staff Sensitivity to the Black Client." *Social Casework* 9(September):419-25.

Lightfoot, O. B. 1982. "Ethnic and Cultural Variations in the Care of the Aged—Psychiatric Interventions with Blacks: The Elderly—A Case in Point." *Journal of Geriatric Psychiatry* 15:209-23.

Lockery, S. A. 1985. "Care in the Minority Family." *Generations* 10(Fall):27-29.

Lum, D. 1986. *Social Work Practice and People of Color: A Process-Stage Approach.* Monterey, CA: Brooks/Cole.

Manuel, R. C. 1982. "The Study of the Minority Aged in Historical Perspective." Pp. 3-12 in *Minority Aging: Sociological and Social Psychological Issues,* edited by R. C. Manuel. Westport, CT: Greenwood.

Marples, M. 1986. "Helping Family Members Cope with a Senile Relative." *Social Casework* 67:490-498.

Martin, E. P. and J. M. Martin. 1978. *The Black Extended Family.* Chicago: University of Chicago Press.

Montgomery, R., ed. 1984. *Family Seminars for Caregiving: Helping Families Help.* Washington, DC: Department of Health and Human Services.

Morrison, J. 1986. "The Church as a Support System for Black Elderly." *Center for the Study of Aging Newsletter* (University of Pennsylvania) 8:7.

Morycz, R. K., J. Malloy, M. Bozich, and P. Martz. 1987. "Racial Differences in Family Burden: Clinical Implications for Social Work." *Journal of Gerontological Social Work* 10(1/2):133-54.

Oliver, R. and R. A. Bock. 1985. "Alleviating the Distress of Caregivers of Alzheimer's Disease Patients: A Rational-Emotive Therapy Model." *Clinical Gerontologist* 3:17-34.

Roberto, K. A. 1985. "Adult Children and Aging Parents: A Report of a Program Design and Evaluation." *Activities, Adaptation, & Aging* 6:89-101.

Silverman, A. G., C. I. Brahce, and C. Zielinski. 1981. *As Parents Grow Older: A Manual for Program Replication.* Ann Arbor: University of Michigan.

Solomon, B. B. 1978. "The Black Aged: A Status Report." In *Policy Issues Concerning the Minority Elderly: Final Report, Six Papers,* edited by R. Valle. San Francisco: Human Resources Corporation.

Stack, C. 1974. *All Our Kin: Strategies for Survival in the Black Community.* New York: Harper & Row.

Stone, R., G. L. Cafferata, and J. Sangle. 1987. "Caregivers of the Frail Elderly: A National Profile." *Gerontologist* 27:616-26.

Taylor, R. J. and L. M. Chatters. 1986. "Patterns of Informal Support to Elderly Black Adults: Family, Friends and Church Members." *Social Work* 32(November-December):432-38.

U.S. Senate, Special Committee on Aging. 1986. *Aging America: Trends and Projections* (1985-86 ed.; DHHS No. 498-116-814/42395). Washington, DC: Government Printing Office.

Wolinsky, M. 1986. "Marital Therapy with Older Couples." *Social Casework* 67:475-83.

Ziter, M. P. 1987. "Culturally Sensitive Treatment of Black Alcoholic Families." *Social Work* 32(March-April):130-35.

About the Authors

Charles M. Barresi, Ph.D., is Professor of Sociology and Senior Fellow of the Institute for Life-Span Development and Gerontology at the University of Akron, Ohio. He has written extensively in social gerontology, on topics including widowhood, the unmarried, male caregivers, Black and White family comparisons, and ethnicity and long-term care. He is coauthor of *Ethnic Dimensions of Aging* (Springer, 1987), and his primary area of research interest is ethnicity and aging.

Linda M. Chatters is Assistant Professor in the Health Behavior-Health Education Department of the School of Public Health and Faculty Associate with the Research Center for Group Dynamics at the Institute for Social Research at the University of Michigan, Ann Arbor. After earning her Ph.D. in psychology at the University of Michigan, she completed postdoctoral study supported by the Rockefeller Foundation and the National Institute on Aging. As recipient of a First Independent Research Support and Transition (FIRST) Award from NIA, she will investigate issues related to the use of survey data among diverse groups of Black American respondents.

Her work has appeared in *Psychology and Aging, Journal of Gerontology: Social Sciences, The Gerontologist, Journal of Marriage and the Family, Social Work, Family Relations,* and *Journal of Black Studies.*

Mary McKinney Edmonds, Ph.D., PT, is Professor of Sociology at Bowling Green State University, Ohio, where she is also Vice President for Student Affairs and Joint Professor in Gerontology for the College of Health and Community Services. At the Medical College of Ohio at Toledo, she is Adjunct Professor in Physical Therapy. She is author of many articles and papers in medical sociology and social gerontology, and she has a particular research interest in the aged Black female.

Cheryl Stewart Gerace, MSSA, is Clinical Specialist for the East Cleveland Neighborhood Office of the Benjamin Rose Institute in Cleveland, Ohio. Drawing on her experience at the Benjamin Rose Institute in working with a diverse elderly population and its caregivers, she has provided field instruction in the undergraduate social work program at Cleveland State University, copresented a workshop sponsored by the university and the Cleveland Clinic Foundation, and authored a paper on the effects of Alzheimer's disease on the elderly and their caregivers. Her special interests include aging and ethnicity, and mental health services to the elderly.

Rose C. Gibson, Ph.D., is Faculty Associate at the Institute for Social Research and Associate Professor in the School of Social Work at the University of Michigan, Ann Arbor. A former National Institute on Aging Postdoctoral Fellow in Statistics, Survey Research Design and Methodology on Minority Populations, she has participated in pioneering national surveys. She is the author of *Blacks in an Aging Society* and serves on several editorial boards of journals in the field of aging. Her major research interest is in the area of sociocultural factors in aging.

Zev Harel is Professor and Interim Chair of the Department of Social Work at Cleveland State University in Cleveland, Ohio. He received his MSW from the University of Michigan and his Ph.D. from Washington University in St. Louis, Missouri. He has conducted research and has written extensively on mental health consequences of extreme stress, long-term care, ethnicity and aging, and vulnerable populations. He has served in leadership roles with local, state, and national organizations concerned with social work and aging.

Harold R. Johnson is Dean of the School of Social Work and Professor of Health Gerontology in the School of Public Health at the University of Michigan, Ann Arbor. A former President of the Association for Gerontology in Higher Education, he chaired the Technical Committee on Education for the 1981 White House Conference on Aging. Currently, he directs an international project designed both to improve health care services for the elderly and to inculcate gerontological content in educational programs for health care professionals.

Cary S. Kart, Ph.D., is Professor of Sociology at the University of Toledo, Ohio. He is author, coauthor, or editor of eight books and many articles and book chapters on aging, health, and long-term care, including *Aging, Health and Society* (Jones & Bartlett, 1988). The third edition of his text *The Realities of Aging* (Allyn & Bacon) will appear in 1990.

Irene Luckey received her M.A. in 1973 from the University of Chicago School of Social Service Administration, and her Ph.D. in social work in 1982 from the City University of New York. She was a postdoctoral fellow in the University of Michigan prior to accepting a position at SUNY—Albany as Assistant Professor of Social Work and Research Associate at the Ringel Institute of Gerontology.

Edward A. McKinney is Professor and former Chair of the Department of Social Work at Cleveland State University in Cleveland, Ohio. He received his MSW from Atlanta University, and his MPH and Ph.D. from the University of Pittsburgh, Pennsylvania. He has conducted research and has written extensively on health care and health planning, religion and social work, ethnicity and aging, and vulnerable populations. He has served in leadership roles with local, state, and national organizations concerned with social work and health care.

Geeta Menon earned a Ph.D. in social gerontology at the University of Akron, Ohio. Her primary academic and research activities are in the area of sociological perspectives on death and dying. Her dissertation analyzed public attitudes toward life prolongation. She is also interested in health care policies for the elderly.

Sharon E. Milligan, MPH, Ph.D., is Associate Professor in Social Work at the Mandel School of Applied Social Science, Case Western Reserve University, where she teaches courses in research and health policy. Her research interests, drawing on extensive experience in nonprofit health systems, include chronic illness, accessibility of health care services, and social support networks.

Linda S. Noelker, Ph.D., is Associate Director for Research at the Margaret Blenkner Research Center of the Benjamin Rose Institute in Cleveland, Ohio. She has published articles on institutional, community, and family care of the aged. Her current research interests are in the areas of the quality of intergenerational relations and the relationship between informal and formal support systems.

Wornie L. Reed, Ph.D., is Director of the William Monroe Trotter Institute at the University of Massachusetts, Boston. Previously, he directed the Institute for Urban Research at Morgan State University, was a faculty member in the Sociology Department and an Associate in Health Care Research in the School of Medicine at Washington University, and held positions in federal government and private industry. Trained as a medical sociologist under a health services research training fellowship, he has taught and published research in criminal justice as well as in medical care and mental health.

John H. Skinner, Ed.D., is Associate Dean and Associate Professor of Health Policy and Management in the College of Public Health at the University of South Florida. For more than 25 years, he has worked in the field of aging, holding research and administrative positions in government (U.S. Department of Health, Education and Welfare and the Administration on Aging) and private nonprofit organizations (National Council on the Aging) as well as in universities. His research interests are in the areas of resource allocation, service access and utilization, information management, quality of care and program outcomes, and minority aging issues.

E. Percil Stanford, Ph.D., is Professor and Director of the University Center on Aging, College of Health and Human Services, San Diego State University. His interests are in the areas of retirement, job satisfaction, health issues, cross-cultural and minority issues, media and aging, and educational training.

Robert Joseph Taylor, MSW, Ph.D., is Assistant Professor of Social Work and Faculty Associate at the Institute for Social Research at the University of Michigan, Ann Arbor. After earning his doctorate in social work and sociology at Michigan (1983), he completed postdoctoral work sponsored by the National Institute on Aging and is currently a recipient of NIA's First Independent Research Support and Transition (FIRST) Award. His research focuses on family and friend social support networks across

the life span, with a particular emphasis on the networks of older adults. His work has appeared in *The Gerontologist, Journal of Gerontology: Social Sciences, Journal of Marriage and the Family, Journal of Black Studies, Review of Religious Research,* and *Social Service Review.*

Wilbur H. Watson is Geriatric Research Associate, Morehouse School of Medicine. He is a graduate of Kent State University, where he earned the B.A. and M.A. degrees in sociology, in 1964 and 1966, respectively, and the University of Pennsylvania, where he earned the Ph.D. in 1972. His major interests are in the sociology of medicine, the social psychology of health and aging, and the history and sociology of science. His contributions to the literature include *The Village* (Village Vanguard, 1989), *Black Folk Medicine* (Transaction, 1984), *Aging and Social Behavior* (Wadsworth, 1982), *Stress and Old Age* (Transaction, 1980), and *Human Aging and Dying* (St. Martin's, 1977).

Michael Williams is Assistant Professor and Field Education Coordinator with the Department of Social Work at Cleveland State University in Cleveland, Ohio. He received his MSSA from Case Western Reserve University, and his MPH and Ph.D. from the University of Pittsburgh in 1985. He has conducted research and has written on health services, income security of African American elderly, ethnicity and aging, and vulnerable populations. He has served in leadership roles with local and state organizations concerned with social work and health care. He has a special interest in social policies that affect the African American elderly and community.